1989

DISC

Gossip, Reputation,
and Knowledge in Zinacantan

Gossip, Reputation, and Knowledge in Zinacantan

CHAMPLAIN COLLEGE

John Beard Haviland

The University   Chicago and London
of Chicago Press

The University of Chicago Press, Chicago 60637
The University of Chicago Press, Ltd., London

Library of Congress Cataloging in Publication Data

Haviland, John Beard.
  Gossip, reputation, and knowledge in Zinacantan.

  Bibliography: p.
  Includes index.
  1. Tzotzil Indians—Social life and customs.
2. Gossip—Case studies.   3.   Zinacantán, Mexico—
Social life and customs.   I.   Title.
  F1221.T9H38   301.2'1   76–8095
  ISBN 0–226–31955–5

John Beard Haviland is a research fellow in the
Department of Anthropology of the Institute
of Advanced Studies, Australian National
University.

Contents

Preface

I first arrived in Zinacantan at the beginning of June 1966,
fresh from college and just in time to celebrate my saint's day
and be christened with my new Tzotzil name, Xun. I was,
I thought, just passing through, in a brief flirtation with
anthropology before getting on with my serious plans (I was
a philosophy student). My name was soon extended to
Xun Jvabajom ("John musician") as I spent that summer
tagging along behind Zinacanteco musicians, who taught
me to play and sing and who began my instruction in talking,
joking, and being polite.

It turned out to be more than a flirtation. I was back
again the next year with my wife Leslie, and a couple of
years later with our daughter Sophie—to stay, by then, for
a year. I had fallen into an easy identity in Zinacantan
(as one of those Harvard anthropology students, but one
who pretended to be a musician and could pass as one in a
pinch), but I had never really *earned* my reputation. As
a musician I could manage the tunes and follow songs, but
I could neither joke nor lead ritual nor advise on procedure.
As a private citizen I could construct grammatical Tzotzil
sentences and conduct myself without offending others
with my clumsiness (though I frequently amused them),
but I couldn't really *talk* to anyone about anything that
mattered (farming, land, politics, cargos, neighbors). I had
friends, ritual kin, and debtors, but I felt that I knew very
little about them (as, indeed, they knew little of me).

Thus began the struggle to penetrate more deeply into
the lives of my Zinacanteco victims. This book documents
a part of that struggle.

By the time I began the studies described here I had
become familiar with current anthropological theory bearing

on the knowledge that natives are said to have of their
cultures. I knew that Zinacantecos were able to manipulate
lexical sets; that they could perform complex calculations
of rank and prestige; that they could classify kin and produce
corn both to eat and to sell. And I had been taught that
whatever they knew, I could learn; that whatever they had
learned from I had access to as well. How was it, then,
that I found their conversation, their gossip, so impenetrable?
This book charts my wobbly entry into the world of Zinacanteco talk, and it ultimately questions received notions
of cultural knowledge or competence.

I eventually came to feel that my studies had brought
me rather far. Studying the language of motives, causes,
reasons, rules—charting people's missteps and disasters,
their miscalculations and failures, as well as their less-
discussed triumphs—through gossip had led me to some
central questions. I began to consider in a new light the
interrelations between rules, as promulgated through conversation, the goals at which people aimed (or claimed
to aim), and, finally, the institutions in which rules are
embedded and which in large measure create the goals and
purposes of men. Gossip—which is ordinarily talk about
rules and goals as much as it is talk about the doings of
others—makes problematic the nature of this embedding:
the standards which gossips summon are themselves inter-
twined with a way of life. The rules justify the institutions of
the society, which in turn promulgate the rules. Conversation manipulates events and opinions to produce order—
an order that agrees with (and is agreeable to) the institutional order.

So far so good: here is a self-validating cultural circle,
which we can penetrate and observe in action by attention to
gossip. And getting even this far is a task whose complexity
and formidableness many theorists have failed to grasp.
This book will, I hope, at least demonstrate that the circle
is hard to enter.

And yet, with this research behind me, I now fear that
my beginnings have been false ones. It is possible to ask
transcendental questions. On the one hand, talk of rules and
codes, of the gossip's cultural competence, and of cultural
grammars (even in fragments) may simply be an elaborate
dodge, allowing us to forget that we have both modeled
away those mechanisms of mind and brain that we do not
understand and also merely skimmed off the abstracted and
manageable regularities from what remains an almost

totally mysterious jumble of behavior. We progress from
real people behaving, to "native actors" who know something
about behavior, to gossips whose only behavior is to juggle
talk about that knowledge. The gossip is quick to interpret
but slow to act.

There is a still more immediate objection to the sort of
study I offer here. In conversation people construct, through
the application of an elaborate cultural mechanism, order,
reason, and meaning from a capricious world; but this
process may also be at the heart of mystification. To enter
the circle of a way of life and the rules and ideas which
validate that way of life is so far not to ask, Why *this* way of
life? Or, What sort of life *is* this, anyway? Perhaps the
elaborate scheme of cultural rationalization is self-contra-
dictory, deluded, illogical, even destructive, in the face of
real constraints on Zinacanteco life. The consciousness of the
Zinacanteco gossip is perhaps as selectively fogged as the
view of the Zinacanteco woman who sees, among the
hundreds of bustling figures in the ladino town of San
Cristóbal de las Cases, only her own hamlet neighbors.
For her, the rest do not exist. In a similar way, for the
Zinacanteco gossip, neither do ladino landlords, government
manipulators, coffee *fincas*, truck-owning monopolies, missionaries, foreign or domestic anthropologists, lawyers,
storekeepers, or multinational corporations exist. They do
not figure in the order he creates in talking, although they
do figure (often decisively) among the constraints which
govern his life.

This book, then, at once strikes deep into the heart of
Zinacanteco culture and ideology and at the same time
simply misses Zinacanteco society as a real part of Chiapas,
of Mexico, and of the rest of the world. A good deal may
occur in the realm of discourse which gossips create, which
people think; but Zinacantecos actually inhabit the real
world, where they live, work, and die. My own worry with
what I have written stems not from a dissatisfaction over
what I have learned about how Zinacantecos think and
talk—I am glad to have gotten as far as I have—but from
the fear that much of this book is irrelevant to the lives
of Zinacantecos and the conditions that underlie those lives.
There is one consolation: Zinacanteco ideas of the forces
governing their lives may be similarly deluded, so that a
central part of future work in Zinacantan and neighboring
communities must be devoted to overcoming these ideas
and forging a new awareness. I hope in my future work to
be a part of such an endeavor.

Acknowledgments

My primary debts are to my family and teachers in Zinacantan, to whom I address the following words. (I write Tzotzil, throughout this book, in a practical orthography described in Appendix 4.)

Kolavalik akotolik yuʔun ti achiʔinikon, ti achanubtasikon, ti ap'isikon ta vinik ta avamikoik. Koʔol ijchiʔin jbatike, lek ijtzak jbatik ta loʔile, koʔol liyakubotik ʔune. ʔAk'o mi chalabanon, ʔak'o mi chavuton, pero yuʔnan saʔbil kuʔun, toj sonsoon. Avalbeikon jp'eluk k'op, avalbeikon jset'uk rason, ijchan ʔo k'u chaʔal chiloʔilaj, k'u chaʔal chiʔabtej, k'u chaʔal ta jchaʔle jba.

Koliyal tajmek li jmol kumpare Xun Vaskis ta Nabenchauk xchiʔuk jkumale meʔel, yuʔun slekil yoʔonik, ijch'amunbe sna ta Jteklum, xchiʔuk ta jnatikotik ta Nabenchauk ʔune. Jal ich'ay jjol ta loʔil xchiʔuk li jkumpare mole, k'alal liyalbe kwentoetik yuʔun ti ʔantivo moletik, ti voʔne krixchanoetik. Mi liʔipaj lek lispoj, liyak'be kantela. Lek lixchabibe li kunen tzebe, li xch'ul ch'amale.

Koliyal li jmol kumpare Petul Vaskis ta Nabenchauk, xchiʔuk jkumale Petuʔ, xchiʔuk sManvel, sChep, yAntun, sLoxa, skotolik. Ta primero ijchiʔin jbatikotik ta pas kobral ta ʔolon. Lavie, koʔol jnatikotik, koʔol jbetikotik, koʔol kaʔaltikotik, koʔol jk'optikotik, koʔol jjoltikotik. Jchanojbe sk'op srason. Lek listzak ta loʔil, ijchan ʔo k'u chaʔal chitak'av, k'u chaʔal ta jpak loʔil ʔune. Ta jp'is ta jtot jmeʔ.

Koliyal li jkumale Paxkuʔ stzeb li jkumpare Petul ʔune. Koʔol kilojbe jbatikotik jnatikotik. ʔIjchan ʔo k'u chaʔal chilabanvan, k'u chaʔal chiloʔiltavan, k'u chaʔal chitzeʔin. Mi liviʔnaj liyak'be yot jveʔ. Mi sik ikaʔi liyak'be jk'uʔ jlap.

Koliyal li ʔanima jtot Petul Buro ta Jteklum xchiʔuk jmeʔ
Mal. Lisp'is ta skrem, ijch'amunbe sk'ob ta vob ʔune.
Lastima mu p'ijuk li jjole, komo vokol ijchan.
Koliyal li jkumpare Chep K'obyox ta ʔApas. Buyuk
jnup jbatikotik, lek ijchiʔin jbatikotik. Koʔol chiʔabtejoti-
kotik, lek chiloʔilajotikotik, lek chkuch'tikotik.
Koliyal li mol Manvel Tulan ta Nabenchauk xchiʔuk
jmeʔ Xunkaʔ. ʔAti chopluk yoʔon li jmeʔ Xunkaʔ
ʔune, solel t'anal chixanav k'al tana, yuʔun lisjalbe jpok'-
k'uʔ jtzotz-k'uʔ li meʔele xchiʔuk sTinik. Liʔay ta ch'omil
ta yabtel li mol Manvel ʔune, ijchan ʔo k'u chaʔal mu
xivayotik ʔune.
Koliyalik li mol Lol Romin ta Nabenchauk, li jkumpare
Xun Sukipan xchiʔuk jmol kumpare jmeʔel kumale, li
jkumpare Maryan ʔAch'eltik ta Nabenchauk, li jmol
kumpare Chep Pulivok ta ʔApas xchiʔuk jmeʔel kumale
xchiʔuk jch'ul ch'amal Mal, li jmol kumpare Maryan
Konte ta Pera, li mol Chep Nuj ta Nachij, mol Xalik ta
Voʔ ta Petej ta Chamuʔ, k'ox Romin ta Nabenchauk,
li mol Romin Teratol ta Jteklum, xchiʔuk skotol jkumpare-
tak jkumaletak kamikotak tzjunul jteklume.

I would never have gone to Zinacantan at all, nor pursued
anthropology, without the Harvard Chiapas Project, per-
sonified by Professor Evon Z. Vogt and Catherine C. Vogt.
Vogtie and Nan opened Zinacantan to us and kept it
open, welcoming my family and me into their home, into
their family, and into the anthropological world. George
and Jane Collier were my first and most valued teachers in
Zinacantan, and they have more than once shared house and
larder with us. Robert Laughlin shared with me vast
amounts of Tzotzil, and I feel I have barely scratched the
surface of his knowledge.
I benefited from the advice and friendship of many people
in San Cristóbal: Maria-Elena and Eva Bermúdez, my
comadrita Maria-Luisa Porras, Don Vicente Reyes, Químico
Agusto Ruiz Bonifaz, Bibiano Luna, members of the
selección de Basquetbol San Cristóbal, Doña Gertudis Duby
de Blom, Frank and Franzi Cancian, Francesco and Phip
Pellizzi, Ulrich Köhler, Richard and Flora Alderson,
Priscilla and Johannus Linn, Rob and Janice Wasserstrom,
Ann Legett, Mimi Laughlin, Dennis Breedlove, and various
generations of Harvard Chiapas Project anthropologists.
My family has shared my life in Zinacantan and made
it not only richer but possible at all. My wife Leslie and my
daughter Sophie have been through all of it and done
better than I. My brother Peter has run me ragged from

time to time and even helped dig out the floor of our house in Nabenchauk.

I have worked on material in this book while supported by various institutions: National Institutes of Mental Health (Predoctoral Research Fellowship #2 F01 MH36381), the Harvard Chiapas Project, Harvard University Summer School, NATO (Postdoctoral Fellowship in Science, Department of Linguistics, SGS, Australian National University), and the Department of Anthropology, Research School of Pacific Studies, Australian National University.

I have benefited from criticisms of earlier versions of this material by David Maybury-Lewis, E. Z. Vogt, Keith Kernan, Robert Laughlin, Tim Rush, and Roger Keesing.

My parents, Morrison Chandler Haviland and Mary Elizabeth Haviland, helped me with the production of the manuscript; and I am especially indebted to Patti Smith and Ria van de Zandt, who typed it.

Finally, Christopher Boehm deserves special mention (a share of the blame?) for inspiring this whole enquiry. One evening in a Cambridge delicatessen, while over cheese blintzes I pondered my research plans for Zinacantan, Chris and Leslie were engrossed in a violent, shocking gossip session. Awakening to what was going on I realized in a flash the fascination of gossip; hence, this book.

A Plea for Gossip

K'al tana mu xpaj slo?iltael.
"Gossip about him will never cease."

Walking along a path I met a group of Zinacanteco men and stopped to join their conversation. Old Xap had just been sent to jail by his in-laws.

"I don't know if it is true, but they say that old Xap was embracing his own daughter."

"He was giving her injections, they say. . . ."

"Yes, young children discovered it—it was little Xun who is always playing nearby. I hear that the old man was tickling his daughter inside the house. When the children came near, they peeked inside—the little brats looked under the rafters, though they didn't know what was going on. 'I'll take a look at what they're doing in there,' said one of the little fuckers. What he saw was father and daughter lifting each other onto the bed, playing one another's music. (Ha ha ha.)"

"The kids probably sat right down to hear how the daughter would sing. (Ha ha ha.)"

"Yes. Then one of those damned kids went right up to the door, and spoke. 'Are you here, mother Paxku??' Are you here, father Xap?' he said. He pretended to ask if they were home. And they were indeed home: they were embracing each other on the bed."

"What happened?"

"Then the kids went home to tell their mother. 'I don't know what mother Paxku? is doing with grand-father Xap,' they said upon arriving home. 'They are sleeping together in bed.'

"When the woman heard what the children were saying, she went next door to have a look. But when she arrived, the old man and his daughter were just seated by the fire. The music was already finished. (Ha ha ha.)"
"But is that Paxku? old man Xap's real daughter?"
"Yes, his own daughter. . . ."
"Damn! So that's why his brothers-in-law jailed him."

For me the task of learning about Zinacantan coincided with the task of learning to understand Zinacanteco gossip. When I first went to Zinacantan I benefited from the extraordinary range of previous ethnographic research there, research documented in Vogt (1969). From the library I brought skills and information whose acquisition would have otherwise been slow indeed. But it was only when I began to listen to Zinacantecos talking with one another that I came to feel any genuine understanding of what was going on around me.

This is a book about Zinacanteco gossip. Much of the book in fact *consists* of fragments of Zinacanteco conversation, rendered into English and robbed of real names. Understanding talk about the world presupposes knowledge about the world; what Zinacantecos say leads to an appreciation of what they do, what they are concerned with, what they find worthy of comment.

Though I shall not be concerned with recounting ethnographic phenomena elsewhere described, some facts of Zinacanteco social life, glimpses of some Zincanteco faces, will emerge from the gossip. I shall try to lead the reader to certain discoveries about Zinacantan by sharing some of what I heard people say.

This is also a book about the *process* of learning about Zinacantan. I intend not a description of my own family's fieldwork in Zinacantan but rather a demonstration of the process by which attention to conversation leads to knowledge. We are able to enter the particular worlds depicted in Zinacanteco gossip by constantly modifying our assumptions that Zinacanteco worlds are like our own. The process is like (and, indeed, includes) learning a second language: we progress from tentative *translations* of new words by old words to direct, unglossed understanding of utterances. There are certainly more direct ways to find out *about* another culture, but we must not confuse what we learn about Zinacantecos by these direct methods with what Zinacantecos themselves know about themselves.

Conversation turned to old Xap's poverty.
"He hardly raises any corn at all. I think he survives by selling charcoal, which he makes in the mountains."

"But is it true, as people say, that one should not sell charcoal?"
"Why not?"
"I've heard it said that charcoal is terribly hot. One's luck will turn
hot from handling it; then one's cornfields will refuse to grow.
Perhaps that is why old Xap has so little corn. . . ."
"But must we believe that? Old Petul's sons sold charcoal after he
died, but it did not sour their luck."

A person's knowledge of his culture has a structure perhaps more
easily learned than described; I shall argue that we can probe the deep-
est levels of this structure by observing people's conversations with one
another, in particular their gossip. Through such a study we can penetrate the tangle of rules we have called "cultural codes" to discover
salient skills, categories, and objects.[1] I am prepared to suggest that
there is an intimate relation between the native's knowledge of his own
society and his ability to gossip (or to understand gossip).

Ethnographers construct, or pretend to construct, or offer suggestions
about how to construct, fragments of cultural descriptions, based on
some particular theory of culture (Keesing 1974*a*). Minimally, the
ethnographer seeks to describe some subset of people's actions and institutions and to *account* for them according to standards that vary from
one anthropological fashion to another. He may argue that underlying
observed actions are certain "standards" (Goodenough 1961, p. 522),
precepts, or rules: "whatever it is one has to know or believe in order
to operate in a manner acceptable to" the members of the culture (Goodenough 1957, p. 167). His account may then consist of a description
of the components of this knowledge and its organization. Or the ethnographer may try to discern meanings which attach to people's actions,
so that his account amounts to an interpretation of sequences of behavior, of acts, and of events (Geertz 1973). Gossip as text and gossiping as commentary, explicit though often severely bounded by context
and convention, are particularly illuminating guides to either sort of
account. In fact, whatever one's views of acceptable analysis, whatever
one's convictions about the ultimate transcendence of anthropological
analysis over native awareness, one quickly discovers that the gossip
knows (though perhaps cannot consciously formulate) more than the
novice ethnographer about what the facts are (e.g., what people are
doing) and what they mean. This is, then, also a book about the nature
of ethnographic accounts; I propose to reconsider, in sketching fragments of Zinacanteco ethnography, the tasks of "describing a culture,"
of "untangling cultural rules," and of "interpreting" or "coming to understand the meanings of" social action.

As conversation continued, someone mentioned that old Xap was also the owner of a talking saint.

"Yes, but for him it is only a pretext to steal money."

"It is the same story with all talking saints. They only lie."

"I have forgotten who it was who exposed Old Xap. Two boys, it was, who went to trick him. They said their mother was sick.

" 'What's wrong with her?' asked old Xap.

" 'We don't know. Please ask the saint for us,' they replied.

"The old man was willing to ask the saint, but the boys had to offer it a bottle of liquor.

" 'Oh, but we have brought no liquor. Please sell us a bottle here,' they told old Xap. 'We'll pay you tomorrow. We were so worried about our mother—What if she were to die?—that we forgot to bring along payment,' they explained."

"So the boys wanted to consult the saint?"

"Yes, that was why they had come. 'Very well,' agreed old Xap, and he had his wife pour out a bottle of rum. 'Here it is, son,' he said, handing it over to the boys.

" 'Thanks,' they replied, 'We'll come back and pay for it tomorrow. Let's drink it. Please, father Xap, do us the favor of asking the saint about our mother who is very ill.'

"In a moment old Xap began to squeal and murmur—the way talking saints sound—you know the sound. He started nodding his head; he arranged his scarf around his head this way. 'The saint is about to start talking,' he said. He started to make little noises now, and seemed to be talking to his saint.

"In a moment he said to the boys, 'Aaaa, tomorrow or the next day, only a few days to wait—she's going to die. Yes, your old mother has been taken very severely ill.'

" 'Aaa, we understand,' exclaimed the boys. 'She's going to die. Well, all right, we understand. We'll come back tomorrow to pay for the rum.'

" 'Think well,' continued old Xap. 'Perhaps if you decide to have a curing ceremony for her, then perhaps the saint will manage to cure her.'

" 'All right, we'll consider well,' they replied. 'We'll come speak to you about it later.'

" 'Agreed,' said old Xap.

"But as soon as the boys were outside they began to laugh. 'Shit, that old son of a bitch, pretending that his saint can talk! The bastard just talks pure lies,' they said to each other. Because, you see, their mother wasn't even sick; it was all a trick."

"Ha ha ha ha."

"She was going to die, but she wasn't even sick. Ha ha ha."

J. L. Austin, in "A Plea for Excuses" (1961), suggests that moral philosophers may profit from examining the excuses people offer for their misdeeds and errors. At the same time, Austin's plea embodies his conception of what philosophy (and philosophizing) must be like, of what it means to unravel certain philosophical tangles by attention to ordinary language. People's excuses are well suited to the analytic methods of ordinary language philosophy. We discover what counts as a successful (or unsuccessful) moral argument by observing how people use critical words to get themselves off the hook. The study of excuses represents a sort of philosophical "fieldwork." The philosopher investigates the logic of moral reasoning through particular bits of actual excuse-making (or by imagining *possible* excuses for hypothetical transgressions).

I wish to make an analogous plea for the study of gossip in ethnography. Just as excuses reveal how people ordinarily think and talk about certain kinds of moral dilemmas (which is in part to show what these dilemmas are), gossip reveals how native actors examine, use, and manipulate cultural rules in natural contexts. Just as excuses point up the aspects of an act or situation relevant to ascriptions of fault or responsibility, gossip dwells on those features of behavior which call cultural rules into play—those items of information that enable people to make evaluations. Finally, just as excuses provide verbal raw material for philosophizing (Austin looks at, among other things, morally tinged adverbs), gossip displays, by example, ethnographically important words. Gossip distills verbal characterizations of significant roles, situations, and behavior.[2] Both gossip and excuses arise with departures from normality —a symptom of the general axiom that people find only such departures worth talking about. Both gossip and excuses occur in natural conversation; people both gossip and make excuses in ordinary, uncontrived language. Hence, as ethnographers or as philosophers, we have access to both gossip and excuses in our favorite form: as words and phrases in context.

But there is a stronger parallel between Austin's plea for excuses and my plea for gossip. Austin urges not simply that excuses are interesting in themselves but further that the study of excuses exemplifies the form of philosophical inquiry; that if we see how excuses can be put to work we shall see how one arrives at solutions to philosophical problems. I argue that while the study of gossip is certainly a powerful ethnographic tool capable of uncovering otherwise inaccessible facts and phenomena, if we appreciate the native actor's ability to gossip and to understand gossip then we must revise our notions of what constitutes ethnography. We must expand our view of the "cultural competence" of native actors and alter our conception of what it is to understand ethnographic phenomena. I argue implicitly for these claims in the last chapters of this book.

Gossip has, of course, been a favorite source of information for anthropologists at least since Malinowski. Field notes and diaries, if not actual monographs, are usually filled with natives' gossip about their neighbors (and often about the ethnographer as well). In communities where news is passed by word of mouth, the ethnographer who fails to intercept at least some part of this stream of talk will remain woefully uninformed.

But gossip has most often appeared anecdotal and scattered, recording only anomalies and missteps, the ripples initiated by disruptions in the orderly flow of social life. Thus, Elsie Clews Parsons begins a chapter on "Town Gossip" in Mitla this way: "In any systematic town survey much detail is necessarily omitted and the life appears more standardized than it really is; there is no place for contradictions or exceptions or minor variations; the classifications more or less preclude pictures of people living and functioning together" (1936, p. 386). Here appears the disconcerting suggestion that "systematic" analysis of society must necessarily impose order and regularity on social phenomena and cannot therefore accommodate certain sorts of information. Parsons goes on to comment on the particular bits of ethnographic detail she hopes to convey by recounting gossip. "From these impressions will be imparted, I hope, some appreciation of the disposition of the townspeople, what they laugh at, what they are willing to talk about, and what they keep to themselves; the kind of behavior they condemn or are indifferent about; how they feel about customs they know are lapsing; their manners and conventionalities" (1936, p. 387). What striking omissions, on this account, would plague an ethnography which failed to include gossip! Far from being superfluous and incidental to scientific description, such details as townspeople's dispositions and propensities to laugh or condemn seem central ethnographic concerns.

Most anthropological attention to gossip has centered on the properties of groups within which gossip occurs; gossip is reckoned a mechanism for social control, able to police the boundaries of the group and to sanction misbehavior. Gluckman's (1963, 1968) early statements on gossip and scandal sound his familiar refrain: gossip is circumscribed by, and in fact helps maintain, the relevant groups within a society. That is, only insiders can gossip to each other about each other. Gossip is incomprehensible to the observer who is unacquainted with the protagonists or inadequately informed about their habits and histories.

Gluckman characterizes a new member of a group as follows: "He may learn the rules of technique which keep the group in being, and he may be on excellent terms with the other members of the group, but he does not belong to the group until it is impossible for him to be rude to one of its members unintentionally" (1963, p. 314). A similar (though perhaps less categorical) criterion applies to the novice gossip; learning to gossip in a group implies, among other things, learning what constitutes *rudeness*, and further learning enough about everyone involved to know, at least most of the time, what to say to whom and what *not* to say. Don Handelman makes a related point concerning the knowledge of workers in a Jerusalem workshop about their fellow workers and the conventions governing talk in that context; in the course of working in a fairly stable (if small) social setting over time workers "developed fairly early good conceptions about the kinds of information which they could use in their interaction without eliciting rebukes" (1971, p. 396). One must learn to respect the dangers of gossip before one can enjoy its virtues.

I suggest in chapter 4 that in Zinacantan in the baldest sense one cannot understand most conversation without information about important "focal individuals." I can attest from personal experience that it is possible to exist successfully in Zinacantan observing most ordinary canons of etiquette and correct behavior without possessing any of the knowledge or conversational skills which allow one to gossip. Gluckman argues that gossip is possible only within the boundaries of a group and, further, that gossip is a "social weapon" by which a group protects itself from incursions by outsiders: how better to snub a newcomer than to demonstrate his alienness by gossiping in front of him? Whether or not people always use gossip consciously in this way (outside of the circles Professor Gluckman mentions), it is clearly possible to chart the boundaries of a social group by the ability of individuals to participate in its gossip.

Professor Gluckman also addresses himself to the elusive relationship between gossip and the "morals and values of social groups" (1963, p. 308). It is easy to suggest that gossip asserts or supports values (whatever these latter may be); in Zinacantan, at least, "values" are implicitly the *subject* of the evaluative portion of most gossip sessions (see chap. 4). Gluckman expresses the nature of the relationship more subtly in other passages. He suggests that among the Makah "values and traditions largely persist in the gossip and in no other way" (1963, p. 311).[3] Again, even when conflicting groups have opposing interests, Welsh villagers "evaluate people as leaders, as good villagers, and the like, so that gossip also serves to bring conformity with village values and objectives" (1963, p. 312). Commenting on Paine's claim (1967, p. 280) that people appeal to group values in gossip only insofar as this furthers their own self-interests, Gluckman observes that "when one man advances his prestige by gossiping against another with allegations that the latter has broken the code of the group, he may value and desire to preserve the code. Even if he does not, the fact that he acquires prestige by defending the code, validates it" (1968, p. 32).

It is at least clear that a gossip group forms what F. G. Bailey calls a "moral community"; that is, a group of people "prepared to make moral judgements about one another" (1971, p. 7). Members of such groups themselves possess reputations and are familiar with the reputations of others; and they consider themselves entitled to comment on and evaluate the behavior of other group members (even behavior that they do not see, but only hear about). In chapter 4 I show that Zinacanteco gossip dwells on the moral dilemmas posed by the narrated events. Gossip in Zinacantan encourages speculation about such matters as, for example, how a girl should behave in courtship or the proper way to raise children. The moral argument in gossip sessions clearly has the *appearance* of being based on a shared set of ethical precepts. It is by such precepts, which we may be tempted to call "values," that people's reputations are reckoned and constituted. And "the relevant values and categories are near to the surface: they rise to people's lips, when they pass judgement upon one another" (Bailey 1971, p. 9). I shall return to these difficult issues in chapter 8.

Paine (1967, 1968) emphasizes the function of gossip as a tool an individual may use to attain certain ends. People "gossip, and also regulate their gossip, to forward and protect their individual interests" (1967, p. 280), which may be (and usually are) in conflict. This view of gossip has implications both about the nature of gossiping groups and about the relationship between gossip and "public morality." First, even if gossip implicitly serves to maintain the boundaries (hence the "unity") of a group, gossip explicitly furthers the ends of some individuals or factions against those of others within the group. A man once gossiped to me about the disobedient and disrespectful behavior of his son (who had moved out of his father's home without making a proper request) specifically in order to influence my willingness to lend money to the boy. The man, it turned out, was involved in a legal dispute with his son and wanted to eliminate the possibility that the boy could hire a non-Indian lawyer with my money.

Gossip is most obviously instrumental in furthering *factional* ends in Zinacantan when a well-spoken person, accomplished in legal argument, is recruited to support one side or another in a dispute. Various individuals bend the man's ear with accounts of their enemies' wrongdoings. Zinacantecos are aware of the power of gossip in this connection. One man told me how two groups of habitual enemies tried to enlist his aid in settling a marriage dispute (which had become the focus of their factional split): a man from one faction would invite my informant for a beer and tell him his side of the story, while a man from the other faction would eavesdrop on what they were saying. As soon as the one left, the other would accost my friend and harangue him with another interpretation of the facts. By convincing this man, one side in the dispute would gain a powerful ally.

Paine remarks that "gossip serves to pattern issues which were but vaguely or confusedly perceived by a local population" and hence that "gossip is a powerful social instrument for any person who learns to manage it and can thereby direct or canalise its catalytic effect" (1967, p. 283). A man gossips to control others and accordingly fears gossip as it threatens to control him. Hence, a man tries to manage the information[4] that exists about others and himself by gossiping about others (and drawing others into gossip-laden conversations), on the one hand, and by trying to limit gossip about himself.[5] Zinacantecos, as will become clear, are passionate in their desire to acquire and spread information about their kin and neighbors, while very consciously suppressing as potentially harmful the dissemination of information about themselves or their immediate households. They often fail, of course, to stay inside the one-way screen. Thus, whatever one's intentions, to advance one's ends through gossip requires a good deal of skill and craftiness in handling the encounters in which gossip occurs.

Nor is the relationship between, say, factional ends and the *content* of factionally motivated gossip necessarily direct. Bruce Cox suggests that, in looking at factional divisions through the mutual gossip of the two sides, "one cannot forget what is being fought over. Since . . . we must focus on the impression the parties wish to give of themselves (and of others), and the way they attempt to manage information in order to do so, we are bound to learn what each thinks important in the dispute" (1970, p. 97). On the contrary, factionally based talk in Zinacantan seems most often to mask rather than to expose the basis of conflict. Thus, for example, the large factions of the hamlet where I lived square off periodically over land boundaries, public works, schools, the presence of motorized corn mills and *cantinas*, and so forth.[6] But the disputes which come to court, result in jailing, and generally proliferate gossip usually have to do with, for example, alleged witchcraft, assassination attempts, or, often, shouting matches and traded insults rather than with the more obvious political issues (Rush 1971). The gossip, that is, has less to do with power and political ends than with the personalities and propensities of the disputants.

Even if we cannot always assume that enemies will reveal in gossip the true nature of the conflict between them, it is nonetheless undeniable that natives as well as observers incorporate talk about their neighbors into the body of knowledge they construct to understand the world in which they live. Various authors have used, in this connection, the metaphor of a map. Hannerz (1967)[7] suggests that where a community makes available a large number of life strategies and value orientations (and, concomitantly, a large number of possible interactional networks, that is, groups of friends and associates), gossip provides an individual with "a map of his social environment including details which are inaccessible to him in his own everyday life. He learns, in the most efficient way possible, what persons are currently desirable or undesirable associates from his point of view, and he also learns something about how one might profitably deal with them, as inferred from their latest gossiped-about characteristics" (1967, p. 57). Thus, generally, "gossip may serve to channel network affiliations" (1967, p. 45) by distributing various kinds of instrumental information by which one decides one's own program of action. Such a phenomenon may be observed in Zinacantan, where economic changes and government policies have provided individual Zinacantecos with alternatives (although limited, heavily constrained alternatives) to "traditional" agricultural or trading careers. Gossip dwells on sources of individual livelihoods, on men well connected to government agencies and outside labor opportunities.

F. G. Bailey argues a more general point, that gossip helps map the community for its members.

> An event or an action is public not only to those who see it, but also to those who hear about it. Indeed it is speech which defines the nature of that event: the moral evaluation, which is what matters, is of its very nature unseeable. Comment relates event and action to the "eternal verities" (egoism, equality, and so on) and just as these abstract qualities are invisible, so also are the events which are judged in their light. The map which a man has of the community around him, of what is going on and of how he should respond to others, is a map created by the spoken word, by the information circulating around his community [1971, pp. 284–85]

Importantly, on this account, gossip not only supplies a raw "description" of certain events but rather an *account* of events, with interpretation and often evaluation attached.

Here we confront again the interdependence of gossip and norms. Paine emphasizes that appeals to norms are motivated by more than the desire to validate them. "Important data concerning the 'moral order' of a group are the manipulations it is possible for individuals to make concerning their interests, and gossip is a device used in these manipulations" (1967, p. 282). If we observe gossips in action we soon understand that one does not just *appeal* to norms or rules; rather, one applies them, manipulates them, and interprets them for particular purposes. Gossiping *requires* such manipulation of rules;[8] its great attraction and potency stem from the opportunity it provides to bend the "moral order" to a particular purpose. And where there are alternative strategies for success, alternative sets of values and ends, gossip allows people to sound out the opinions of their associates and to influence the values and assumptions of their neighbors.

Discussion shifted from old Xap's talking saint to his own abilities as a curer.

"At least he is a good curer. He's not a witch, is he?"

"He may not be a witch, but he gets too angry when he is curing. He wants too much liquor during curing ceremonies."

"Wasn't he responsible for the death of Maryan's child?"

"Yes, yes, he was called to cure illness at Maryan's house. But all he said was: 'You have been fighting too much among yourselves; you scold one another too much. That is what has brought this illness; it must be turned around.' Then he asked for half-litre bottles of liquor to be brought out. 'Quarter-litre bottles will not cure the illness,' he said."

"Indeed, when old Xap goes to cure, all the helpers, all the assistants must each be given half-litre bottles."

"But this time everyone got so drunk, even the patient, even the husband, that they got into a fight. The curer even struck his patient. Ha ha ha."

"Damn!"

"Yes, they had to settle the affair at the town hall. 'It's all your fault,' old Xap was told, 'for asking for so much liquor.'"

"So, you may say that he is a good curer if you like. But he has his little stupidities as well."

In chapter 3 I propose a loose working definition of gossip which circumscribes an area of activity (conversations between Zinacantecos about absent third parties) which I took as the object of study. I discovered that, although there is no native single-word equivalent of "gossip," Zinacantecos have clear ideas about gossiplike conversation, its dangers, and the considerations that motivate it. Moreover, I discovered that such conversation displays a recurrent structure, which I shall detail in chapter 4. Briefly, a gossip conversation typically consists of three segments: (*a*) an introduction, in which the protagonists are identified; (*b*) an account of the events, a story; and (*c*) a series of evaluative comments. My field research revolved around these components: I needed a systematic way to elicit gossip in a more or less natural form and to supply myself with the peripheral information which would render the stories intelligible.

My family and I set up housekeeping successively in two different Zinacanteco villages, first in a borrowed house in the ceremonial center and later as guests in a large house compound in the outlying hamlet of Nabenchauk (map 1, chap. 2). I made notes on all the conversation I heard in the ordinary course of life. (In fact, I kept "gossip notes" rather than ordinary field notes.) As I stayed longer in Zinacantan these notes became fuller. I learned to understand conversational Tzotzil better, and I began to know my neighbors and other notables by name. I supplemented these notes on naturally occurring gossip by asking my various acquaintances to provide the details of half-heard or misunderstood conversations.

I had hoped to work exclusively with talk which arose in natural contexts, but I found that my presence in conversations tended to inhibit gossip; that Zinacantecos who felt themselves responsible for me tended to avoid certain sorts of social contact with other Zinacantecos, in an effort to keep me invisible. To a large extent, Zinacantecos avoided topics of conversation they thought I would not understand; and without the expertise to ask appropriate questions, I remained in the dark. It was only when I had devised other means for expanding my sources of information that Zinacantecos began to treat me as an appreciative and knowledgeable interlocutor and began to include me in their natural gossip sessions.

In an effort to provide myself with background information about my neighbors in Zinacantan Center (where my family and I borrowed a house for a year), I recorded conversations with an experienced anthropological informant in which I asked about the residents of each house in the neighborhood. These conversations were especially notable in that they demonstrated the "interanimation" (Quine 1960, sec. 3) of Zinacanteco belief. The reputations of Jteklum residents were best described not only in terms of their past behavior, but with respect to items of belief (about the nature of the world, supernatural forces, etc.), theories of personality (about, for example, motivation and evil propensities), and causal arguments masked by obscure leaps of reasoning. Stories about particular people were more than gossip: they were rife with tidbits of cultural knowledge and lore which I had always imagined to be inaccessible.[9]

I supplemented these stories and checked on the consistency of reputation by collecting "gossip texts" about particular individuals living in Zinacantan Center. That is, I asked several literate Zinacantecos to select cards from a pile containing the names of individuals taken from my house census of the hamlet and to write stories about them, if any were known.

I still had found no satisfactory solution to the problems implied by the identification segment of gossip conversations. I had no means to penetrate the pathways Zinacantecos used to identify people in ordinary talk. I needed, at the very least, a list of all "focal individuals" in the *municipio*—all the people whose names are well known to every Zinacanteco; better still, I needed some list of individuals who were known (or could be described) not just by name but by cargo performance, civil office record, professions, and so forth—who could be identified by formulas that occur in gossip sessions. In short, I needed a *Who's Who* for Zinacantan.

With the encouragement and the financial and practical assistance of George A. Collier I undertook to create such a Who's Who during the summer of 1970. We reasoned that panels of Zinacantecos, selected to be representative and knowledgeable, could produce lists of the well-known people in each hamlet and then supplement these lists with basic identifying information about each person.

We found that it was indeed possible to elicit lists of names for each hamlet. The work had two stages. First our panels (of three to five Zinacanteco men) would respond to the question

Much'u mas x?ojtikinat tzkotol parajel?
"Who is best-known in each of the hamlets?"

When we had exhausted this question, we asked the panel to name people from the hamlet who fell into various categories (e.g., curers, moneylenders). (Cf. Appendix 2 for a complete description of the categories.) For each name we elicited a cargo history, a record in civil office, age, and some rudimentary genealogical information, and we noted short descriptions which occurred while the men on the panel tried to identify individuals among themselves. We realized that we had managed to capture the skeletal forms of reputation—that we were dealing with incipient gossip, as the men on the panel discussed each man at length, argued over his past performance, and joked about his nickname.[10]

The format of Who's Who eliciting sessions was amenable to gossip as well as to the census-taking we were doing. Therefore, I used the same panels of Zinacantecos to generate stories about each of the people on the Who's Who lists for three hamlets. The stories were tape-recorded and either edited or fully transcribed in Tzotzil. This was by far the richest source for gossip: I recorded and transcribed more than forty hours of such gossip sessions, replete with wild laughter, joking, and mocking as the panel considered the reputations and exploits of Who's Who notables. Losing its initial inhibition, the panel gradually warmed to the task. Professor Collier and I frequently withdrew from the conversation completely and let the men talk naturally. Conversations often continued long after we had left the workroom and turned off the tape recorder. Except that we asked the group to talk about one man at a time (a restriction we could not always enforce), the panel was self-directed: the participants decided what stories to tell one another. The dynamics of the group determined which one of a number of men who might know a particular story told it.

Armed with this meaty material, I myself became a formidable gossip partner when my family and I moved into the hamlet of Nabenchauk. I found myself in the embarrassing position of knowing about a person's dirty linen when I did not even know his or her face. But throughout the daily routine of life in the house compound I found myself able to follow the fragments of stories, the veiled allusions, the secret jokes about hamlet neighbors. Our family no longer assumed us to be uninformed and thus suspended the protective censorship we had noticed earlier during our stay in Zinacantan. (In fact, periodic absences from the village often meant that my information about the doings of its residents was dated, so that our hosts' confidence in our knowledge-ability was often unjustified.) They merely appended to disclosures about their neighbors certain cautionary instructions to insure that I not blurt out what I knew to the wrong person.

The stories I collected from these different sources form the basis of this book. When I refer to "Zinacanteco gossip" I mean this varied corpus. When I speak of "ordinary usage" or "ordinary conversation" I mean occurrences of words or phrases transcribed from natural speech. Zinacantecos converse, exchange information, and sharpen their cultural expertise in a variety of situations which I characterize as "behind" or "inside the fence," *ta yut mok*—that is, within the confines of the house compound, in private, and sheltered from unwanted ears. I use "gossip" as a convenient and suggestive gloss for conversation in such circumstances—a gloss which must not obscure the fact that stories people tell about their neighbors may go well beyond what we should be inclined to call "gossip" in ordinary English usage.

It is true that not all that can be learned from gossip can be learned from what I heard. During my time in Zinacantan I participated in and overheard a good deal of gossip, but my corpus may well not be representative. It is, at least, *genuine*. It preserves natural interactive constraints on talk. And it exposes the ordinary ambivalence toward gossiping: an uneasiness about saying nasty things, coupled with an eagerness to be entertained and entertaining. Finally, as I hope to show, this corpus of gossip reveals a good deal about Zinacantecos and their exploits.

I have arranged my argument to proceed from some general ethnographic background (chap. 2) to a more detailed look at what gossip is in Zinacantan (chap. 3) and how gossip interactions are organized (chap. 4). I then catalog the subject matter of Zinacanteco gossip (chap. 5), with particular attention to the aspect of public identity that derives from performance in the religious hierarchy (chap. 6) and to the lexical resources Zinacantecos have at their disposal for describing and evaluating their neighbors (chap. 7). In the final two chapters I consider wider issues surrounding "cultural rules," their relation to action, and their place in ethnographic description. Throughout I have found it illuminating to proceed from particular examples (of gossip, conversation, or Tzotzil usage)—all inextricably rooted in an ethnographic context—to reflect on the nature of the surrounding rules, the ideational and semiotic structure within which people act.

Down the path someone spotted a young man named Xun, whose reputation as a drunkard made everyone anxious to be on his way.

"If you meet him drunk on the path, he has no mercy. He won't listen to what you say, that Xun."

"He doesn't understand what you say; you're right. If he's just a bit tight when you meet him on the path—*puta*, 'Let's go, let's go,' he'll say. You will be forced to drink."

"But doesn't he get angry?"

"No, no. He'll just say, 'Let's go have a little soft drink.' "

"He's good-natured."

"But he doesn't bother to ask if you're in a hurry to get someplace. . . . (Ha ha ha.)"

"No, he's good-hearted. (Ha ha ha.)"

"If you find yourself in a hurry to get somewhere and you see him coming the best thing to do is hide. . . ."

". . . or run away."

And with that, the various men went on about their business.

The Ethnographic Context

Te to jk'opon jbatik ti bu jnup jbatike.
"We'll talk again wherever we happen to meet."

2

The municipality of San Lorenzo Zinacantan lies along a ridge and adjacent valley in the highlands of the State of Chiapas, in southeast Mexico. Zinacantan lies slightly to the west of the ladino (Spanish-speaking) town of San Cristóbal de las Casas, and just to the south of Chamula, another Indian community whose inhabitants, like Zinacantecos, speak the Mayan language Tzotzil. The *municipio* lies for the most part at an altitude varying from 2,100 to 2,500 meters (Vogt 1969, p. 4); the weather is therefore cool. The summers are rainy and damp; the winters are dry, warm in the day and frosty at night, with a clear sky marred only by a haze of smoke during the months when fields are burned off in preparation for planting.

Zinacantan is composed of hamlets scattered through the municipal territory, with a ceremonial and political center, or Jteklum, at its northeastern corner (see map 1). The political and social factors which govern settlement contribute definitely to a Zincanteco's conversational *resources*: the people he has to gossip with, the people he knows well enough to gossip about, and the things he has to say about them.

Vogt describes hamlets as "subdivided into three basic social units of ascending size: the domestic group living in one or more houses in a compound; the SNA, consisting of two or more domestic groups; and the waterhole group, composed of two or more SNAS" (1969, p. 127). A man's domestic group includes the people he commonly eats with—with whom he shares a house com-

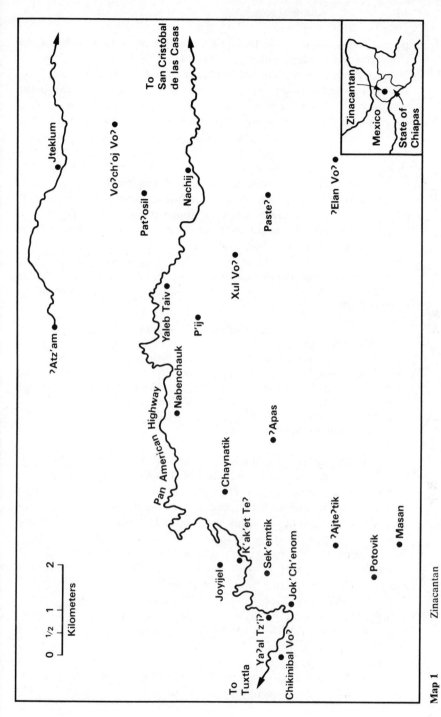

Map 1   Zinacantan

pound and a house cross, the symbolic point of entry to a house for ritual functions (Vogt 1969, pp. 127–28).

At a given moment a household may include a man, his wife, and their unmarried children. He may share his house, or at least his house compound, with his youngest son after marriage; and as he grows older he retires as the central figure of the domestic unit. The household thus defines the smallest pool of shared information. The recipient of an old man's knowledge of the past is likely to be a son or grandson who lives in the same domestic unit. And the household creates a continuous context for talk. People perform domestic chores, wash, and farm most comfortably within the privacy of their house compound—*ta yut mok* ("inside the fence"). Here conversation can proceed in confidence. At mealtime a family commonly exchanges the day's information and discusses the doings of neighbors and kin.

I was sitting by the fire at dinnertime with Old Petul. His daughters had just returned with jugs of water which they had filled near the town hall.

"Father, Xun is at the town hall. He is drunk and shouting."
"Your brother Xun?"
"Yes. They say he fought with Mikel from the corner store."
"They both had mud on their clothes."
"How stupid! That wife of his is ruining him. She's just playing with his money. He told me that she had encouraged him to buy twelve beers there drinking with his friends."
"Yes, she is leading him wrong."

The larger "units" of a hamlet, the *sna* and the waterhole group, are counters in a geographical code which Zincantecos employ to map the *municipio*.[1] Often houses cluster in such a way that their location may be labeled by the name of the predominant family in the cluster. Thus an *area* at the edge of the valley of Zinacantan Center is known as *sna Muchiketik* (the home of the Muchiks), though men from other families live there or nearby (particularly sons-in-law living uxorilocally).

Similarly, groups of houses whose inhabitants draw water from a common waterhole form a "waterhole group" named after the waterhole itself. For the more dispersed hamlets these waterhole names serve to identify the significant locales in which people live. (Zinacantecos sometimes use the Spanish word *lugar* ["place"] to describe the area identified by a waterhole name.) Vogt (1969) describes various ritual activities based on these groupings.

In fact, natural landmarks (trees, rocks, notable formations) mark the map almost as frequently as do house groups or waterholes. The

latter are transitory, in any case, as families move from one site to
another (one fifty-year-old acquaintance of mine has lived in about ten
different houses in four distinct locations during his life) and as they
dig or affiliate themselves with new waterholes.[2] A hamlet like Nabenchauk, where my family and I lived, falls into several natural areas (the
"first curve" in the road, the ridge "overlooking low country," the "central water tank," etc.), each of which contains several house groups,
some notable landmarks.

In conversation a man may be asked about the doings of other people
in his neighborhood—in his *sna*, if he lives in one, or in his waterhole
group—though he is not expected to be as well informed about those
living farther away.

> "What about Petul? Does he have any faults?"
> "Eh, I haven't heard anything."
> "What do you mean? Why haven't you heard anything? *You* are
> his neighbor, but we know nothing about him, living far away as we
> do. But what do people who live nearby say about him?"
> "Well, just that he is an ugly drunk, that he beats his wife—treats
> her just like a *burro*."
> "Ha ha ha. There, you see. . . ."
> "Ha ha ha. Perhaps you've given the wife a few blows yourself."

The hamlet, or *paraje*, in some cases represents a unit well defined
both geographically and politically, grouping together several waterhole
groups. In other cases, hamlet "boundaries" split waterhole groups, and
living "in" a hamlet represents only an affiliation with certain institutions such as tax rolls or a school committee.[3] Moreover, there is considerable variation between hamlets in density of settlement. These
factors complicate the relationship between one's hamlet of residence
and the pool of neighbors about whom one can gossip. A man from
Nabenchauk—a rather compactly settled *paraje* with a tightly focused
political, social, and ceremonial life—will be likely to know about nearly
everyone else in Nabenchauk, whereas a man from the section of Nachij
called ʔAvan Chʼen may be better versed on the doings of his nearby
neighbors from the hamlet of Pasteʔ than those of his hamlet-mates from
the opposite end of Nachij.[4]

Geographical and historical considerations suggest further divisions
of Zinacantan above the hamlet level. George Collier (personal communication) reported disproportionately frequent ties of ritual kinship
(*compadrazgo*) between certain hamlets, indicating a higher-level grouping of "superhamlets" as shown on map 2. The routing of important
roads through the municipal territory perhaps accounts best for these

Map 2   "Superhamlets" of Zinacantan

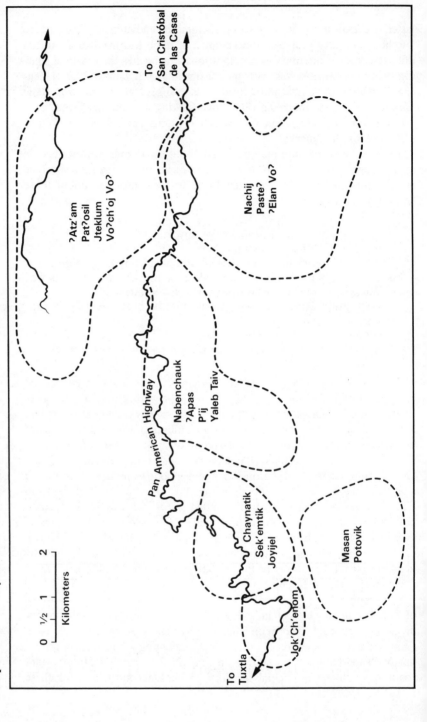

close affiliations between *parajes*. Zinacantan Center (Jteklum) and ?Atz'am both lie on the old main road from Tuxtla to San Cristóbal. Nabenchauk and ?Apas share a common access point to the Pan-American highway—the major paved road linking highland Chiapas to the rest of Mexico, linking the *municipio* of Zinacantan to markets in San Cristóbal and Tuxtla and to lowland cornfields—as do, for example, Nachij, Paste?, and ?Elan Vo?.

People in Nabenchauk use these superhamlets in a kind of geographical shorthand. The ceremonial center and its surrounding hamlets are often simply called ?Ak'ol ("higher"), whereas hamlets to the west down the mountains are often called collectively ?Olon ("lower") or Chobtik ("cornfields")—a reference to the reputation of these warmer areas as good corn-growing lands.

Moreover, these larger divisions of the *municipio* seem roughly to coincide with *gossip areas*. A man from Nabenchauk could be expected to know a good deal about his neighbors in ?Apas. A resident of Nachij might take me aside to dispute an account of events offered by a man from Paste?, and so on. Gossip seems to follow the same paths that men walk (or ride).

Given this expanded notion of "area" within Zinacantan, I agree with Jane Collier:

> Individuals in Zinacantan appear to be closely tied to a single area. Few people move from one hamlet to another, and marriage partners are usually found among neighbors. Zinacanteco women know few people beyond their own kin and close neighbors, but men have opportunities to form a wider circle of acquaintances. Young boys, like the women, know few people, but as they grow older and serve in the religious hierarchy, they meet office holders from other hamlets, while a politically active man can participate with other hamlet leaders in making community-wide decisions. [1973, p. 7]

In the rest of this chapter I shall enumerate institutions which allow Zinacanteco men to extend their circles of gossip.[5]

Just as most of a Zinacanteco's life revolves around corn, corn provides the focus for much of his contact with others. A casual visitor to San Cristóbal could not fail to notice circles of Zinacanteco men near the market, often near the corn-selling stalls, weaving hats and talking prices and politics. But selling corn gives less opportunity for conversation and joking than does growing corn. Work in the cornfields is grueling, especially during the long weeks of weeding in wet season; yet Zinacantecos look forward to these periods of labor.

> "I want to learn how people talk together, how they joke with one another." [Conversation with a *compadre*]

"Ah, but compadre, if you want to hear the best gossip, the best joking—then you must go where we work, in Hot Country, in our cornfields. When we have finished work late in the day, we eat. That is when the real joking starts. Then people have verbal duels; they mock each other. People will say whatever comes into their heads; they will make lewd jokes. It is too much!"

Farming groups are usually composed of kin, but friends and ritual kinsmen may often share in the cultivation of rented plots. As elsewhere in Latin America, Zinacantecos acquire *compadres* by asking other Zinacantecos to become godparents to their children (see Vogt, 1969, pp. 230–39). Friends and *compadres* often lend each other money and associate at fiestas, drinking together and amusing each other with conversation.

When work in the cornfields slackens during the winter many Zinacantecos seek work on government road-building and agricultural projects. Robert M. Laughlin has remarked to me that myths and other stories are likely to be recounted in the context of such roadwork. Similarly, in recent road-building projects within Zinacantan, the *j'abtel ta be* ("workers on the road") are notorious gossips, whose sharp eyes and tongues are to be avoided.

These days young men spend increasing portions of their time in wage labor, often far from Zinacantan. The fifteen-year-old son in the family with whom I lived had a one-year contract for work with a lowland road crew and was home only on weekends. His brothers helped his father with corn cultivation, and he brought home cash wages. His circle of acquaintances at home was severely restricted, while the number of non-Zinacantecos—both Indian and ladino—he knew was unusually large.

The religious calendar and the system of religious cargo positions which supports it multiplies a Zinacanteco's opportunities to widen his circle of friends and his store of knowledge about other people. There are four hierarchical levels of cargoholders, or *jpas ʔabtel* ("work-doers"); the "work" they perform is a year of service to a particular saint—caring for the saint's image through regular ceremonies and holding calendrical church fiestas. A man serves one year at the lowest level, then progresses through higher levels of ritual "work" as he gradually accumulates sufficient resources (Cancian 1965). Passing through all four levels of the system represents the pinnacle of traditional success; only older men who have enjoyed considerable wealth attain the status of *pasaro* ("one who has passed").[6]

Entering the cargo system brings a man into close contact with men from other hamlets and of various ages. Senior cargoholders and their formal ritual advisers are often respected powerful older men, while cargoholders on intermediate levels are generally men with considerable economic success. At the lower cargo levels, and serving in the capacity of helpers, scribes, *sacristanes*, and so forth, are young men with ambitions for success through traditional religious service.

Performance in the ritual hierarchy is one of the most frequent topics of conversation in Zinacantan. Men are constantly calculating a cargoholder's outlay of money and reexamining the schedule of incoming and outgoing offices. Other indexes of personal ability and success are related through conversation to cargo performance.

"Didn't old Maryan spend 12,000 pesos in his cargo?"
"Yes, but they say he owes 25,000 to the bank in Tuxtla."
"30,000 I heard."
"Yes, he may be rich, but they say it was from all his sons that he got that way. They do the work. The old man himself doesn't work at all anymore."
"What about old Petul, the musician?"
"People say that he also doesn't work much himself. He just passes cargos through the labor of his daughters. Perhaps it is from selling tortillas that he passes his cargos—so some people say. Or maybe from selling feathered wedding gowns. But he hasn't ever planted much corn—just one *almud*, or perhaps two."

Men take pride in their mastery of correct procedures and orthodox behavior in cargos. They must learn to pray, sing, and joke.

"But let me tell you, that ʔAlperes Trinirat just cannot joke. He doesn't know how to do it."
"*Kere.*"
"If you throw him a challenge, an insult, he doesn't know what to respond. He just says 'hmmm, hmmm' and hides his head in his kerchief."
"Ha ha ha. He just bows his head."
"When I was *ʔalperes*, the musicians wept when I left my year in office. Maryan, the musician, said to me. 'It will not be the same without you here to joke with us.' "

Political activities open to a Zinacanteco man further widen his knowledge of other Zinacantecos and their doings. Men gain political influence in Zinacantan by controlling important decisions, through skill at dealing with outside forces, or both. Thus, each hamlet has elders "known for their wisdom in settling conflicts, who can be approached by a person involved in a dispute" (J. Collier 1973, p. 26). It is easy to discover the names of such powerful men in each hamlet and to identify them with factional groups: to identify them, that is, as decision-makers on questions important to the hamlet and *municipio*. Moreover,

people remember past political leaders and give vivid accounts of the
disputes in which they were involved and the alignments of power.

"*Puta*, there was a big fight over it; they made a lot of trouble over
it. . . ."
"Hiiii, that was a long time ago."
"They grabbed old man Okotz. They even managed to arrest old
Sarate and old Chep Krus—that was when he was *presidente*, or
maybe treasurer—I've forgotten which. *Puta*, they tied him up anyway. Soldiers went to his house. And they brought out the money, too;
the embezzled money was found in his house. . . ."
"Yes, you're right, that's the way I heard it."
". . . it was soldiers who found the money and recovered it. Any-
way, as for old man Okotz—he fled; old man Sarate also fled. They
ran off into the woods to sleep, they couldn't sleep at home anymore."
"Who brought the accusations?"
"Well the ones who started the trouble were that old Petul Tzu, old
Papyan Chayna, old Maryan Xantis and his brother Palas, as well as
old Antun Okotz. They were the real leaders; they were behind it all.
But they had their men, their supporters. . . ."
"Sure, probably lots of them."

Mexican law provides for the existence of certain civil officials to
serve three-year terms at the town hall, the *cabildo*, in Jteklum and
peripherally in the *agencias* or hamlet-level governments. Though they
have other duties as well, these officials—chief of whom is the *presidente*
—are most often called upon to decide questions of a certain gravity
(e.g., murder accusations) or to rule on disputes which have not been
resolved by hamlet elders. Serving in such a civil office, most anthropologists have argued, does not in itself lend prestige and political power;
but such people are considered to have become skillful at settling disputes and may therefore be asked to help settle disputes after their terms
have expired (J. Collier 1973, chap. 1).

"That's just the way it is: when a man has a civil office people
slander him behind his back. There are always two sides."
"That's right."
"One side likes him if he has agreed with what they want. The
other side, with whom the *agente* doesn't concur, will say, 'See, he's
no good.' "
"But there can only be one side for whom the quarrel turns out
well. For the others it doesn't go so well. They come out the
losers. . . ."
"What people want is always to get to the town hall first; they want
whoever is going to settle the affair to listen to them first, so that they
won't be made to look at fault."

"That's what they want. But when the official assigns guilt equally to both parties, even if one party has spoken first—well, then they say he's good for nothing."

"They're annoyed."

" 'It didn't do any good, my talking to him, my giving him good strong rum,' they say. 'He didn't settle the dispute for me,' they say."

"But it's because the *agente* hasn't favored them. Instead he has settled the dispute evenly."

Some ambitious Zinacantecos acquire power and influence outside the schedule of religious and civil offices. This is often a matter of learning to manipulate or extract advantage from non-Zinacanteco institutions. Just as post-Conquest *naguatlatos* (native translators) used their linguistic skills and familiarity with Spanish ways for power and gain (Heath 1972), in recent times politically strong Zinacantecos have been those men able to accommodate themselves to ladino authorities. Notably, since the Revolution, control of land reform under *ejido* laws has been the basis of political power. The most recent clear political boss on a *municipio*wide scale came to control Zinacantan's *ejido* through a unique series of circumstances. His power stemmed not only from his control of the land itself, but from the network of subordinate *ejido* officials upon whom he could count for support in other issues (Vogt 1969, p. 286). More recently a man rose to political prominence in ?Apas and Nabenchauk by heading a movement to obtain a new tract of lowland cornfields under present *ejido* laws. He gained prestige (as well as the hostility of some of his seniors) by rapid progress through the cargo system; but he took advantage of his knowledge of Spanish and personal charisma to manipulate ladino authorities with skill and persistence.[7]

There is a small group of men who are reputed to be clever representatives before ladino courts, a class of Zinacanteco lawyers. These men are fluent in Spanish, and they have experience in confronting ladino authorities. Such men are in increasing demand as Zinacantecos become aware of the discrepancies between traditional rules of dispute settlement and Mexican law—and try to exploit these discrepancies to their own advantage (Cf. J. Collier 1973, pp. 239ff.). Mexican authorities have only recently come to suspect these legal "brokers" (W. Freeman 1974).

"But that is really evil, to charge such interest on a loan. If someone borrows one hundred pesos, the interest soon reaches one hundred, and first he must pay off the first one hundred pesos he received."

"The principal."

"Then the one hundred pesos of interest remain, and that amount in turn gathers new interest."
"It doesn't end."
"The years go by. . . ."
"If someone is stupid he will lose his lands that way."
"Or perhaps he will have to sell his children. . . ."
"Or his horse will be sold. . . ."
"Yes, but that's only for those who aren't clever. The one who knows how will come into San Cristóbal; he'll hire a lawyer and avoid paying."
"It doesn't occur to all of us, you see, to do that. All we can think of is the jail waiting for us in Jteklum."
"That's right: it's off to jail for us stupid ones."

As men amass supporters and learn to manipulate the various agencies of coercion—from the hamlet elder to the San Cristóbal court—factional arguments arise over a broad range of specific issues: road placement, government projects, communal labor, and so forth (cf. Rush 1971). It is these factional disputes, as well as the domestic fights and cases of violence made public at open hearings at the town hall, that provide the juiciest input to the gossip stream in Zinacantan.[8]

"What's happening to Antun and his wife?"
"I don't know. Is anything?"
"I saw him standing at the *cabildo* this morning, but I didn't hear what was going on."
"Here comes Maryan. Let's ask him. He's always hanging around the town hall." [Conversation overheard on path]

The day-to-day flow of talk in the hamlet where my family and I lived reflected these various sources generating and radiating gossip. Even though the town hall where disputes were settled was in a distant part of the village, by the end of the day accounts of virtually every case had filtered back to the compound. Women on routine errands were the vehicles of this talk. Gathering firewood, tending sheep, carrying boiled corn to the mill to be ground into tortilla dough, women set aside time to exchange news with their friends and cousins. In our household, much gossip originated with a cousin whose father held a civil office at the municipal town hall and who spent two weeks out of every month hearing court disputes. The daughter was a much sought-after companion, always ready with some fresh scandal.

Men in the compound made somewhat more distant forays into the world and accordingly brought home more esoteric news, from other hamlets, from San Cristóbal, from the lowlands. During the several days of community labor to clear roads directly after the Fiesta of Todos

Santos, all the men of the hamlet gathered together into work gangs and caught up on recent events between swings of machete and hoe. But outside of such infrequent occasions of public work, or sporadic visits to other hamlets, or chance encounters on the path, men did not have regular opportunities for gathering rumor and gossip.

Instead, people in the house compound kept a constant watch for the doings of their neighbors. At least one pair of eyes was constantly focused on the main paths near the house, ready to spot and identify passersby, and their cargos or companions, and to prompt speculation about their business. A gathering of people, an untoward noise, was excuse enough to dispatch a young boy, or, lacking that, a girl or young woman as a spy to find out what was going on.

> A funeral passes: "Who was the dead girl? I didn't
> know Old Papyan had another daughter."
> A drunk shouts on the path: "Has Lol finally been
> kicked out by his wife?"

And all this with a conspiratorial air, dripping with secrecy and muffled giggles: for even in such a compactly settled hamlet, where most neighbors are also kin, people in our compound maintained only very limited friendly contacts with other households. Of some ten other households of aunts and uncles, open, regular contacts were maintained with only two. People were interested in the others, but acquired their information only through espionage.

The corollary is privacy and circumspection at home. Members of the family were obsessed with secrecy, constantly running to hide when strangers appeared, evasive and hedging when forced to talk to outsiders, always apprehensive lest I, a clumsy incompetent, might reveal too much about the family's doings.

> "Is Xun Tontik going to pay you back the money he owes you?"
> "Well, yes, he promised to give me corn."
> "When?"
> "He says he doesn't have enough corn. He says his harvest was poor."
> "Ah, but is he telling you the truth? Yesterday I saw him leaving for Tuxtla with two big bags to sell."
> "Well, he says he can give me half in corn, half in cash."
> "Ah, in that case, won't you sell me one bag of the corn he gives you? I have almost none left, and I won't finish my harvest for another month."
> "Um."
> "And try to get him to give you all he owes in corn. Tell him that you have run out. Tell him that you need corn to feed your animals. But don't say anything to him about your selling some corn to me."

The Domain of Gossip

*Pero mi yech xal ʔo mi
loʔil no van?*
"But is he telling the truth,
or is it just gossip?"

3

It will be apparent that what I am calling "gossip" in this book includes a somewhat wider conversational realm than one might ordinarily understand from the word. From all the talk I heard in Zinacantan, I selected for particular attention conversations about absent third parties.[1] I hypothesized that such conversation would not be open: that it would neither range over all subjects nor dwell on all actions. Conversation has its own rules: not all facts are worth repeating; not all speculation is (or can be) mouthed. Or at least an audience will not be interested in every disclosure. Thus I was willing at the beginning to take as my subject (as "gossip in Zinacantan") all conversation of the following form: A tells B about an absent C. Moreover, I gathered any information which rendered such conversation intelligible to its participants. Gossip rests on reputation. And in English it leaks into "spreading news" at one end and "slander" at the other. I have included in the study of gossip elements of news, report, slander, libel, ridicule, insult, defamation, and malicious and innocent gossip.[2] In my discussion I use the word "gossip" as a convenient gloss to label a wide range of conversational phenomena.

Two issues arise from this usage. First, a certain ethno-scientific tradition seems to require that I show that "gossip" labels some coherent class of phenomena in the Zinacanteco scheme of things. When I speak of "gossip in Zinacantan," am I talking about an activity that Zinacantecos recognize? Second, calling various sorts of Zinacanteco conversation "gossip," even if the term is

loosely applied, suggests that Zinacantecos do something that we ourselves should recognize as gossiplike; it suggests, further, that Zinacantecos feel about such activity what we might feel: nervous and anxious,
but fascinated—doubtful about the propriety of talking behind someone's back, but secretly eager to hear some deliciously awful tidbit; and
so on.

Rather than argue for the universality of gossip (in some well-defined
sense), I shall concern myself in this chapter with Zinacanteco native
theorizing about the nature of talk about one's neighbors and country-
men. Zinacantecos do recognize a domain of verbal behavior that resembles gossiping. Despite the fact that no Tzotzil word is adequately
glossed "gossip," a considerable body of native speculation and theory
surrounds the sort of conversation I have described above. This constitutes what we might well call a Zinacanteco theory of gossip. In this
chapter I shall concentrate on native intuitions regarding these matters
and avoid the thorny and fruitless search for a monoleximic domain
label, for a neat taxonomy, for an unambiguous eliciting frame, and for
Gossip.[3]

Various ethnographers have offered taxonomies of verbal behavior
or verbal genres in Tzotzil. The results, however, are disconcertingly
indecisive. (In Appendix 1 I present some of these taxonomies in detail.) It seems unlikely that a single hierarchical lexical structure is
adequate to characterize Zinacanteco conceptualization of verbal behavior. A diagnostic test is the possibility of using labels from tree-
diagram nodes to initiate further eliciting. Will a word which seems to
correspond to "gossip" prompt a Zinacanteco to gossip? Will a phrase
glossed as "myth" encourage a storyteller to tell the desired sorts of
stories? Wasserstrom (1970) had little success:

"I tried to elicit tales concerning the Virgen del Rosario using the
question,

Mi ?oy ?antivo k'op skwenta jch'ulme?tik rosario?
Is there a story about the Virgen del Rosario?

Much to my surprise, I often had difficulty in conveying to informants
my desire to hear such a story. Not only was this fact due to the
artificiality of contrived eliciting situations (I was invariably more
successful when I went to the spot at which something had happened
and then asked about it), but also I believe that the domain of
?antivo k'op is not well-defined in the minds of Zinacantecos. Thus I
was better understood by some informants when I asked the simple
question,

Mi ?oy k'opetik skwenta . . . ?
Are there words about . . . ?" [p. 27; orthography altered]

Certain nominal expressions in Tzotzil suggest to otherwise reluctant Zinacantecos stories which might legitimately be called gossip. However, a taxonomy based on nouns fails to exploit the rich vocabulary of verbs which denote activities that resemble gossiping. These activities are grouped into a coherent domain by a body of theory about the origin and consequences of conversation about one's neighbors. This theory is implicit in language; talk about talk draws heavily on the grammatical and semantic resources of Tzotzil. The semantic properties of key expressions having to do with talk, stories about others, truth, and intent are evidence for the existence of a Zinacanteco conceptual domain even where more ordinary lexical structure is absent.

The two relevant Tzotzil noun roots for speech, -*k'op* ("word") and -*lo'il* ("speech") combine with a number of affixes to form stems from other surface structure "word classes"; they co-occur with other nouns and verbs in patterned contexts. In the examples that follow, all drawn directly from actual ordinary speech, I mean to present not a semantic analysis of the terms but rather data enough to lead the reader to an understanding of this segment of Tzotzil vocabulary.[4]

Consider first the root -*lo'il*, which means "talk" or "conversation." Ordinary usage includes the following forms and contexts:

1.   j-koj *lo'il*
          "one *story*"

Lo'iletik are discrete and can be counted; in Tzotzil the same numeral classifier (cf. Berlin 1968; Haviland 1970*a*) is used to count "stories" as is used to count steps, layers, curing ceremonies, levels in the religious hierarchy, songs, floors of a building, and crimes. When someone says in the midst of a discussion of another person's reputation

2.   ʔOy ʔotro jkoj *lo'il* ikaʔi . . .
          "I've heard yet another *story* [about him]. . . ."

he conjures the image of piling one story on another.

3.   Vinajem *lo'il*.
          "The *story* is apparent."

4.   Mu xa k'usi k'op yilel pero syempre ilok' *lo'il*.
          "It seemed that there was no longer anything wrong, but the *story* came out anyway."

When *lo'il* occurs with certain intransitive stems, notably -*vinaj* ("be apparent, visible, audible") or -*lok'* ("exit from, leave, go out"), it implies a story which is liable to become public, and hence to induce scandal: scandalous gossip.

5.   Lek yilel tzeʔej loʔilik yaʔel chak k'u chaʔal liʔ chotolotik.
"It seemed just like friendly *conversation*, just as we are having sitting here."

6.   Mu noʔox *loʔil*-k'opuk.
"It wasn't just ordinary [innocent] *conversation*."

The word *loʔil* can express the quality of a conversation. In (5), the word *tzeʔej* ("laughing") indicates talk that is all smiles, friendly: some men accosted another on the path and, while appearing to engage him in friendly conversation, murdered him. In (6), two enemies meet each other; one tries to act naturally. The other immediately picks a fight, unwilling to ignore their enmity; he will not allow their meeting just to be ordinary *loʔil k'op*.

7.   Tztzak sbaik ta *loʔil*.
"They engaged each other in *conversation*."

8.   Ilik s*loʔi*lik.
"A *conversation* arose between them."

9.   Mu xbak', muʔnuk stak' *loʔil*, muʔnuk stzeʔin, te nijil.
"He doesn't make a sound, he doesn't answer *when you talk to him*, he doesn't laugh; he just sits with bowed head."

One can *-tzak* ("grab") another in conversation, often to initiate some joking sequence. Or such conversation can just *-lik* ("arise") naturally. But it is considered antisocial and rude not to respond to invitations to friendly talk.

10.   Lek yamiko sbaik ch*loʔi*lajik.
"They *converse* just like friends."

In fact, the best sign of a good nature is the ability to carry on conversation, to *-loʔilaj*, and to avoid

11.   pukuj x*loʔi*laj
"*speaking* ill-temperedly."

Loʔil contrasts with adjectives *melel* ("true, right") and *yech* ("true, so, thus") in the following interesting way:

12.   Muʔnuk *loʔil*uk yuʔun chkal ta abail ta asatil.
"This is not just *talk*, for I'll tell you to your face. . . ."

13.   Mi yech van; mi *loʔil* no van.
"But is it true? But is it just *talk*?"

14.   Ta melel kere.
"Boy, that's the truth!"

15.   Mu *lo*ʔ*il*uk kaʔuktik.
             "That's not just *hearsay*, you're right."

When activated by such a contrast, *lo*ʔ*il* clearly has the sense of simple hearsay, of stories and rumors that are not verified.[5]

Finally, there is a transitive stem formed by adding the modestly productive suffix *-ta* to form *-lo*ʔ*ilta*. Consider the following examples of transitive stems formed with *-ta*.

ʔ*anil*	*-anilta*
"race, running"	"make run"
ʔ*ov*	*-apta*
"shouting"	"shout at"
*tzo*ʔ	*-tza*ʔ*ta*
"excrement"	"shit on"
chikil	*-chikilta*
"a tickle, ticklishness"	"tickle"
pom	*-pamta*
"incense"	"cense"
xuk'um	*-xuk'umta*
"elbow"	"elbow"
*lo*ʔ*il*	*-lo*ʔ*ilta*
"story, conversation"	"tell stories about, gossip about"

To *lo*ʔ*ilta-* someone is to tell a story in which he is involved, usually to his disadvantage.[6]

16.   Yuʔnan ʔilbil, k'u ma chaʔal ti x*lo*ʔ*il*taat.
             "It is probably the case that he was seen [doing it];
             otherwise why would he be *reputed* [to have done it]?"

17.   I*lo*ʔ*il*tabat stzebal.
             "He had *stories told* on his sister."

This is clearly a verb which would be felicitously rendered "gossip" in English; moreover, it is accompanied by the same connotations of sneakiness, enjoyment at another's discomfort, behind-the-back snideness, and so forth, that we associate with gossip—even as we enjoy it. In fact, in ritual couplets[7] *lo*ʔ*ilta* is paired with *laban* ("mock"):

18.   Mu jk'an cha*lo*ʔ*il*taon, mu jk'an chalabanon.
             "I do not wish you to *slander* me, I do not wish you to
             ridicule me."

From *-lo*ʔ*ilta* comes the deverbal noun *-lo*ʔ*iltael*, which is always possessed, and which translates as "the gossip about _____" or "what is said about _____."

19.   Stalel li buch'u ʔo yabtel yech ʔo sloʔiltael.
           "That's the way it is with people in [civil] office: there is
           always *gossip* about them."
20.   K'al tana mu xpaj sloʔiltael.
           "And ever since then the *gossip* about him hasn't ceased."

One is often able to elicit gossip in Zinacantan by asking with regard to
a specific person whether there are sloʔiltael ("stories about him"). Such
a question prods Zinacantecos to recount those parts of a man's reputation that would be appropriate "stories" to "tell on" him—that is, to
ridicule him with. In natural gossip contexts, however, conversation
begins not with particular individuals but with particular noteworthy
events, with unusual behavior. The resulting gossip accrues to individual
reputation and is subject to recall later—for example, when the anthropologist asks about it.

To summarize these semantic properties of loʔil:

a.   loʔil
           represents a discrete story, which can be known or not
           known, which can remain hidden or suddenly become
           public (examples 1–4);
b.   loʔil
           stands for friendly conversation and can be used to
           emphasize the quality of an interaction (5–11).
c.   In certain contexts
           loʔil
           can represent the extreme of unverified (and dangerous)
           hearsay, as opposed to verified truth (12–15); and
           finally
d.   loʔilta
           labels storytelling activity which is conceptually related
           to ridicule, slander, and gossip (16–20).

The root k'op has more complicated properties. Laughlin (1975, p.
196) gives the following formidable gloss:

           k'op:
           "word, language, affair, matter, situation,
           argument, dispute, war, curing ceremony."

Jane Collier (1973, pp. 94ff.) discusses the notion of k'op as legal dispute, court case, or argument presented for settlement to various hamlet
or municipal authorities. A plaintiff can saʔ ("search for") such a dispute until it reaches a conclusion:

           Ilaj k'op.
           "The *dispute* ended."

Imeltzaj *k'op.*
"The *dispute* was settled."

Similarly, the ordinary verbs derived from the root, *-k'opon* ("talk to") and *-k'opoj* ("talk, speak"), have a formal sense.

21.   Ba s*k'opon* preserente.
             "He went to *petition* the presidente."
22.   Sna⁷ x*k'opoj*, lek xtojob ta *k'opojel.*
             "He can *speak*, he can successfully *speak* for one [as a lawyer]."

K'op—as dispute—can "be eased," "appear and become public," "arise," "worsen," "be multiplied," "cool off"; and it is possible to "hush up," "settle," "take responsibility for," "accuse another of responsibility for," and "exaggerate the seriousness of" such disputes.[8] The root *k'op* probably occurs most commonly in ordinary speech to indicate this sort of legal dispute. By contrast with *lo⁷il* it suggests formal or public language (see Appendix 1).

Certain other contexts are of more immediate interest.

23.   Isko⁷oltasbe sba *sk'op.*
             "They agreed on the same *story.*"
24.   Ko⁷ol *sk'op*ik.
             "They are in *agreement*; they share the same *position.*"
25.   Ik'ejp'uj *sk'op*, isok xa ye.
             "His *word* went astray; he made a slip [he changed his story]."

One's "word" is conceived as one's position on a matter, one's story. Zinacantecos are aware that it is possible to manipulate such stories. *K'op* appears in several couplets with a related meaning.

26.   Vo⁷ot ⁷onox ta apwersa vo⁷ot ⁷onox ta a*k'op* li x⁷elan inupun li jtzebe.
             "It was at your demand, at your *urging* that my daughter got married as she did."
27.   Mu⁷yuk a*k'op* mu⁷yuk arason. [Laughlin 1975, p. 96]
             "You have nothing to *say*, you have no thoughts."
28.   Muk' bu s*k'op* muk' bu smantal.
             "He has no *word*, he has no authority."

In each of these couplets, *k'op* represents the verbal element in some decision. In (26), it is a matter of *pwersa* ("force") and argumentation; in (28) a child goes wrong because a parent fails to exercise his *mantal* ("authority") and his spoken *k'op*. And in (27) someone is criticized for failing to speak up and exercise his *rason* ("reason") in suggesting a course of action. In each of these examples *k'op* appears in possessed form: someone's *k'op* is his verbal contribution to an argument, an inquiry, or a decision.

I remark above that conversation allows social interaction in Zinacantan to proceed. The man who cannot or will not talk with his fellows is considered antisocial as well as ill-tempered.

29.   Mi ja'uk s*k'opon* jp'eluk i stote.[9]
           "He didn't even *say* a single word to his father."

30.   Yu'van xaval ti 'o jset'uk xchikin xa*k'opon*.
           "Don't try to tell us that he'll lend you the slightest ear
           when you try to *talk* to him."

31.   Lek 'amiko j*k'opon* jba jchi'uk.
           "I *get along/talk* with him like a friend."

Example (29) concerns a son, estranged from his father, who no longer accords his father even minimal respect and courtesy. Example (30) describes a man with whom it is impossible to reason. The man charges outrageous interest on loans; his brother by contrast is described as follows:

32.   Mas yo jtz'uj ja' mas xa'i *k'op*.
           "He's not as bad; he is willing to listen to *reason*."

Though the ideology reflected in these examples resembles that of sentences (5)–(11), the occurrence of the root *k'op* implies talk for a specific purpose, discussion of some problem or plan, rather than aimless *lo'il* or conversation. In this connection I may cite the ordinary usage[10] of the phrase *lekil k'op* ("good words").

32a.   Yu'van *lekil k'op* ana'oj.
           "Don't tell me you think this is a *proper* thing to engage
           in!"

32b.   'Ak'o yik' ta *lekil k'op* litzebe.
           "Let him marry the girl *without a fuss*."

32c.   Timi chavak' jpastik preva lavajnile chakol ta *lekil k'op*.
           "If you let us try out your wife, then you will be set free
           unharmed."

When something is done *ta lekil k'op* parties are agreed; calm prevails; no rules are broken, and no dispute arises from the matter. *Lekil k'op* represents the triumph of reasoned argument over impulsive, rash action.

Finally, the noun *-k'oplal* is derived from the root *k'op*. The word is used in a legal context, as described by Jane Collier (1973): "When it is said that someone went to the *Presidente* or an elder to *saʔbe sk'oplal* it means that he is looking for a settlement. *K'oplal* means 'a plan,' and the plaintiff who goes to *saʔbe sk'oplal* is literally 'looking for a plan' that will be agreeable to all parties to a dispute" (p. 95). But *-k'oplal* is commonly used to mean "news [of _____]," "the affair [in which _____ is involved]." It is always possessed, and often occurs in couplets with *-loʔiltael*.

33.   Mas chabal toʔox *sk'oplal* sloʔiltael.
           "He used to have less of a *reputation*, less gossip about him."
34.   Mu xlam *sk'oplal.*
           "This *affair* about him will not be hushed up."
35.   Jaʔ to inopoj ti k'alal ch'abal mas *sk'oplal.*
           "He only came near again when the *affair* was mostly forgotten."

Just as *loʔiletik* can be counted with the numeral classifier *koj*, so we can speak of *jkoj sk'oplal* ("one story about him"). Similarly, some-one's *-k'oplal* can "be made public," can "come out," and can "pass" (i.e., be forgotten, blow over)—as can gossip. A person's *-k'oplal* is the gossip about *k'opetik* in which he has been involved: arguments to which he was party, ventures in which he participated, and so no. No-tably, when a man dies it is possible to say

        Laj *sk'oplal.*
        "He died [lit., his *story* ended]."[11]

At death, the dossier on a man closes, even if gossip about him persists.

It is possible in interviews to elicit gossip about an individual by asking for *-loʔiltael* or *-k'oplal* about him. But in ordinary conversation Zinacantecos generally initiate gossip with more leading questions. That is, Zinacantecos realize that it is easier to evoke an interesting response by asking "Has Xun done anything stupid recently?" than by asking "What has Xun been up to recently?" No one ordinarily talks about (remarks upon) unmarked behavior.[12] And nothing marks behavior more than positive badness—than transgressions of one sort or another.[13]

Tzotzil has a rich vocabulary for describing mistakes, faults, sins, crimes, stupidity, failure, and so forth. But there is a small set of par-ticularly potent words which prod gossipy tongues into action. The key words are italicized in the examples that follow.

36.   ʔOy nan *sbolil* jutukuk ʔonox.
           "I guess he has his little *stupidities* after all."

37.   Mi chatz'ikbotikotik j*bolil*tikotik.
            "Will you endure our *stupidity*?"

38.   ʔAʔibil *sbolil*, yech'o ti ikom ta jwera.
            "People have heard about his *stupidity* and he has
            therefore been left out."

I successfully elicited gossip by asking about a person's -*bolil* ("stupidity, foolishness"); a man with a particularly bad reputation may be
described as having a "great amount of foolishness." Similarly, a person
(typically a wife) may disclaim responsibility for another's transgressions by saying:

39.   Mi ta jnaʔ k'u jʔelan *sbolil*.
            "How should I know the extent of his *stupidity*?"

Similarly, Tzotzil uses a loan word from Spanish, *maña* ("a defect or
bad habit") (J. Collier 1973, p. 93).

40.   Lek vaxal mol yilel xchaʔle sba pero te nan yunen *manya*
            jset'uk.
            "He seems like a well-behaved old man—or he tries to
            act that way—but all the same he probably has his little
            wickedness."

41.   Kavron toj *manya* molot.
            "Son of a bitch, you are a *wicked* old man!"

Zinacantecos use questions about a person's -*manya(il)* to prompt tales
of sexual misconduct or promiscuity. Men rarely utter the word without
a smile in ordinary conversation (although the technical implications of
the word in, for example, a legal dispute are not humorous; cf. J. Collier
1973, pp. 92–94).

Finally, references to jailing tend to stimulate conversation. The
Tzotzil root *chuk* means "jail, tie up, tether." Zinacanteco men are
fascinated to learn that someone *sta chukel* ("went to jail"); frequent
jailing is a sure sign of evil propensities.

42.   ʔAyem ta *chukel* jayib bwelta xchiʔuk taj xryoxe.
            "He's been to *jail* who knows how many times with his
            [talking] saint."

43.   Koʔolkoʔol sk'upinik *pus*.
            "They have equal desire for the *sweatbath* [the jail]."

Let me review the linguistic argument so far. Though no single noun
in Tzotzil can be adequately glossed "gossip," there are numerous ex-

pressions, mostly based on the roots *lo?il* and *k'op*, that refer to a cluster of activities, speech genres, and properties of speech. This cluster has a clear kinship with the constellation of ideas we associate with "gossip" in English. Coming to understand an expression or a lexical domain in Tzotzil depends more on learning ordinary usage, common verbal collocations, and contextually activated lexical contrasts than on, say, the position of the expression in a single formal structure.

Consider the two verbs *-lo?ilta* ("tell stories on") and *-laban* ("mock").[14] Both words contain elements of the English "gossip about," though the precise semantic relationship between the two is not easily stated. When the two words occur together in a formal couplet, the meaning of *-lo?ilta* stretches to include a touch of mockery. Yet, when to describe the shrewish public ridiculing of a man by his wife a speaker chooses *-laban* over *-lo?ilta*, he emphasizes a contrast. (*-laban*: "She wanted the world to know how awful he was—that she wanted no more to do with him. She mocked and ridiculed him"; *-lo?ilta*: "She let everyone in on his transgressions.") Understanding the conceptual mechanisms of a language leads an ethnographer to the salient domains of a culture, even when such domains are not otherwise labeled. I shall return to this question in chapter 7.

But the evidence for a native Zinacanteco idea of gossip is not limited to the existence of certain Tzotzil expressions. Zinacantecos talk, and talk about talk, in ways that suggest a definite theory of the properties of talk, the motives that underlie it, its consequences and dangers. In the remainder of this chapter I shall present evidence for this native Zinacanteco theory about reputation and the transfer of information through gossiplike conversation.[15]

Gluckman (1963) remarks that belonging to a group entails knowing the gossip of a group, knowing about other people (and their ancestors). He writes that in Zululand "I found myself excluded from groups because I did not know enough gossip. Gradually I learnt the gossip; but I never acquired enough certainty in knowing when and, more importantly, when not to use it, ever to become a member of Zulu society" (p. 309). My work in the field was aimed explicitly at overcoming at least in part the lack of knowledge that excluded me from Zinacanteco society. When I first arrived in Zinacantan gossip was meaningless to me not because I did not know enough about the people involved, but because I didn't know them at all. Through such devices as the Who's Who I gradually began to recognize names and associate them with reputations, until eventually I could respond appropriately to new revelations, or ask informed questions, or even offer tidbits of gossip myself. Zinacantecos found my acquired expertise amusing, but my friends began to talk to me in a new way. They came to expect me to know the background to their gossip; and they showed a new eagerness to share news and comment with me.

The difference between the inside and the outside was demonstrated one afternoon when a notorious slattern approached my wife at the waterhole and asked a favor. In all innocence, my wife agreed; she was bewildered by the giggles of our *comadre* who observed the exchange. When the women returned to the house my *comadre*—knowing that I knew the girl's reputation— could not restrain herself from rushing up to tell me what had happened, giggling behind her hand; she knew that I knew who the girl was and that my wife did not.

Much of what a Zinacanteco knows about his fellows has practical value; it is what Hotchkiss calls "useful information": "Useful information about others, however, is obtained in contexts that most often are not neutral, that is, in affectively charged conversations with others— gossip. Useful information about someone is conveyed along with evaluations of him. New bits of information are continually added to a body of knowledge, a dossier, that a person has for each of many of his fellow townsmen" (1967, p. 713). In Zinacantan such instrumental knowledge typically includes information about what men are good for loans and how much interest they charge, if any; we have already seen this explicit subject in gossip. Similarly, it is important to know which men are curers and which are powerful. Because of the constant danger of witchcraft, a Zinacanteco must know which men can reverse witchcraft and which are capable of sending sickness in the first place.

Not all information carried by gossip (or, as Gluckman might urge, presupposed by gossip) is of this instrumental sort. Not all such information is fact. Zinacantecos are aware of the questions surrounding the nature of the information conveyed in informal conversation. What I have called their "native theory of gossip" concerns: (*a*) the separation of public from private (privileged) information; (*b*) the question of truth versus hearsay; and (*c*) the general ethics of telling tales on people.

Zinacantecos are aware that the facts of court cases brought to the town hall become public knowledge, and that others are likely to talk about one's misfortunes if they result in public hearings. People draw an explicit parallel between the town hall and other modern mechanisms for disseminating information (with which Zinacantecos are essentially unfamiliar: there are no newspapers, no relevant radio broadcasts).[16]

Cep remembered hearing that a man under discussion had been up to some mischief. No one could remember the details.

"Maybe it never became public knowledge; perhaps it was a secret affair."

"Well, if the *agente* settled the matter in his house no one would have heard about it."

"Yes, when a story comes out at the town hall, then a newspaper report goes out to every part of the country."

"It comes to every streetcorner; we hear about it on the radio. . . . (Ha ha ha.)"

"But when it doesn't come out (at the town hall), then nothing shows up on the radio; no newspaper is published. (Ha ha ha.)"

"Is it true that the old lady divorced old Manvel?"

"Yes; she says she woke up each morning with a wet skirt. The old man would piss on himself at night. Just like a child. . . ."

"At night? Wasn't that just when he was drunk?"

"No, no, according to her he didn't have to be drunk. Even when he was sober. 'What a rank odor his urine has! Not like a child's,' she would say."

"That's right. The old woman even said such things right out at the town hall!"

Zinacantecos realize that children are often the carriers of gossip; there is an attempt to exploit children's apparent harmlessness to find out about one's neighbors. Hotchkiss reports that in the nearby ladino town of Teopisca children have access to otherwise unavailable information by virtue of being "nonpersons." "Children . . . are not subject in the same way as adults to conventions that insure privacy, and they can also be used to breach the walls of secrecy. The child who brings a condolence message to a family where there has been a death is sent by his parents not only to express his family's sympathies, but by this ruse to gain access to a household's inner or "back region" (Goffman 1959), where he can act as a spy . . . children are always underfoot in situations like these, and adults act as if they were not there" (1967, p. 714). A similar situation obtains in Zinacantan; children are frequently cited as the first ones to report some juicy bit of news. A newcomer to Zinacantan finds the inquisitive, touchy children the most visible and ubiquitous people in the *municipio*, even as he tries to ignore them. In the story of chapter 1, little children first reported that the lewd old man was fiddling with his own daughter. The case is not unique.

A man was divorced for embracing the daughter of a neighbor during a curing ceremony.

"Well, listen, while they were in the midst of preparing the candles, old Maryan went outside. The old fucker was drunk, you see. It was children who saw it all, according to what was said at the *cabildo*. They were out embracing each other behind the house—old Maryan and Mat's daughter. That's what came out later at the town hall."

Similarly, one of my friends in Zinacantan was estranged from his brother-in-law because the latter's son had made slanderous remarks at a public hearing. My friend was angered, even though the boy was only five years old.

In conversation Zinacantecos reveal that other factors limit the availability of public information suitable for gossip. Geographical boundaries limit certain transfers of information; and some people, despite their evil desires and many transgressions, may be able to cover their tracks.

> "But that man has always been a big woman-grabber."
> "I know. He had such an experience when his brother was *marto-morey.* . . ."
> "His older brother."
> "He was simply beaten up terribly; it was all due to his woman grabbing. But I don't know the whole story. . . ."
> "That's true, we don't know who the woman was. . . ."
> "Now that you mention it, I think it was one of his brother's helpers, there together with him. . . ."
> "Ah, but if it happened over in Jteklum, that is why it never became public knowledge here."
> "Right, the affair never came out. It happened in Jteklum and that's why we didn't hear anything about it."
> "The man is a ritual adviser today."
> "He's a holy elder now, but he gave injections. (Ha ha ha.)"
> "He made a holy child under the pine trees. (Ha ha ha.)"
> "But that's about all I know about him."
> "That man has had lots of foolishness; there are probably other things like this that he's done, or maybe there were other times [when he got girls pregnant] that never came to light."
> "No. It's just that in this case we all heard about it."
> "If there were other times, it was all secret."

I have shown that the contrast between *lo?il* ("hearsay") and *yech* ("true") or *melel* ("true"), as well as the contrast between a plain declarative sentence and a sentence containing the particle *la* ("quotative evidence"), can draw attention to the unverified quality of a story or statement. Zinacantecos believe that gossip *must* contain a grain of truth; yet they know from direct experience that some gossip is unreliable. The opinion that all officeholders are subject to malicious gossip ex officio appears above. The tension between the "hearsay" and "whole truth" positions is illustrated in the following excerpts.

> "The man is a curer, but he also knows how to send sickness. He talks to the Earth Lord; he transforms himself into a [supernatural] goat."

"Well, has anyone actually seen him doing that, or is it just gossip?"
"He must certainly have been seen, otherwise why would he be reputed to do it?"
"Whoever says he does it must have seen him."
"When our faces aren't seen when we do what we do, then we aren't gossiped about."

"Listen, old lady Xunka is the most quarrelsome old lady there is."
"She's always taken to the town hall; and it's all the fault of her mouth, of her gossip. If she hears any story she immediately goes to tell other people about it."
"But she doesn't just tell the story the way she heard it. She always thinks up new things to add. She has gossiped about lots of her companions, but never the truth. That's why she got into such trouble —all because of the stories she told."

Zinacantecos present their versions of events as true; but they rarely hesitate to discredit conflicting accounts.

Gossip is often especially useful to the ethnographer, since it sheds light on the "exotic beliefs of the natives." Stories about people who transform themselves into supernatural creatures or who witch their relatives illustrate the different constraints in Zinacantan which allow people to believe "apparently unlikely" stories.[17] In a tradition which accepts witchcraft as a prime source of disease, allegations that someone is a witch are at least plausible; moreover, skepticism about such gossip can take two forms: (1) a denial of the existence of witchcraft; (2) an assertion that the person in question is unlikely to be a witch. An elaborate instance of witchcraft gossip involves a man who was estranged from his elder brother and father. Several stories relate to their quarrel:

a   The younger brother, Yermo, was unwilling to obey his father's wishes about how to farm and work. Thus he moved out, violating the ordinary rule that the youngest son stay with his father while the older sons move out to set up their own households.

a' The father, old Manvel, was a domestic tyrant who gave his sons very little land to work independently, and who commandeered most of the household resources. Smarting under the yoke of his father's will, Yermo moved out.

b   Yermo treats his father badly and no longer accords him the respect that he deserves. He also avoids and speaks angrily to his older brother Antun, even though Antun lent him money and support during a recent religious office. He is just waiting for his father to die so that he

can dispute the land division his father made between his
children.

b'   Old Manvel, being displeased with his youngest son, has
systematically cheated him out of his inheritance, giving
him only inferior tracts. He has effectively disowned
Yermo.

c   Yermo got involved with some disreputable men in the
ownership of a corn mill. He placed the mill on a corner
of his land where it polluted one of his father's waterholes and caused people to tread and throw trash on his
brother's cornfield.

c'   Antun has tried to cause official trouble for his brother
Yermo by claiming before civil authorities that the land
on which Yermo put his mill was not his to use. The
claim is false and was made only to get Yermo jailed.

d   Yermo's daughter died of measles, during an epidemic
which also brought two of Antun's children close to
death. Antun even contributed money toward the burial
expenses of Yermo's daughter. The fault for this ill-
feeling rests with the curer who slandered old Manvel;
but Yermo should never have believed the curer's diag-
nosis—or should, at least, have confronted his father
directly with the charges.

d'   Yermo's eldest daughter—almost of marriageable age—
contracted a disease and, after a long illness, died. The
curer discovered that the disease was due to witchcraft
activity by old Manvel himself, a well-known curer.
Yermo feels that his father caused his daughter's death as
part of a general campaign of evildoing against his
youngest son.

I have heard all these stories in different conversations. Note that
story (*d*) may take two forms: some say that old Manvel was unlikely
to witch his own granddaughter, while others claim that witchcraft itself
is suspect. Two *compadres* of mine have, over time, changed their alli-
ances with the two sides of this family, and their willingness to repeat
different versions of these stories has accordingly changed. The first
was a nephew of Yermo's wife who was for a time planning to move
onto land Yermo was to provide. At first he willingly told all of the
stories marked with a prime; he was eager to talk about old Manvel's
ill-temperedness and Antun's propensity for scolding. Later, after fighting with his mother and consequently with her sister (Yermo's wife),
this man switched to story (*d*) to account for the fact that the two sides

of the family don't get along. My other *compadre* is, at least in conversations with anthropologists, a skeptic with respect to witchcraft. He first was closely allied with Antun; when I asked him about the dispute between Antun and Yermo he told me story (*d*), emphasizing his conviction that suspected witchcraft was never sufficient grounds for such a dispute. More recently, this *compadre* has cooperated strongly with Yermo on a land deal, and his version of the family conflict in question has changed predictably. He now suggests that stories (*b'*) and (*c'*) are most likely to explain the schism, and the witchcraft story has totally dropped from view. (I shall return to these questions in the next chapter.)

Zinacantecos' awareness that gossip is rarely "the whole truth and nothing but the truth" leads to a last element of "native theory" about gossip. There is a general ambivalence about gossip: it is a powerful and hence dangerous tool. An individual can use gossip to control others by managing (Goffman 1959) the impressions his listeners have of him and of the person about whom he gossips. At the same time, he fears corresponding control by others who gossip about him. But there is no Sicilian "law of silence" in Zinacantan; Zinacanteco men seem to have a genuine passion for gossiping—so long as there is no possibility of retaliation. In recorded gossip sessions at my house, informants were often reticent and obviously nervous until someone jokingly said: "You know, of course, that Xun here is not going to play these tapes at the town hall, that he just uses them here for his work." Such an assurance amazingly allowed most men to shed their reservations and join in with gusto.

The deep-seated ambivalence over the ethics of gossip is a recurrent theme in gossip itself. Zinacantecos emphasize the potential for danger in telling stories, true or not; they know that bad feelings may follow well-intentioned disclosures.

A boy saw his older brother's fiancée in a compromising position under a bridge with another man.

"He saw them embracing each other near the waterhole. He couldn't see who the boy was, but he recognized his brother's sweetheart. But evidently he went to tell his brother.

" '*Kere*, who knows if you're telling the truth. I don't believe it,' said the older brother to his younger brother.

" 'Well, see. You don't want to be told. I guess you'll be satisfied if you get a bit of his cast-off leavings,' Chep told his older brother.

"But the older brother just wouldn't believe; neither would the parents. '*Kere*, don't break your brother's heart with your babbling,' said the old man and his wife.

" 'See, you just won't listen,' said Chep."

Gossip travels its own paths with sometimes disconcerting swiftness. The bad feelings that arise must often be settled by formal procedures: giving liquor, formally asking pardon, accepting the mediation of an elder.

"Didn't she quarrel with Xun the Musician during her husband's cargo?"

"Yes, she would gossip about him. 'What a disgusting way that musician has! He has cut off lots of my apples and peaches. He has taken ears of corn to eat without asking.' That's what she would say. And she complained that he would say lewd things even when women could hear. She said, 'That old twisted-leg man; he can't restrain his tongue!'

"But the musician's wife heard what had been said. The musician had been called a thief, but he denied it. 'I just cut some peaches to eat; I just had the desire to eat a few.' He offered to pay for them, but the woman would take no payment. Finally they settled the affair over a bottle."

"But Xun must have been embarrassed; for he was maligned as a thief."

Zinacantecos also understand that people spread damaging gossip for different kinds of reasons. Factional disputes engender long exchanges of gossip and slander as each side tries to revenge itself on the other through ever more serious accusations (cf. Rush 1971). Realignments within factional disputes may cause onetime allies to turn informer. Tzotzil uses the root *pak* ("fold") to mean "reciprocate": as when a person slandered in turn slanders his opponent; or when a jailed man devises a pretext to jail his jailer.

A famous attempt to get wealth in exchange for selling souls to the Earth Lord was revealed through treacherous gossip.

"The way it was revealed was through the gossip of Chep. He was the one who told all."

"I didn't know which one of them told. . . ."

"But didn't Chep tell Antun from *Chaynatik?*"

". . . That's right. First Chep had friendly conversations with Antun. They were good friends. . . ."

". . . Chep probably told him that this was what they had done, this was where they had been. . . ."

". . . maybe Antun was thinking of going along with them."

"Anyway, at first they were friendly. But later they quarreled. After that, old Antun came to Nabenchauk and told what he had heard. That's how the story came out."

"They fought over a plan they had together; that's what Antun said. 'We had borrowed money from a bank, but when it came time Chep gave up. He couldn't pay back his debt. I had to pay it off for him.' After Chep backed out of the bank plan, Antun said to himself, '*Puta*, I guess I'll just tell all about their [witchcraft] plans. Let the rest of the people decide what to do. You can't tell me that they will get away with it.' That's how the whole affair was revealed."

"There is a story about the old man's son Chep too, when he divorced his wife."

"Ah, so he divorced her."

"Yes, she didn't stay married to him long, because she claimed Chep was too ill-tempered. She couldn't bear being scolded all the time and having no corn to eat. Also, she didn't want her husband to slander her; when she heard what he said about her she started to gossip about him, too."

"So the husband first slandered his wife?"

"Yes, he would say why he divorced her. He told his friends that she was no good; she didn't want to sleep with him. She wouldn't let him embrace her. 'I don't want to have you in my bed; I'm too little and you can't yet enter me,' she would say even though the man wanted her. The man got angry; he beat her and wanted his bride payments returned.

"But when the girl heard that she had been gossiped about, she started talking herself. Whereas the man said that she wouldn't sleep with him, the woman claimed that the man would just pester her for nothing. He was useless; he would just wake her up and then do nothing. He wouldn't let his wife sleep, but would fidget in the bed. That's what the woman said at the town hall. That is how everyone knows that Chep is impotent."

I suggest that the examples of native speculation I have presented show that Zinacantecos are aware of a domain of behavior similar to that we call "gossip." Despite the unhappy lexical fact that no Tzotzil word glosses cleanly as "gossip," and despite the unfortunate situation that prevents us from uniformly eliciting gossip with a single question or frame, Zinacantecos in fact seem to treat certain sorts of talk and conversation as a coherent body of phenomena. Gossip in Zinacantan includes more, perhaps, than gossip elsewhere: it is conversation which bears on reputation; it is scandal and slander as well as ridicule; it can be friendly and amused, but also hostile and serious. The sort of domain it is can, I caim, be judged from the sort of thing Zinacantecos have to say about gossiping in the examples above.

I began this chapter by suggesting that all conversation about people and their alleged actions is fair game for a study of gossip. (Zinacantecos do, in fact, follow our convention of not gossiping about another to his face, though they may mock him in his presence.) I presumed the possible subjects of such conversation to be limited in range (and see chap. 5). Moreover, native theory on the matter further constrained the sort of conversation I was able to elicit—Zinacantecos have, as we have seen, their own ideas about what it means to tell interesting stories about people.

The Structure of Zinacanteco Gossip

Mi ?oy slo?iltael le?e?
"Is there any gossip about him?"

4

When I first began to pay serious attention to gossip in Zinacantan, although I could understand people's *words* (having acquired some competence in Tzotzil during previous stays), I could not understand the gossip itself. It took me some time to discover what knowledge and skills I was lacking. I heard a good deal of interesting conversation—at meals, at fiestas, near the *cabildo*, or in the San Cristóbal market—but I was unsure how to record it (the words themselves were only part of the conversation); and I was often completely at a loss to appreciate its significance, not knowing the protagonists, their histories, or the background of convention that rendered their exploits noteworthy.

The relative importance of the three sorts of questions I could ask about a given story (Who? What? So what?) became clear as I unraveled the elements of gossip sessions. I found that the immediate conversational conventions were invariant in all gossip situations, and that most gossip "texts" shared a common structure.

There are essentially two participants in a gossip exchange in Zinacantan: the storyteller and his interlocutor.[1] Even when there are more than two persons involved in a gossip session—more than one person who knows the story, and more than one who wants to hear it—a single primary storyteller emerges, and a single listener takes over the responsibility of answering for the whole audience. Others may make comments, but at any given moment it may appear that one man is talking to one other and that the rest are merely eavesdropping.

But the interlocutor is more than a listener. He actively participates in the story, interjecting appropriate comments, exclamations, questions, and so forth. He has a fairly standard repertoire of phrases, words, and grunts to be used more or less for rhythm at neutral points. The storyteller talks in short phrases, pausing between them for the interlocutor's response. He too has a set of fillers from which to draw while he collects his thoughts.[2] Here, by way of illustration, is an excerpt from a two-man gossip session in which all the interlocutor's remarks are included. (The interlocutor is person B, the storyteller, person A.)

B Mi ʔo spasik yech krixchano?
"Have people done anything like that near you?"

A ʔOy spas yech ʔach' toe.
"There was a recent case of that kind."

B Aaaa.
"Oh."

A ʔAli ja? x . . .
"Uh, it was . . ."

B Much'u?
"Who?"

A Stzeb li ʔanima mol Manvel ʔIyene.
"The daughter of the late old Manvel Guillen."

B Aaaa.
"Oh."

A Jaʔ stzeb li ʔanima mol Manvel ʔiyen liʔ ta . . .
"Yes, old Manvel's daughter from . . ."

B Aaaa . . .
"Yes . . ."

A . . . ta ʔAtz'ame . . .
". . . from Salinas . . ."

B Aaaa.
"Oh."

A . . . ta ʔon teʔtik xalike.
". . . from the Madron Grove, as they call it."

B Manvel ʔiyen ʔati iʔech' ta bolomale?
"Was this the Manvel Guillen who was a Jaguar [at the fiesta of San Sebastian]?"

A Jaʔ ʔun bi.
"That's the one . . ."

B Aaaa.
"Oh."

A Pwes, jaʔ primero isk'uban skrem li mol Maryan Kontzarese.

"Well, first she was engaged to old Maryan Gonzales's son . . ."

B   ʔali . . . rejirole?
"You mean . . . the third-level cargoholder?"

A   Jaʔe.
"That's right."

B   Aaaa.
"Oh."

A   Isk'uban baʔyi.
"His son first asked for her hand."

B   Bweno.
"Okay."

A   Bweno, pwes iyak' matanal yaʔel.
"Well, he gave her gifts . . ."

B   Aaaa.
"Yes."

A   Ba yak' jset' juteb yaʔel ta na ʔune.
"He went to give a bit [of liquor] at her house . . ."

B   Li mol Maryan ʔune?
"Who? Old Maryan [and his son]?"

A   Mol Maryan ʔune.
"Yes, old Maryan."

B   Bweno, mi itak'av yaʔel ti smeʔ li tzebe?
"Okay, but did the girl's mother answer [favorably]?"

A   Smeʔ li tzebe, itak'av.
"The girl's mother agreed."

B   Bweno.
"Fine."

. . . .

A   Bweno, solel tey ispak'alin sba toʔox li vinike, cheʔe, porke slok'el yoʔon . . .
"Well, anyway the man just offered himself [to the girl] because he really desired her."

B   Ispas kasto yaʔel?
"He went to some expense then?"

A   Ispas kasto yaʔel, ibat ta vulaʔal.
"He had expenses; he went to visit her . . ."

B   K'usi jalil ismak yaʔel?
"How long did he court her?"

A   ʔIii, te nan chibuk jabil ʔun.
"Mmm, it was about two years."

B   Chib jabil?
"Two years?"

A Chib jabil.
   "Two years, yes."
B ʔIjola!
   "Son of a bitch!"
A Chibuk.
   "About two . . ."
B Bweno, li chib jabil ʔune, chak' matanal.
   "Okay, so those two years he gave gifts . . ."

The storyteller talks in short phrases with considerable repetition. The interlocutor responds with: (a) neutral grunts, (b) exclamations (e.g., ʔijola, from Spanish hijo de la chingada), (c) questions on the identity of the indefinite subject or object of a sentence,[3] and (d) questions of clarification (about the identity of one of the actors in the story or about matters of fact). Drawing out the storyteller without intruding on his style involves considerable skill; and the man who has to face a dumb audience is thrown into confusion and finds it hard to speak at all.[4]

The exchanges from this story illustrate one of the recurrent structural segments found in all gossip stories. If two men begin to gossip in a natural context the resulting conversation will have three parts: (a) identification, (b) story, (c) evaluation. The excerpt above begins to show how the storyteller identifies the people about whom he is gossiping so that the interlocutor can understand from some personal vantage point who they are. He offers a sequence of "identifying formulas," each time responding to a probe from the interlocutor. He identifies the girl in the story by means of the following sequence of formulas:

1.   daughter of Manvel ʔIyen (now deceased);

2.   who lived in the hamlet of ʔAtz'am;

3.   in the particular section of ʔAtz'am called ʔon teʔtik;

4.   and who had passed a particular religious office which entailed performing as a "jaguar" at the fiesta of San Sebastian.

This sequence is sufficient to identify the girl's father and hence the girl. (It turns out later that the interlocutor was well acquainted with the father—had held a different religious cargo simultaneously—though he did not know the daughter in question.)

The first boy mentioned, the girl's first fiancé, was identified as

1.   the son of old Maryan Kontzares;

2.   who [the father] had been rejirol, a third-level religious official.

Again, primary identification of the father is achieved by reference to the religious hierarchy. In this case the interlocutor turned out to know the boy himself; he was able to name him after a further disclosure:

3.   Yu'un chopol jp'ej ssat.
                "One of his eyes is bad."

The interlocutor was then able to say

4.   Ja' li Telexe.
                "Then it was Telex [a particular son of the old man]."

Occasionally the interlocutor is left in the dark and can ask no pertinent questions to identify a character. The storyteller ordinarily makes a concerted effort to establish some pathway which will lead the interlocutor to the person in question. He may use kinship ties. Another suitor who appears later in this same gossip session is identified through the following sequence:

                Interlocutor: "Whose son was that?"
1.   "He was the son of a man they refer to now as the
                late 'Antun."
                Interlocutor: "I don't know him."
2.   "Well, he was also the son of old Maryan Kontzares's
                younger sister [if that helps]."

These long sequences of identifying formulas are extremely important parts of all Zinacanteco gossip; in fact, gossip sessions often break down into lengthy genealogical discussions. Some people seem to pride themselves on their knowledge of kinship and family history, not only for their own families but for those of their neighbors. Similarly, people have fantastically accurate memories of the cargo careers of other Zinacantecos, even from distant *parajes*. It became clear that to begin to understand gossip, I would need to tap the shared knowledge that people had of others throughout the *municipio*, which made identification possible. I compiled the Who's Who precisely for this reason.

A limited number of schemata recur in identifying formulas; the nature of these schemata hinted at the information I needed to gather. To establish a pathway the storyteller need only show kinship relations between the person he has in mind and a well-identified person. Identifying formulas commonly move down generations or stay at the same generation. That is, the beginning of a path may be an older person, well known; the individual being identified may be his sibling, child, or son- or daughter-in-law:

> Yik'oj stzeb li mol Petule.
> "He's the one who married old Pedro's daughter."

Hence, the set of kin relations which occur frequently in such identifying formulas includes child, sibling, spouse, and sibling-in-law (particularly brother-in-law). (The Tzotzil categories are somewhat more specific.)

The following features often appear to identify an individual from whom a kin-based path can proceed:

1. Focal individual (a well-known name); e.g., *mol Maryan Sarate* (the political boss); *mol preserente* ("the municipal president").

2. Religious cargo position; e.g., *mol pasaro* ("elder who has completed the heirarchy"); *ʔech'em ta santa krusal* ("was a mayordomo in charge of the saint called Santa Cruz").

3. Civil office; e.g., *lik'em komite* ("used to serve on *ejido* committee"); *mol jwes* (town hall official).

4. Talent or skill; e.g., *jʔilol* ("curer"); *jvabajom* ("musician").

5. Place of residence; e.g., *ta ʔon teʔtik* ("from Madron Grove"); *yolon mukenal* ("who lives below the cemetery").

6. (By far the least frequent) reference to past gossip and reputation; e.g., *jmilvanej* ("the murderer"); *xch'akoj yajnil* ("the one who divorced his wife").

An identifying formula can involve just these features in combination, or it may utilize kinship pathways, as I show above. In order to make sense out of such identifying sequences a Zinacanteco must have at his disposal a vast array of information about others in the community— their relatives, their cargo careers, and their past transgressions.

After all the characters have been identified, a gossip session proceeds to the story itself. But the story is not simply a narrative. The interlocutor can ask about particular points of interest, providing the analyst with explicit evidence about what counts—what actions and words are crucial to the situation and its outcome. The basic plot of the story I have been examining in this chapter is this:

> Old Manvel's daughter is courted by Telex, son of old Maryan. She rejects him and is hauled into court after running away to avoid him. Despite the presidente's arguments she continues to reject him; she agrees to pay back the money he has spent in courting her. Telex

persists and finally rapes the girl, with the encouragement of her mother, who has favored the boy's suit all along. The girl still rejects him and ultimately marries someone else.

The interlocutor is particularly concerned to establish the form of the courtship; did the suitor act properly so as to insure that the girl was obligated? Did the girl reject him wrongly? Was anyone's behavior extraordinary? The nature of the interaction makes it possible for both interlocutor and storyteller to emphasize the relevant aspects of the affair; the gossip session serves as a practical moral lesson by allowing participants to reflect on particular behavior and observe its outcome before making explicit evaluations.

Here are some examples of questions that the interlocutor asked regarding this story:

During the original courtship petitioning, did the girl's mother *tak'av* ["answer favorably"]?
When the girl rejected her suitor, was she already *k'oponbil ta yan* ["spoken to—i.e., propositioned—by another"]?
How long did the courtship proceed? How much expense did the unsuccessful suitor incur?
When the girl fled, where did she spend the night? [The implication of the question is, Did the boy have grounds for suspecting that she had eloped with another?]

Another feature of Zinacanteco narrative is the liberal use of dialogue.[5] Gossip audiences seem particularly to enjoy what amounts to a dramatization of conversations which the characters in the story are alleged to have had—especially if such conversations are heated.

" 'Will you marry this boy?' said the presidente.
" 'I don't want to,' she said.
" 'Well, if there is some other person who has already proposed to you, say so, admit it openly,' she was told.
" 'No one,' she said.
" 'Well then you should marry him for a while. See if he is able to feed you; gradually you will become accustomed to one another,' said the presidente.
" 'No,' said the girl.
" 'Perhaps it would be better for you to have a civil marriage [which makes divorce more costly],' said the presidente. He started to go into his office [to issue the papers].
" 'No, I don't want him,' said the girl. 'Why don't you just give him your own daughter if you have one?' "
"Son of a bitch!"

"The fucking girl!"
" 'Listen,' said the presidente. 'What gives you the right to talk to me this way? Are you superior to me? You are nobody, but I am a settler of disputes. I didn't just take my seat here at the town hall yesterday; I've had years in this office. Now are you going to tell me to give my own daughter? Are you going to give me orders? You are just acting pretty snotty,' said the presidente."

After the story is told, the gossips begin to evaluate what occurred. When all have heard of a man's transgressions or misfortunes, storyteller and interlocutor are moved to comment on the moral implications of the story. Sometimes such comments are tossed off sarcastically. After hearing about a case of adultery or even a murder, a Zinacanteco is likely to say

> Batz'i lek spasik krixchanoetik yo'e.
> People over there do the nicest things.

Often there is more to be said. In the story I have been discussing, participants in the gossip session laid much of the blame for the girl's misconduct on the fact that her father was dead and could not discipline her.

a.   Ja' xa ti k'u spas ta stukike, komo ch'abal xa stot cha'ie.
      "That is how she acts when she is alone, for she realizes she has no father [to control her]."

b.   Li sme'e, mu xa sp'is ta vinik.
      "As for her mother, she does not respect her."

c.   Sme'e, mu xa baluk.
      "Her mother is not enough."

d.   'Ati kuxluk ti stote, xch'un mantal nan bi a'a.
      "If her father were alive, then she would obey."

e.   K'alal sme' xa no'oxe, mu xa xak' ta kwenta.
      "When only the mother is there, then she will pay no attention."

f.   K'alal kuxul li totil ya'el che'e, syempre ja' mas chak' xi'elal, komo vinik chava'i.
      "When the father is alive he always gives more cause for fear because, you see, he is a man."

There is a clear sense in which this part of the gossip session is the most active part: people build ethical theories on evaluations of such situations. Zinacantecos, through gossip, continually test ordinary rules and evaluative words against actual behavior.

Let me recapitulate, from a somewhat different perspective,[6] how a single gossip session relates to a widespread set of ethnographic facts and phenomena not bounded by one particular story or a single instance of its telling. I mean to point out the ramifications for an ethnographer of the gossip's ability to gossip or of the interlocutor's ability to understand what gossip is about (see fig. 1).

Fig. 1

```
┌─────────────────┐
│      Story      │
└─────────────────┘
```

At the heart of a gossip session is a story—a verbal narrative which we may in principle write down. (A gossip story is no more an abstraction than, say, a myth for a nonliterate people.) To the uninitiated ethnographer, in fact, gossip is barely more than text: unadorned and uninterpretable accounts of events. This is not to say that such texts are useless; in chapter 5 I shall take an inventory of the frequent themes of gossip stories I heard in Zinacantan and put forward this inventory as a catalog of those departures from ordinary behavior sufficiently notable to result in gossip.

A gossip text necessarily offers an "emic" description of behavior, which goes beyond ordinary observables. I have in mind here Popper's (1972, p. 72) notion that observation is "theory-impregnated," and this is true of both native's and ethnographer's observation. An ethnographer may observe behavior and not know even *what he has seen*[7] until he hears it described. The ethnographer may not, that is, be able to cut the behavior stream into words—a feat which a gossip text has already accomplished. To give a deeper example, gossip frequently alludes to motivation, state of mind, emotion, intent, and so on—"inner states" whose outward manifestations ethnographers necessarily find difficult to recognize. Thus, gossip stories lead directly to the normatively salient aspects of behavior. We learn what constitutes sufficient excuse to break off a courtship; we learn how Zinacantecos express anger; we learn how it is possible to justify running away from one's husband, one's wife, a religious cargo, and so forth. Gossip always draws our attention immediately to the important facts, and it never fails to draw appropriate conclusions: deciding who is to blame, who acted badly, when things began to turn sour, etc.

Gossip, furthermore, continually alludes to generally inaccessible bodies of native theory and belief.[8] On Quine's (1960) familiar account of "interanimation," the logic of all argument or the import of even a single word in discourse may be tied to a large body of sentences (a theory) which relate to it. Gossip leads the ethnographer to (and draws on the native's knowledge of) pieces of such native theory. Two examples will illustrate my point.

A woman from a particular hamlet was said to be living now with her third husband, her first two husbands having died. One participant in the gossip session suggested jokingly,

> "Perhaps she has a red scorpion on her hand. Who knows when this husband of hers now will also die? (Ha ha ha.)"

The comment rides on a folkloric item: that people with a particular pattern on their palms said to represent a *tzajal tzek* ("red scorpion")[9] will find a mate who survives only after three have died.

Correspondingly, only an understanding of Zinacanteco belief about the earth and the Earth Lord, about the formation of the world and the characteristics of treasure, will render comprehensible the gossip that surrounded a project to exhume a supernatural bell in Nabenchauk. The project failed, seemingly thwarted by a variety of natural obstacles. The gossips agreed, finally, that the project was doomed from the beginning, since

> Kuxul li balamile.
> The earth is alive.

Gossip alludes to otherwise inaccessible beliefs about "hot" and "cold" foods and diseases, about fertility and luck, about buried treasure and supernatural means to gain wealth, about the medicinal efficacy of various herbs and preparations, and so on. I call these beliefs inaccessible because they are infrequently expounded in other contexts; gossip, as the most common form of narrative, is almost uniquely responsible for keeping alive speculation about such matters.

Gossip stories raise a large class of problems surrounding the notion of "cultural rule" (or "norm" or "value"), which I shall consider in some detail in chapter 8. Here it is worth pointing out that from gossip we can extract certain rulelike propositions which underlie evaluative statements. When someone remarks in gossip that a particular awful boy "does not respect and obey his father," and that if his own sons treated him like that he would throw them out, it seems possible to formulate some kind of a "rule" about filial obedience. Similarly, from accounts of cargo failures we learn "rules" surrounding proper cargo performance; from stories of jailing, poverty, or divorce we learn about upright behavior, farming techniques, guidelines for successful marriage, and so on. Such a procedure, at least, seems justified if we accept the view that gossip is itself a (perhaps feeble) social sanction: native actors learn how to behave by observing what sorts of misbehavior are sanctioned (by being gossiped about).

I argue in chapter 8, against this facile view, that the fact that we can often draw morals from the transgressions of others tells us little about the "rules" that purportedly "govern" behavior. Talk about rules raises but does not settle questions about their status: are "cultural rules" explicit or tacit? may there not be conflicting orderings of rules (so that one function of gossip is to achieve agreement between participants about which rules dominate in a particular case)? Here we confront again the plaguing distinction between behavior and accounts of behavior; it is far from clear that principles which underlie the accounts also constrain the behavior.[10] In any case, there is a clear sense in which these underlying rulelike propositions amount to a statement of the *semantics* of behavior: they allow native actors to discuss and interpret the behavior of others; they legitimize and inform speculation about motives, intentions, second thoughts, regrets, and so forth, insofar as these are available to cultural scrutiny and insofar as they are relevant to evaluations of behavior. (Consider the highly psychologized gossip which characterizes American student circles: the rules of gossip permit [and in fact demand] discussion of the personalities and psychological states of gossip victims. In this respect, gossip reflects a native theory of behavior: that the prime determinants of action are individual psychological factors.)

I have shown that by various identifying formulas gossip leads participants to understand exactly who is involved (see fig. 2). In Zinacantan it was necessary to collect the information in the Who's Who to understand the gossip itself, not only to identify the protagonists. What is there to understand about the identities of the characters in a gossip story?

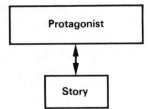

Fig. 2

Gossip relies on reputation while at the same time it expands on it. The fact that a man is known as a murderer certainly affects the way others treat him and the distance they maintain; and a story about a past murderer may easily trade on the man's reputation without explicitly stating it. Here is one basis for Gluckman's argument that gossip excludes outsiders. A man's proper name may even come to connote aspects of his reputation. One woman, for example, was reputed to seduce men with the object of stealing their good luck and wealth; she used a certain magical trick to take their good luck:

> "That's what she would do you see; she would get her riches from receiving just one thrust of the penis."
> "That is wicked!"
> "And our compatriots would end up just like Mat."

The speaker refers to a person named Mat, a notorious crazy man who wears a beard and refuses to work, living instead by begging.

Similarly, two men were once discussing the crooked land deal being arranged by another man. They talked about how the affair would end in assassination if it came out publicly:

> "If this is true, *kavron*, you'll see, he will end up like Lol C.; he will finish sitting behind a rock just like Lol C."
> "It will come out, *kavron*, the whole affair won't be settled easily. This argument will be decided with bullets."

Lol C. was murdered in an ambush as a result of his alleged witchcraft activities.

In a slightly different way, gossip identifies its protagonists not only by past reputation but in terms of culturally defined roles. For example, an observer must be familiar with the cargo system and individual cargo-holders before he can understand references to cargo positions. And so on. The seemingly simple ability to talk about people presupposes considerable knowledge about who people are and how they may be described.

Similarly, to use nicknames speakers must have mastered considerable native lore. A man's nickname in Zinacantan often seizes on an outstanding feature of his past identity. Thus a man is called *komite* ("*ejido* committee") because he served for a long time on the committee responsible for overseeing lands gained under land-reform laws; he has retained a reputation for abilities in dealing with ladino authorities. Another man is called by the name *kapon* ("capon, castrated animal"). He inherited the name from his grandfather, whose older brother never married and who himself married late. The present generation has similar characteristics; the man in question married very late, and his brother is not married at all. In one gossip session everyone said: "Well, they are aptly named even now!"

Gossip often draws on its protagonists' personal associations and factional affiliations. Information about a person's friends, or about the groups with whom he is *jp'ej sjol xchi'uk* ("of one head with"; i.e., in agreement with) is significant only to someone who knows the factions, who is familiar with peculiarities shared by certain groups. Thus, to say that a man is "there with the Valik family" is to imply where he stands on a number of disputed issues in the hamlet of Nabenchauk. And to remark that a boy is a good friend of one Antun K. condemns him as a rake, a licentious misuser of women. Identifying formulas in gossip are rarely neutral.

Nor is a man's gossip about someone else's factional ties or moral state likely to be disinterested (see fig. 3). Gossip reveals a set of relationships between narrator and protagonist. If the narrator is himself involved in a factional dispute with which the protagonist is also connected, we obviously expect the gossip to reflect whether the two are

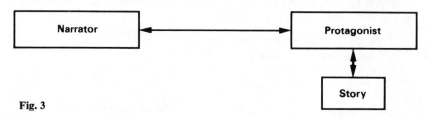

Fig. 3

on the same or opposite sides. Moreover, gossip often draws an implicit moral contrast between the protagonist and the narrator. Some Zinacantecos take advantage of others' misfortunes or misdeeds to draw attention to their own successes and otherwise to give themselves airs.[11] Thus the man who criticized another for letting his son be disobedient went on to declare that if he himself were treated that way he would throw his sons out, let them find their own food. At a wedding, one Zinacanteco told me how the proceedings disintegrated whenever he wasn't there to tell everyone what to do. He said: "Old Petul is supposed to be the adviser, but he doesn't give orders the way I do."

Again, one ex-cargoholder used gossip about another cargoholder as a thin disguise for his own self-aggrandizement:

"In the middle of our circuit of all the *alfereces'* houses, we stopped to rest. Our musicians went to sleep. The time came for us to leave, and I said that we should wait. But Chep said that we should leave:

" 'We'll never finish our rounds if we don't go. We are already overdue at the next house.'

"I said: 'But we can't leave without the musicians. We had better wait until they sober up.'

"But Chep wanted to go. He said he would play the violin and old Xun would play the guitar. He used to be a musician. I told them to wait. I said I would stay behind and bring along the musicians when they awoke.

" 'But why should you do that? You are supposed to be playing
the part of the Jaguar. Let them sober up by themselves.' "

Eventually the musicians did awaken. They were angry to find the
party of ritual entertainers gone. They decided to go home. Only after
strenuous pleading did my informant convince them to return to the
group and continue to play. The moral of the story, which I heard the
man repeat four or five times to different people, was clear: "Chep, for
all his good qualities, knows less than I do about the correct way to
handle cargo duties."

I suggested above that a gossip story represents an "emic" description
of behavior; but the fact that a gossip story originates with a particular
narrator makes it more than an "emic" description. A narrator is a
complex filtering mechanism; telling a story involves both selecting and
construing events, motives, intentions, and so forth. We know from
conflicting versions of the same story that people gossip about the same
event for different reasons; and part of the task of understanding gossip
is untangling these reasons.

Rush (1971) demonstrates how people on opposite sides of a major
factional split in Nabenchauk tend to give almost unrecognizably different accounts of the events which led to particular manifestations of factional disputes. On a smaller scale, I followed the progress of a dispute
between two men, Xun and Lol, centering on Xun's wife.

Here are two versions of the story, one from a friend of Lol, the other
from a friend and ally of Xun.

Version 1   (from Lol's friend):
Lol stole Xun's wife. Before she was married, Lol
courted her, since she was very pretty. But Xun elbowed
in and was the first to get the consent of the girl's mother.
Lol went to the girl to ask whether she would marry
Xun. The girl replied that she must. So Lol decided to
marry the girl's younger sister. But Xun was a bad
husband. He did not provide his wife with corn; he was
often drunk; he beat her. The wife and children suffered
from hunger. Luckily the wife was industrious, and she
wove clothes to sell, buying the thread from her own
labor. She was unhappy, and finally she went to Lol
(who was then an official at the town hall) to ask him
to help her find work as a maid somewhere in San
Cristóbal? She wanted to leave her husband. Lol thought:
"Why should I send her off to San Cristóbal? I might
as well marry her myself." So he sent her out to collect
firewood, as his own wife was feeling ill. Soon Xun
arrived and, as he came near the house, he caught a

glimpse of his wife there. He said to Lol: "Where is my wife? Have you seen her?"

Lol replied that he had not. "Why should she come to me?" he asked.

"Well," replied Xun, "I got drunk and scolded her, so she ran away."

"If you've lost your wife, don't come to me; go tell the presidente," was the reply.

Xun did take the case to the presidente, who summoned Lol. But Lol waited several hours before going to Zinacantan Center, and during this time Xun got very drunk and was no longer able to plead his case at the town hall. The presidente scolded Lol for not having admitted that Xun's wife had come to see him. But Lol said he was willing to marry the woman, although he had not himself solicited her attentions—she had, after all, been driven out by her husband's ill-treatment.

Xun tried to have Lol jailed, but since the whole affair was his own fault, he was unsuccessful.

Eventually, Lol's first wife grew angry and threatened to leave. Lol told her: "Go on if you want to." Now Lol just has the one stolen wife, the older sister (who is prettier anyway); and Xun just sits all alone at home.

Version 2   (from Xun's companion):

Xun's wife was always dissatisfied with her huband's bad luck, and she took it ill when he would drink with his friends and scold her. However, he never beat her. One day she simply took it into her head to run away. She went to Lol's house, where her sister lived, and asked to stay. Lol agreed to keep both women.

Soon Xun's wife said to Lol: "You must murder my husband; otherwise he will come to murder you."

Lol agreed, and he hired a friend named Petul to shoot Xun. Petul was a powerful *ejido* official with many lawyer friends in the ladino world.

Petul hid by the path and tried to ambush Xun. He shot at him twice and put a hole in Xun's shirt, although Xun managed to escape. Xun knew that since Lol was an official at the town hall he would have no success pleading his case in Zinacantan; so he went to the municipal town hall in San Cristóbal and had both Lol and Petul jailed for attempted murder. He brought in his shirt with the bullet hole as evidence, and he produced witnesses who had seen the attackers shooting and brandishing machetes.

> However, after only a few hours in jail, both Lol and
> Petul managed to secure their releases. And they were
> walking the streets again that very same day.
> That's how it is when you have money and friends.
> You can always bribe your way out of trouble.

Although in my fieldwork I did not systematically collect variant
accounts of stories, I am aware that all the gossip I heard is likely to be
as selective and as biased as these two versions of the same story clearly
are. The stories must be understood as coming from particular narrators,
each with his own interests and allegiances, and natives regularly reckon
with such factors.

The identity of the narrator intrudes on gossip in another way. Different people are variously well-informed about the events in gossip; more
interestingly, they may have different preoccupations. A man named
Lukax was discovered in an adulterous relationship with the wife of a
high town hall official. Men from his own hamlet, when telling the story,
were most interested in the history of the liaison and in Lukax's previous
evil tendencies. A man from another hamlet, who is incidentally extremely concerned with his own public image, related only the circumstances through which the guilty couple were punished and shamed by
having to perform hard labor in the middle of a large fiesta. Similarly,
the fact that a particular man is himself reputed to have fathered several
illegitimate children and possessed several dozen mistresses lends extra
significance to the large number of gossip stories he tells about such
womanizing behavior in others.

The interaction between the storyteller and his audience involves
considerable manipulation of ideas, opinions, and information (see fig.
4). Paine (1967) and Cox (1970) use the term "information-manage-
ment"—after Goffman's "impression-management" (1959), which itself
characterizes gossip sessions—to describe a narrator's use of gossip to
influence his interlocutor's opinions, and, in fact, to control the other's
access to information—either by giving information or by withholding it.

Clearly, the identity of the interlocutor will influence what a narrator
says. One never gossips directly to one's victim; and one is reluctant to
gossip to those who are in a position to blab.[12] Contrariwise, Zinacantecos at first seemed reluctant to gossip in front of me as an outsider;
only when I showed some familiarity with the people in question (by
letting slip some bit of gossip I had heard elsewhere) and when they
were familiar with me would Zinacantecos decide it was possible to talk
freely in my presence.

Gossip is plainly *aimed* at the interlocutor. People try, through gossip,
to convince their interlocutors, to arouse their sympathies, or to recruit

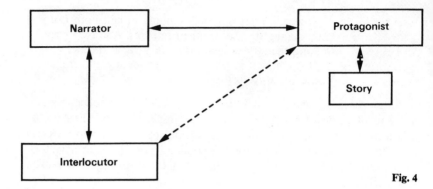

Fig. 4

their support. During the preparations for a wedding in the hamlet of Nabenchauk, members of both the groom's family and the bride's family took time to gossip with the godfather, who is ritually charged with the care of the souls of the couple (Vogt 1969, p. 216) and who will "mediate between the couple in any disputes that arise" (J. Collier 1970, p. 159). Before setting out for the church in Zinacantan Center the groom's family told the godfather how uncooperative the bride's father had been, how the mother of the bride had continually sent messages to her daughter (who had for several weeks been living with her fiancé), trying to lure her home on some pretext. They shook their heads and said, "This wedding is not going well. The relatives of the bride are too ill-tempered."

Later, while the godfather and the bride's family rode together to Zinacantan Center, the bride's father complained of the boy's misconduct. He alleged that the boy got angry with the girl and beat her whenever she went home to visit her mother and her sick grandmother.

The godfather tried to soothe both sides, urging them to wait until after the wedding to see how the couple got along.

The object of all this gossip was quite specific. The bride's family wanted to avoid a civil marriage and to have only the church wedding. If the girl eventually decided to leave her husband, she would be required to pay a large sum to expunge a civil marriage from the Zinacantan records. Without a civil marriage, she would be free simply to leave. The groom's family, on the other hand, planned to insist on a civil marriage to bind the girl. Therefore the bride's family gossiped to convince the godfather not to insist on the civil marriage after the church ceremony. (In this case, the godfather's own interest was to make the marriage permanent; though he listened sympathetically to the pleas of both sides, he nonetheless made sure that the civil marriage occurred.)

Ironically, when this particular marriage fell apart after two years, gossip was again aimed at the godfather, but the strategies of both sides had backfired. The wife had left her husband, complaining of mistreatment and frequent beatings, of never being allowed to visit her mother. The man claimed that he was glad to see her go, that she had been lazy and ill-tempered with his mother. Several points of contention festered during a year-long separation. The woman returned in secret one afternoon and abducted her year-old daughter whom she had left behind when she ran away and who was being cared for by the man's mother. But the wife was unable to regain her own clothes and possessions (weaving and cooking implements). In turn the husband accused the woman of having stolen not only the little girl but also some cash which had been in the house. He accused the woman of having a lover, who had never ceased to meet with her during their married life.

The godfather had the duty to try to reconcile the pair. The wife's family now argued to him that the boy was acting badly, was refusing to care for his own child; that he had robbed the girl of her personal belongings and had never made a proper attempt to reconcile the matter by approaching his father-in-law in a formal way. They urged the godfather to force the boy to settle the matter.

The boy gossiped to the godfather about the wife's wretched behavior and retold the rumours about her having a secret lover. Moreover, he disclosed confidentially that he could never live with the woman again, that she had accused him of having a bent penis. He wanted to enlist the godfather's help in dissolving the civil marriage (that he and his group had insisted upon at the marriage ceremony!).

In the end the godfather withdrew entirely from the matter, saying:

"If you plan to reconcile your differences and begin living together again, then I will help you. But why should I stand before the presidente as godfather of your marriage and be shamed if you divorce one another once and for all?"

Because of his formal duties and responsibilities as godfather he was able to accept the gossip from neither side, despite the sympathies he might have felt as a private citizen. He was forced to be a quite unsatisfactory interlocutor, neither assenting to nor openly opposing the moral interpretations of events suggested by the gossip of one side or the other. (In fact, as the divorce began to seem more and more inevitable, the godfather actively sought to avoid conversation with either side.)

Gossip clearly propagates factions in Zinacantan; much of the informal talk between Zinacanteco men who are in San Cristóbal for business purposes has to do with the latest developments on issues that are the focus of disagreement and hostility. Recently, such factional issues have included the introduction of (and payment for) schools, electricity, all-weather roads, potable water, and so forth (cf. Rush 1971; Haviland 1974b).

Zinacanteco narrative style, and the nature of the interaction between narrator and interlocutor, gives gossip its power as catalyst of factional disputes. Perhaps gossip can be said to "reaffirm cultural values" in the sense that in gossip events are discussed and their outcomes rationalized.[13] But this is more than reaffirmation: the narrator tries to manipulate his interlocutor's opinions; he not only makes statements with which the interlocutor will necessarily agree, but he actively solicits agreement and sympathy. The patterned responses of an interlocutor, the interjections and grunts between the narrator's phrases, are morally charged. Far from being merely neutral, they express agreement, surprise, acceptance, or discomfort over the narrator's conclusions. The skillful gossip appeals selectively to rulelike propositions to create and deliver the desired impression.

Moreover, a prudent gossip often elicits as much information from his interlocutor as he himself is prepared to divulge (if not more). A woman in Nabenchauk whom I had frequent occasion to visit always grilled me about the doings of my neighbors—people whose affairs she knew well enough herself—simply to discover what my reactions were and how much I knew. She delighted in scoring points against her rivals by revealing to me details about them of which I was unaware. She also tried to elicit allegiance from me, at the expense of other Zinacantecos with whom I had some relationship. (She wove my clothes, and she constantly fished for declarations of the form: "I ask you to weave this for me because my *comadre* X cannot weave as well as you!")

Similarly, during the Who's Who sessions for one hamlet, a particular old man who knew the histories of all concerned often feigned ignorance. He could thereby hear someone else's gossip and observe someone else's opinions.

Finally, I may extend my diagram to include the salient groups to which protagonist, narrator, and interlocutor belong and to relate the particular story recounted in a single gossip session to the entire "cultural code" which "governs" behavior (see fig. 5). One might study what groups can (or commonly do) gossip with what groups about what other groups. That is, in the most general sense, gossip can be understood as a phenomenon taking place between individuals who belong to groups,[14] just as the particular transgressions of individuals (which provide the material for gossip) can only be fully understood as departures from some general standards of appropriateness. The striking thing about gossip is its absorptive capacity; it contains clues to an unlimited set of ethnographic facts. Despite particular uses to which we put it—as, for example, the survey of the subjects of gossip stories in the next chapter—we are able to master gossip as an activity only when we have, essentially, mastered the whole culture.

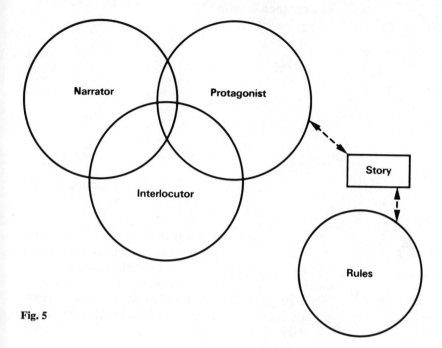

Fig. 5

5

What do Zinacantecos gossip about? I have hypothesized that Zinacantecos' conversations about their neighbors will not, in fact, range over all possible subjects but will center on selected topics of interest—a wide but limited range. I suggest that a corpus of Zinacanteco gossip could be organized to form an encyclopedia of Zinacanteco social life; that what Zinacantecos gossip about is a good index of what they worry about.

A survey of the gossip I heard in Zinacantan turns up just such a limited range of topics and preoccupations. To give the reader a glimpse of this range, in this chapter I consider the information about people that surfaced during Who's Who sessions, including those offhand remarks clearly designed to lead into more elaborate stories as well as the recurrent themes of the gossip I heard in less restricted settings.

The Who's Who of Zinacantan captures part of the shared knowledge available about well-known and notorious Zinacantecos. Starting with lists of people generally well known, George Collier and I added to the lists by asking for the names of people who fitted certain categories. The categories themselves, in turn, grew out of short characterizations and descriptions which occurred when members of the Who's Who panels identified people among themselves. If, for example, a man was identified as

"Xun from Pasteʔ, the curer"

we added the word *jʔilol* ("curer") to the set of categories.

Table 1 shows the entire category list (which is discussed in more detail in Appendix 2). This set of descriptive phrases, I reasoned, was a kind of catalog of Zinacanteco social personae. The most common identifying labels, I suspect, mark precisely those macroidentities (at some gross analytical level; see Keesing 1970) which are most culturally or practically salient. Especially in a society where names are often insufficient to identify an individual unambiguously, the best identifier will be a person's most significant feature, the source of his widest reputation: for example, Xun, the *curer*.

Often more suggestive information emerged from the Who's Who. In the midst of discussions about a man's nicknames or his cargo history someone might interject a remark like,

"He fights with his elder brother," or
"His wife is a Chamula, not a Zinacanteca," or
"He tried to murder his neighbor."

Most such comments constitute *incipient* gossip. They demand amplification, hinting that there is more to be said, if others are willing to take the time to gossip. A few such remarks, all of which arose spontaneously during Who's Who discussions of a single hamlet, show what sort of conversational tease will pique a Zinacanteco's interest. I have arranged the examples into several rough categories.

a. Courtship, marriage, and sexual habits

Ibat ta pojbel slekom.
"He had his fiancée stolen away."
J-poj-tzeb.
"He is a girl thief."

Many courtships fail because an engaged girl takes up with another boy (J. Collier 1973, pp. 211ff.). Since courtship involves considerable expense, losing a girl to another man is both an affront and an economic setback. News of fractured romances and illicit liaisons kept our own household constantly entertained. The wronged suitor is thought a fool, whereas the girl thief is considered laughable for failing to curb his sexual impulses.

Conversations start, as well, with intimations of promiscuity or sexual deviance.

J'elek' mis, j'elek' 'antz.
"He is a pussy stealer, a woman stealer."
Lek chak' matanal.
"The woman gives many free gifts."
Ispas preva xchi'uk sni' me'el.
"He had a try with his mother-in-law."

Table 1   **Who's Who Category List**

Tzotzil	English
Cargoholding	
1. jpas?abtel	cargoholder
2. pasaro	man who has finished cargo hierarchy
3. totil-me?il	ritual adviser
Religious service and auxiliary personnel	
4. ch'ul mol	holy elder
5. jk'echnomal	saint-bearer
6. pixkal	sacristan
7. chk'ot ta ch'omil	serves as ritual helper
Civil offices	
8. ?abtel ta kavilto	work at town hall
9. preserente	municipal *presidente*
10. ?ajensya	hamlet-level *agente*
11. krinsupal	hamlet representative, *principal*
12. komite	member of *ejido* committee
13. lukasyon	member of school committee
14. jtzobtak'in	tax collector
15. jjunta	*fiesta* committee member
Ritual specialists	
16. jchik'pom	incense burner
17. jjapkantela	candle-bearer
18. jvabajom	musician, flutist, drummer
19. j?amarero, jtampolero	
20. jtenkamaro	cannoneer
Curing	
21. j?ilol	curer
22. jtamol	midwife
23. jtz'akbak	bonesetter
Dispute settlement and secular skills	
24. jmeltzanejk'op	dispute settler
25. sna? rason	wise
26. xtojob ta k'opojel	capable talker
27. sna? k'op ryox	prays well
28. sna? kastiya	speaks Spanish
29. sna? vun	literate
30. ?ep xpetomaj	often chosen as godfather
31. jva?anejna, j?alvanil	house builder, mason
32. jtz'ispixalal	sews hats
Economic indicators	
33. jk'ulej	rich
34. ?oy skaro	truck-owner
35. ?oy smulino	owns corn mill
36. ?oy styenta	store-owner
37. ?oy svakax, ska?, xchij	owns cattle, horses, sheep

38.	xak' ta ch'om stak'in	lends money
39.	xak' ta jolinom stak'in	lends at interest
40.	jchonʔatz'am	salt-seller
41.	jʔekel-ʔixim, -turasnu, -nichim	reseller of corn, peaches, flowers
42.	snaʔ slakan pox	distills liquor

Negatively evaluated characteristics

43.	ʔoy sryox	owns talking saint

Witchcraft

44.	jʔak'chamel	witch
45.	snaʔ xchonvan ta balamil	sells souls
46.	snaʔ xk'opoj ta balamil	deals with Earth Lord

Aggression

47.	jmilvanej	murderer
48.	jmakbe	assassin, bandit
49.	jʔelek'	thief

Troublemaking

50.	jsaʔk'op	troublemaker
51.	jchukvanej	man who jails others
52.	ʔep sta chukel, lek xaʔi pus	often jailed, enjoys jail
53.	pukuj yoʔon	ill-tempered

Poverty, drunkenness

53.	jyakubel	drunk
54.	mu sut yuʔun yil	unable to repay debts
55.	meʔon	poor
56.	ch'aj, mu snaʔ xʔabtej	lazy

Mental incapacity

57.	chuvaj	crazy
58.	jvoviel	madman
59.	xchujil	feeble-minded
60.	sonso	stupid
61.	sovra	worthless, good-for-nothing
62.	ʔumaʔ	dumb, with speech impediment

In a slightly different vein, it is noteworthy for an adult to be unmarried.

Te stuk, ch'abal yajnil.
"There he is, all alone, without a wife."

No man, and few women, in Zinacantan can survive unmarried. For a
man to grow old without a wife is considered, at best, unnatural; and
the widower is truly pitiable, turning from one female relative to another for his food.

b. Wealth and poverty

Comments about another Zinacanteco's riches or lack of riches are rarely idle. Sometimes the attribution of wealth is accompanied by sinister suggestions:

> Jk'ulej tajmek, ʔolon staoj.
> "He is very rich; he found his wealth in the lowlands" [i.e., by witchcraft].

Similarly, to comment on another Zinacanteco's poverty is often to complain about debts unpaid—

> Tzinil ta ʔil.
> "He is tightly entwined in debts."
> Mu ʔaltikuk tzpas yil.
> "He just incurs new debts without a thought."

—or to moralize archly about the failings of humankind:

> Ch'ajch'ajtik yilel.
> "He seems a bit lazy."
> Ibat ta burdel stak'in.
> "His money went to the bordello."

c. Temperament and physical peculiarity

Some people depart from the even-tempered, sociable ideal. The observation that someone

> pukujtik yoʔon timi saʔbat sjole
> "is evil-tempered if provoked"

invites an anecdote to prove the point. In the same way, though deformities and physical oddities often prompt nicknames,[1] certain disclosures obviously lead into further interesting stories.

> Staoj k'aʔel, solel xtuet.
> "She contracted rot and became simply foul."
> Lajem ta bala snutiʔal-ʔat.
> "His scrotum was ruined by a bullet."

d. Religious and civil office

Most offhand remarks about cargo performance or civil office deal with failure, through reluctance or inability, to carry through the responsibilities of a job.

> Ch'ayem smartomoreyal.
> "He lost his opportunity to be *mayordomorey.*"

Te toyel toyel batel yuʔun.
"He kept putting off and putting off [his entry into public office]."[2]

Other remarks highlight the incongruity between failure in ritual duties and respected old age.

Tol xvay ta totil-meʔilal.
"He sleeps too much when he is ritual adviser."
Mol ta yech.
"He is an old man good for nothing" [i.e., despite his age he never finished the cargo system or became a ritual adviser].

Cargo performance, both successful and unsuccessful, is a preoccupation of gossips in Zinacantan. I shall discuss the ethnographic content of the great volume of resulting talk in chapter 6.

Offhand remarks of the kind I have called incipient gossip demonstrate a clear link between identifying schemata—taken as standard formulas by which gossips pinpoint and identify protagonists—and frequent gossip topics. A particular man may, in certain circles, be recognized as, say, "Xun from Nabenchauk," whereas in another context his name will be unknown, while part of his reputation—as, say, "the man who was jailed for drunkenness on the first day of the Fiesta of San Lorenzo last year"—will be sufficient identification. Identifying schemata thus form a rough continuum, ranging from highly specific and neutral (names, kin relations, places of residence, etc.), to identifying items of information, often with evaluative overtones, that draw on wider parts of the audience's knowledge of reputation and past gossip. Hence, frequent gossip topics, sometimes in the form of reduced "incipient gossip," feed the corpus of characterizations which can be used, in turn, to identify individuals. It is for similar reasons that a person's "good name," in our society, consists of a good deal more than his or her name.

Soon the Who's Who panelists stopped alluding to gossip stories and began telling them. The resulting tales, and all the gossip material I gathered in other situations, both formal and natural, during my stay in Zinacantan, form a corpus of texts whose recurrent themes can be extracted, if not properly quantified. By means of a flexible coding system[3] I arrived at a categorization of themes and subject matter, which appears in full in Appendix 3.

Table 2 shows twenty common gossip subjects, raised frequently in stories told during Who's Who sessions as well as in other contexts. These twenty categories include all those topics which occur in 5 percent or more of the (roughly one thousand) discrete stories in the corpus.[4]

Table 2   **Most Common Gossip**
                     Themes

Subject	Number of Stories in Who's Who	Number in Other Gossip	Total
1. Drunkenness, drinking, and drunken behavior	64	68	132
2. Divorce, child support	69	42	111
3. Illicit sexual relations, incest, fornication	68	48	116
4. Jail, other punishment	66	35	101
5. Wealth, poverty	52	38	90
6. Kin disputes	45	45	90
7. Courtship	33	46	79
8. Adultery	34	40	74
9. Fighting, beating	44	28	72
10. Stealing, embezzlement	41	29	70
11. Cargos	36	32	68
12. *Cabildo* scenes, dispute settlement	32	40	72
13. Witchcraft	48	19	67
14. Promiscuity	32	31	63
15. Scolding, quarreling	37	24	61
16. Sickness and death	24	30	54
17. Curing	35	20	55
18. Marriage disputes	33	21	54
19. Murder	36	18	54
20. Fleeing	22	28	50

Table 3 shows further topics which occur with notable frequency in either Who's Who gossip or other gossip, but not both. In what follows I give examples of the sorts of stories Zinacantecos tell involving some of these frequent conversational topics.

1. Drunkenness

It would be easy to select from conversational texts all passages having to do with drunkenness by cueing the root *yak*, which occurs, for example, in *-yakub* ("get drunk"), and a few others. The category is unambiguous, and the topic is omnipresent: more than one story in ten contains at least a reference to some sort of drunken behavior. Consider the following stories.

> Several drunken men terrorized an innocent tourist who had the misfortune to stray into a Zinacanteco village off the Pan-American highway. The ladino authorities dragged the drunken offenders from their beds in retaliation, taking them to jail without their pants.
>
> A woman curer is known as a heavy drinker when she cures; when drunk she rants and raves and has even been known to curse the saints.

Table 3   **Additional Frequent Topics**
                     in Gossip

Subject	Number of Stories
Frequent Topics in Who's Who Gossip	
Borrowing and lending	36
Factional and land disputes	33
Troublemaking, *saʔ-k-op*	30
Past and ancient events	28
Miscellaneous violence	25
Frequent Topics in Other Gossip	
Rape	34
Nicknames	26

> A man is so accomplished at sewing the traditional style
> hats that he could surely support himself at this trade
> were it not for his propensity to drink. Sometimes he will
> sew an entire hat for just one litre of liquor.

> A man recently died in Hot Country after falling into a
> river while stone drunk.

Conversation is scattered with remarks like

> Batz'i lek xaʔi pox leʔe.
> "He really likes his liquor."

and observations about a man's drinking habits, even when stories are
not explicitly about the consequences of drinking and drunkenness.

2. Divorce

Zinacantecos talk a lot about divorce: the circumstances leading to it
and its terms—including the provisions for child custody and support.
Some gossip is about particular cases.

> The son of a powerful man divorced his first wife. The
> husband's family thought the girl was too lazy: she
> wouldn't get up early to grind corn for her husband's
> tortillas; she spent too much time at her parents' home.
> The woman was sent packing with her child.

> A man abandoned his wife and child to take up with a
> mistress. Since the marriage had included a civil
> ceremony—and was thus listed on official *municipio*
> records—the wife went to San Cristóbal to demand a
> civil divorce and support for her child. The man was
> jailed for not producing the money, and he eventually
> made up with his wife and returned to her.

Other gossip relating to divorce has to do with the habits of people while divorced (bereft men sitting in fireless houses; gay divorced women seeking multitudes of lovers, etc.). And the following story is about a divorce-monger.

> An old woman used to serve frequently as a mediator between married people having fights. But she tended to encourage the woman not to make up with her husband and, instead, to seek divorce. She fanned the flames of disputes.

3. Illicit sexual relations

This category includes stories of sexual relations between unmarried people and incest. (Adultery, having slightly different legal consequences, is listed separately below.)

> A cargoholder was chagrined when his daughter was caught fornicating with a sacristan while she was supposed to be washing the clothes of a saint image.
>
> A notorious witch is reputed to have screwed his own mother in front of a cave in which he had performed witchcraft ceremonies—this in order to render his spells especially potent.
>
> A man was glimpsed having intercourse with an unknown girl in a dry creek-bed. Passersby pelted him with rocks.

Zinacantecos feel that sexual mores are degenerating. Whereas in past times unmarried boys and girls could be whipped for merely talking to one another, according to a man from Zinacantan Center nowadays one frequently comes upon couples embracing in the shelter of trees and bushes near paths. Gossip turned so often to illicit sexual relations during the Who's Who sessions that the panel coined a new euphemism for intercourse: *ʔak' ʔinyeksyon*: literally, "give injections."

4. Jail, and other punishment

Almost every gossip story about a public dispute ends with the jailing of one of the principals. And a frequent source of gossip is the news that springs from a fresh jailing. There are other sorts of punishment:

> A man had planned to enter an expensive and prestigious first-level cargo. However, because he beat his wife so often, he was made into a *mayol* by the presidente. [A *mayol* is a very low-prestige first-level cargo, and its duties amount to little more than serving

as errand boy and occasionally as policeman at the
service of town hall officials.]

A man and a woman caught as adulterers were not only
given jail terms but also were forced to perform public
labor clearing the waterways of Zinacantan Center
during a large fiesta when crowds gathered to watch and
mock them.

5. Wealth and poverty

Much gossip is devoted to the acquisition and outward manifestations
of wealth. Similarly, gossips often cluck their tongues over the loss of
wealth and the hardships endured by the poverty-stricken.

A wealthy man claims to have started out as a poor
farmer. He got his first money from distilling cane liquor
and "taking money from drunks." He and his wife went
to the church in Zinacantan Center and prayed to San
Lorenzo for wealth. In a dream the wife saw herself
before a woman inside the church who handed her a bag
full of gold coins. From that moment, the man claims,
he has prospered.

The son of a wealthy man, who used to own a "ranch"
with cattle and horses, squandered all his money on
whores in Tuxtla after his father died. He is now
poverty-stricken.

A man who has for a long time claimed to be sick, and
who walks with a limp, is so poor that he sometimes
goes to Tuxtla to beg.

A woman from Nabenchauk was divorced by her
husband and faced the prospect of raising three children
with no means of support. She sold one of her sons to
work as a *mozo* [indentured laborer] in San Cristóbal,
and used that money to survive.

Zinacantecos argue that acquiring wealth requires diligent work, good
luck, and piety. Extreme poverty, on the other hand, is most often due
to laziness and dissipation; Zinacantecos take the selling of children or
property as a sign of desperation induced by lack of money.

6. Kin disputes

Jane Collier (1973, pp. 169ff.) characterizes public legal disputes between kinsmen as "usually presented by both parties as disputes over
land or other physical property."

She distinguishes three general categories: problems that arise between a boy and his guardians or parents (pp. 171–73); disputes between siblings (pp. 173–76); and problems that arise over property held by women (pp. 176–78). Though conflicts between kinsmen may ultimately take the form of property disputes if they reach the town hall, gossip is able to dig more deeply into the motivations of kin conflict and its immediate manifestations.

> Two men from different hamlets who share a common grandfather were cooperating in building a house in Zinacantan Center to be used by members of the family and friends for their cargos. One man, the owner of the land in question, had lent money to the other; when the money was not repaid in time the two men quarreled. The first man calculated how much his cousin had contributed to the building of the house; he deducted this amount from the other's debt and thenceforward excluded the other from use of the new house.

> A respected old man is estranged from his daughter. His sons, after marriage, all moved out, leaving him only two daughters. He invited the elder girl's fiancé to come live in his house compound in order to have another man there to work with him. But the boy also crept into bed with the man's younger daughter and deflowered her. The old man married the younger girl off immediately in an inferior match, and he threw out the offending son-in-law. But the first daughter, longing for her husband, finally herself abandoned her aged father and went to live with the husband. Now the old man has hardened his heart against the daughter and will no longer speak to her.

I have also included gossip about disputes between a man and his in-laws under the category of kin disputes.

> A young man who quarreled with his father-in-law over the performance of his new bride has recently tried several times to implicate his father-in-law in theft. He accuses the old man of having gotten him drunk and having stolen a one-thousand-peso bill from him. Everyone agrees, however, that the story is a lie concocted "so that he could get his father-in-law jailed."

> A man who had moved in with his wife and his widowed mother-in-law after his marriage argued so much with the old woman that she eventually moved out, even

though the land was hers. "He couldn't live in the same house with her so he drove her out."

7. Courtship and courtship disputes

Most gossip about courtship has to do with broken courtships requiring court settlement (cf. Jane Collier 1973, chap. 10). One informant told me with great glee about the troubles that a respected elder in Nachij had over his sons' courtships. The first son lost his fiancée to an interloper after several years of courtship; then the second son himself broke up another courtship and was forced to marry the girl and pay back the injured suitor's expenses. Both cases were ultimately settled at the town hall with great scandal.

The gossip covers a range of events that did not necessarily end at the *cabildo*. In one story the bad performance of a suitor had drastic consequences.

> A boy had asked for the hand of a fierce old man's daughter. He was accepted as a suitor, but the girl's family was not pleased with the boy's evident poverty or the fact that he had no hat [or other proper young man's furnishings]. The boy went down to Hot Country with a bottle to get into the good graces of his future father-in-law and brothers-in-law who were working there. But the others turned on him and murdered him by throwing him off the mountainside.

In other cases the suitor is simply rejected outright.

> A man whose mother was known to be evil-tempered had a hard time getting a second wife after his first wife divorced him. He approached one girl, but her family refused to let her go off "only to be scolded, only to be scorned and beaten" by the boy's mother.

> A boy born in a now-abandoned hamlet had difficulty finding a wife. Girls mocked him, saying, "this is not your hamlet; you cannot take a wife from here."

The gossip also includes stories in which a boy and girl elope, thereby denying the girl's family its rightful bride-price; cases in which a prospective bride flees marriage at the last minute; cases in which a boy abandons a courtship (when he hears that his fiancée has "gotten injections from another" or when he tires of the expense); and stories of excessive bride-prices (one man even charged interest on a delayed bride-payment for his daughter). Very rarely does gossip touch on courtships which seemed outwardly successful.

One of an old man's several daughters was considered
remarkable because only she, of all her sisters, *tuk'
inupun* ["got married correctly"].

8. Adultery

Adultery is by far the most frequent topic of gossip about married couples. Jane Collier (1973) states the formal position regarding charges of
adultery as follows: "Although gossip implies that many Zinacantecos
indulge in extramarital affairs, a formal accusation of adultery, by either
husband or wife, is a serious matter usually leading to divorce. Unless
the accusation is dismissed as false at a hamlet hearing, the case goes
to the town hall, where the aggrieved husband asks his wife's lover to
recompense him for the bride-price and has the guilty pair jailed, or the
aggrieved wife demands a divorce and a substantial share of her husband's property" (p. 189). Gossip about adultery does not wait for a
husband or wife to make a public complaint. Furthermore, there is no
doubt about the bias in men's gossip about adultery: a cuckold is made
foolish by his adulterous wife; a man committing adultery is simply
following his natural (if excessive) impulses (Can you blame him if he
is a man?), even if he wrongs his wife in the process.

> A man who spends considerable time in Tuxtla working
> as a bricklayer's apprentice is mocked for not visiting
> his wife more often. Everyone suspects, though, that the
> woman gets a bit of sexual satisfaction on the side;
> her husband can't know about such adultery "because it
> doesn't leave marks the way, say, sandals do."

> A woman once asked her neighbor to help her fix
> up the corn bin while her husband was away. She then
> complained to the visitor about her husband's lack of
> ingenuity and pluck. The neighbor, seeing his oppor-
> tunity, offered to take care of her in still more ways, and
> the woman agreed. She made arrangements to leave her
> door open at night; and he told his wife that he had
> to go out to make a deal with a truck owner about
> having corn delivered. The adulterous liaison went on
> for some time until the man was spotted climbing out of
> his neighbor's window.

> A powerful elder has an illegitimate child, product of an
> adulterous union from his youth. He had approached
> an old man about borrowing a horse; the old man sent
> his daughter along to help catch the animal. The girl,
> once they were out in the woods, solicited the man's
> attentions, and finally he agreed to oblige her. Later the

girl kept pestering the man despite the fact that he had a wife; when she got pregnant she charged that he had raped her. He denied it and related the whole story, defending his action before the presidente saying, "Would *you* refuse such a gift?" He made up with his wife and simply gave money to have his child reared.

9. Fighting, beating

Casual observation in Zinacantan would reveal little overt violence; only drunks are sufficiently uninhibited to punch and push each other. This is not to say that ambushes and sober fights do not occur.

The hamlet *principal* was walking near the gate of a girl who was known to have several lovers. Suddenly a group of men jumped out of the bushes, beat him up, and stole some money from him. He accused several boys later, but all agreed that the leader was probably Antun, the girl's most jealous lover.

Two well-known witches once got into a fight. One hit the other about three times. The beaten man then threatened to kill the other by witchcraft, but nothing happened. "Perhaps their powers are equal."

Two brothers have long been fierce enemies. "They almost bite each other when they meet on the path."

Still, men rarely come to blows; aggression is usually covert, as when a man resorts to secret witchcraft. Thus, it is always news when two men actually square off.

10. Stealing

Not all theft is punished by the town hall; in fact, few petty thieves are caught in the act, and there is usually no way to prove theft after the fact.

A young man is now known as "Turkey Thief." He used to round up his neighbor's turkeys, put them in a white flour sack, and carry them to Tuxtla to sell. He was discovered when an old lady neighbor went searching for a turkey that had strayed into the cornfield; she looked in his house and couldn't see anything because her turkey was inside a bag hanging from the rafters. But she heard it, and the boy was made to pay.

An *agente* from Nabenchauk was removed from office and forced to flee after it was discovered that he had

> embezzled leftover funds from various fiesta taxes and
> school levies and spent the money himself. He eventually
> returned about one thousand pesos, though rumor has
> it that he stole considerably more.

As I mentioned above, a few old women and lazy young men have reputations for light-fingeredness: they pick up clothes set out to dry on house compound fences, grab fruits or tools left unguarded in other people's yards, and steal squash as they walk through cornfields. Other men steal more systematically.

> A good-for-nothing man (who used to take his whole
> family to visit his father, when he knew the old man
> would be eating, just to be given a free meal) hired
> himself out as a laborer when his father was harvesting
> corn. But instead of picking all the corn he saw, he left a
> considerable amount on the plants; later he went back
> to collect what was left for himself.
>
> Another good-for-nothing married a clever woman who
> had her own money. He forced her to lend him large
> sums of money which he squandered on his own projects
> —lending to enhance his prestige, buying a liquor still,
> building a large brick house with a lock on the door—
> never repaying a *centavo*. He walks around in a warm
> woolen tunic, but he bought it with money stolen from
> his wife.

Thus, despite the fact that relatively few cases of theft come before the presidente, the idiom of "stealing" (Tzotzil root *-elk'*) is frequently used in describing unearned gain.

11. Cargo performance and failure

Because of the general interest in cargo affairs much conversation has to do with the schedule of officeholding, the identities of future cargoholders, and so on. Such conversations are neutral; they concern unevaluated matters of fact.

The cargo system contributes to more highly charged gossip when a man's performance—good or bad—comes under scrutiny. Gossip recounts how men fail to enter their cargos on time because of wrongdoing or insufficient funds; it scorns men for incomplete cargo service, for leaving their cargos in the middle, or for serious misconduct in office. The cargo system gives rise to gossip about other peculiar situations.

An extremely old man has asked for a first-level cargo. Everyone considers it odd, indeed, that he should begin his service so late.

People laugh about the apparent fact that in the whole hamlet of ʔElan Voʔ nearly no one has passed any cargo except the low-ranking *mayol*, the presidente's errand boys.

In the next chapter I shall examine cargo gossip in some detail.

12. *Cabildo* scenes, dispute settlement

Table 2 shows that more than 7 percent of the stories in the gossip corpus include accounts of formal dispute settlement, either by hamlet elders or at the town hall. Many stories, that is, have to do with events which ultimately lead actors to conflict that must be formally resolved; the gossip includes the settlement as part of the story.

13. Witchcraft

Gossip about witchcraft dwells first on different techniques for sending sickness and death. People are interested in the details of petitions to the Earth Lord to exchange souls for wealth, and in the ghoulish remnants of witchcraft ceremonies found in caves or dug up in the cemetery. Zinacantecos are fascinated, horrified, and amused all at once by stories like the one in which a witch has intercourse with his own mother to make his spells irreversible. There is a morbid, half-joking narrative style which characterizes accounts of supernatural powers.

> "People just say that he goes out at night and becomes a goat."
> "*Carajo!*"
> "That's what I hear, that he has singular habits."
> "Something of a witch, eh?"
> "Yes. He turns himself into a goat, and then wanders about on the path. He has frightened lots of people there near his house, I hear."
> "But how did the people see him? Did he just transform himself while they were watching?"
> "I guess that they saw all right."
> "While they are just this far away, why then he just comes at them shaking his whiskers and his furry hide from side to side. . . ."

"Aha!"

". . . and then when he gets up close; "Bee ti bee ti bee bee," he says. He stamps his front hoof."

"Indeed!"

"And if they try to get him—if they've brought their shotguns, or if they have machetes perhaps, they say to themselves, 'Let's see if he can be hurt at all. . . .' But that old goat refuses to be hurt. He just goes on terrifying people. That's why they call the old man 'the Goat'."

Another large segment of witchcraft's gossip is concerned to pin the blame for individual cases of sickness and death on particular witches. Circulating the rumor that a particular man is a successful witch helps Zinacantecos to know which witches are dangerous enough to avoid and which only make empty threats.

During an argument a self-confessed witch said to his opponent: "We'll see how things turn out tonight or tomorrow"—a veiled threat of witchcraft. His opponent replied: "If you really know how to do it, go ahead, eat [me, my soul] if you have no meat of your own." But no harm came to the man who had quarreled with the witch, leading others to speculate that he is not a witch, but just "says so with his mouth."

And sometimes during gossip sessions Zinacantecos speculate about the credibility of alleged witchcraft phenomena.

"*Kere*, you musn't believe that there are witches! No, sickness comes by itself."

"That's what I say, too: that sickness comes of its own accord. Sickness is ubiquitous."

"I don't believe in witches; they exist according to curers, but I say that is one of their lies. (Ha ha ha.)"

"Well, okay, but—you see we all contract sickness. As for witches, they just torment us; we just get sick from them. But we don't die of it. We will only die one day when sickness comes and, well, we die. But that is according to the command of Our Lord."

"Yes, that is how it is. If we have only a small time, if our destinies are not long, then if we have made enemies and at the same time get sick, well then we conclude that we have been witched."

"Ah, yes, that's what we say. . . ."

"Even if it isn't true."

14. Promiscuity, womanizing

In some moods Zinacantecos will claim that sexual moderation is desirable; that husband and wife ought to remain faithful to one another; that promiscuity is bestial, doglike. Yet a high percentage of gossip has to do with loose women (whom I have arbitrarily labeled "promiscuous") and insatiable men (whom I have called "womanizers"). The metaphor of "giving" pervades descriptions of the sexual act.

> When a notorious woman was first divorced she "gave freely," it didn't matter where or to whom. She "made a gift of it" to other people. "She went to be doctored elsewhere, got lots of injections."

> A man is ridiculed for divorcing his wife to marry his mistress. "But she wasn't only *his* mistress; she had lots of masters. She gave alms to any man who wanted."

Men with insatiable sexual appetites are likely to suffer from their propensity for *tzak-ʔantzile* ("woman grabbing"); whereas promiscuous girls are labeled *loko* (literally, "crazy").

> "And after he told me how he had seduced old Petul's wife I said to him, "But you are just a wicked old fucker, *compadre*."
> " 'Ahh, but I am a *man*,' he replied. (Ha ha ha.)"

During gossip sessions Zinacantecos are eminently able to conceal their own histories and join in moral speculation. (One of the men who gossiped most actively about the sexual exploits of others is reputed to be the father of at least ten illegitimate children!) Similarly, dispute-settlers may not practice what they preach.

> An ex-presidente was mocked for being self-righteous while on the bench. He would say to rapists and adulterers: "*Puta*, but what kind of behavior is that?" But he had his own wicked tendencies, and was beaten once by the mother of a girl he had violated.

A man with two wives may ridicule the sexual appetites of his neighbor who has three.

There is a considerable native theory about sexual desire. "Itchy" women are supposed to have red-colored bugs in their pubic hair. It is considered natural for young women to have as much curiosity about sexual contact as young men.

> Several eligible young women of Nabenchauk have failed to attract suitors. People worry that if no young men

appear to ask for their hands properly, their "heads may
stop functioning" and they will search out lovers
in secret.

Old women are considered to retain sexual sensitivity until their sexual
organs shrink away.

People joke about an old woman who was recently raped
while tending sheep. Her son asked her, "Did you see
who it was?" "It was Chep," she replied. "How was it?"
"It was enough, it was enough," said the old woman.

15. Scolding, quarreling

A feature of all conflict and dispute is the verbal dueling and skillful
scolding of which Zinacantecos are capable. Special words appear in
scolding, and occasionally a man will be moved to speak in couplets
when he rails against another. Laughlin (1975, p. 28) distinguishes the
speech categories of "scolding speech" and "denunciatory speech," the
former being an informal mode "used characteristically when one wishes
. . . to upbraid another" and the latter being the use of formal couplet
speech "in self-righteous declamations at home or at the courthouse"
(p. 28). I assigned gossip stories which included bits of indirectly quoted
scolding to this relatively large category.

The remaining categories listed in table 2 are largely self-explanatory.
Stories of "sickness and death" (category 16) have to do with the circumstances of illness, especially fatal illness. Gossip takes special interest in venereal disease ("rot") and in the loss of life force engendered
by extremely violent sexual intercourse (called "losing one's *chon* ['animal']"). Category 17 contains stories having to do with curing ritual,
the curing powers of certain individuals, and even a few recipes for
potions to cure exotic diseases. (One Who's Who session contains a long
discussion of how to make an aphrodisiac.) Category 18, "marriage
disputes," contains all stories about marital discord except cases of
adultery: wife-beating, husband-scolding, sexual incompatibility. Category 19 includes stories of murder or attempted murder. Finally, category 20 includes stories in which people run away, from their hamlets
or from Zinacantan, to escape punishment or to avoid marriage or
cargos. (Appendix 3 lists and describes all the topic categories which
figure in the gossip corpus.)

I have sampled the most common gossip themes to arm the reader
for considering the following hypothesis: the ability to gossip is a general
manifestation of cultural competence (i.e., the knowledge one has of a
culture) and, hence, as a corollary, the collected gossip of a community

contains the germ of the ethnography of the place. I shall be concerned in the last chapters of this book with the ramifications of such a hypothesis for the theory of ethnography.

Consider first the relationship between the thematic concentrations of gossip and the results of other ethnographic analyses of similar topics.[5] Do people gossip about the same sorts of things which cause conflict and result in legal settlements? Do they gossip and joke about the same topics?

Victoria Bricker (1968, chap. 4) isolates "two main humor complexes" in Zinacantan. She defines the complexes in terms of "cultural categories" as follows:

Class 1   Self-Image Complex
Clothing
Filth
(of body or clothing)
Awkwardness
(i.e., stumbling, falling down)
Caught
(i.e., tied up, limbs imprisoned)
Losing
(when it appears with *clothing,* refers to loss of articles of clothing)
Violence
(hitting, beating, fighting)
Drunkenness

Class 2   Male-Female Relations Complex
Marriage
Lust
(illicit intercourse, seduction)
Efficacy
(when it appears with *Marriage* or *Lust,* refers to sexual prowess)
Exchange
(when it appears with *Marriage* or *Lust,* refers to exchanging women)
Violence
(hitting, fighting, beating)
Deceit
(lying, tricking)
Drunkenness
[p. 54]

Bricker found that the norms governing these ethnographic categories were "implicit in the deviant behavior which Zinacantecos seem to regard as humorous" (p. 52). That is, Zinacantecos are most likely to laugh at people who fumble the rules for maintaining self-image or to ridicule deviance from the standards governing the relations between men and women (cf. Bricker 1973a, pp. 145–49).

The reader has no doubt come to understand that most gossip in Zinacantan is funny, at least to Zinacantecos, and that gossip sessions are occasions of laughter and joking. It would be comforting, then, if the humor complexes Professor Bricker describes were familiar to us as students of Zinacanteco gossip. In fact, the humorous complex having to do with male-female relations seems to lend itself well to gossip; consider the frequent gossip topics of divorce, illicit sexual relations, courtship problems, adultery, promiscuity, marriage disputes, and rape.

As for the Self-Image Complex, gossip seems at least to be looking nearby. A few stories mention clothing deficiencies as a device to highlight other objectionable qualities a person may have.

> "I said to the girl, 'Well, won't you marry Petul since he was the first to ask for your hand?' "
> " 'Why should I bother to sew up his rotten pants for him?' she replied. 'Do you think that's the kind of man I want? He has barely covered his asshole. I want a good man, one who wears his pants a bit longer.' (Ha ha ha.)"
> "Because that guy just wore his pants right up to here. . . . He really had to squeeze himself in. . . ."

Gossip emphasizes the deviant actions which accompany drunkenness rather than the foolish, mud-stained image of the drunk. Bricker finds that drunkenness is the object of humor insofar as consumption of alcohol is an "obstacle to the Zinacanteco's desire to present himself with demeanor in public" (1968, p. 76).

Similarly, fighting and beatings create juicy gossip, just as drunken brawls engender laughter (Bricker 1968, p. 79). Fights prompt gossip, especially when they mark preexisting hostilities or some inherently scandalous underlying situation, for example, adultery.

Nonetheless, gossip is not simply concerned with the demeanor and physical state of individuals in the way Bricker describes for Zinacanteco joking. A large component of joking takes place in contexts where the most available source for a good put-down is appearance or demeanor: the musician who mocks a drunken cargoholder (and thus reprimands him) during a ceremony is joking, but not gossiping. And gossip growing out of the incident emphasizes not simply the man's stupor but his ritual failure.

Table 4   Categories of Conflict

1. Witchcraft
witches who send sickness by themselves
witches who ask for sickness
witches who perform specific actions (e.g., burying meat, cutting candles)
witches with supernatural powers
talking saints
petitions to the Earth Lord
?ok'itabil chamel ("sickness called down by crying")

2. Aggression
threats of witchcraft or murder
false accusations
drunken insults
fighting
beatings
causing sickness (e.g., by frightening)
rape
forcible entry
theft
attempted murder
murder
malicious curing (i.e., hastening the death of patient)

3. Kin disputes
boy vs. guardian or parents
disputes between siblings
disputes regarding women's property

4. Marital disputes
wife-beating
adultery
divorce

5. Courtship disputes
breaking a courtship
elopement
third-person interference in a courtship

6. Disputes between neighbors
debt
unfulfilled curing contract
damage to person (by nonrelative)
damage to property
accidental damage to property
intentional damage—theft
unintentional damage—drunken destructiveness
long-term neighbor fights
political battles

7. Disputes between individual and community
hamlet-level wrongs (failure in obligations to hamlet)
wrongs against entire *municipio*
accusations against high officials

Source   Jane Collier 1970.

Jane Collier (1973) categorizes conflict leading to legal battles; I have extracted her categories in table 4. Again, since gossip draws heavily on the public scandal which flows from town hall court cases, it would be reassuring if conflict categories resembled gossip themes.

It should be clear from inspection that there is a close parallel between what Zinacantecos find interesting to gossip about and what they find worth fighting about.[6] We know that gossip often deals explicitly with town hall settlements and with the jailing that follows a dispute. Gossip precedes the courthouse; gossips may be aware of a dispute and its causes before a pubic conflict erupts. The corpus of gossip contains stories on each of the conflict themes Collier lists. Indeed, Collier reports some famous cases which enjoyed *municipio*wide notoriety; these stories reappeared almost word for word in Who's Who gossip sessions. For example, she lists as a case of "wrongs against the community" the story of a trip to lowland caves by a group of men who wanted to exchange the souls of their neighbors for wealth from the Earth Lord (J. Collier 1973, case 8, pp. 142–43).

It seems clear that the gossip corpus points to areas of Zinacanteco life which are interesting enough to talk about. What comes up in gossip parallels cases at the town hall, behavior that Zinacantecos ridicule. I suggest that the implicit subject of gossip is rules, somehow understood, underlying proper Zinacanteco behavior.

Gossip and the Cargo System

Pero mi yora ch²ech' ta ²abtel timi ilaj i tak'ine?

"But can he survive a cargo if his money is finished?"

6

In the last chapter I reported that cargo service was a frequent topic in the gossip I heard in Zinacantan. People continually discuss the schedule of officeholding in the hierarchy, the performances of cargoholders past and present, and their own plans and experiences in the cargo system. Less directly, men often use the cargo system to locate and identify particular people—as, say, the *martomorey* of a particular year—and to comment on them in a telescoped but significant way:

> "the man who was *martomorey* three years ago but who ran away halfway through the cargo."

This conversational preponderance is a symptom of the importance of the cargo system to most of the Zinacantecos with whom I gossiped. Zinacantecos, like other people, talk about what interests them; the best clue—though not the only one—about what is on their minds is what is on their lips.

Contemporary ethnographers of Zinacantan have been similarly fascinated by the cargo system, a religious hierarchy characteristic of communities throughout the Maya area (and, indeed, a widespread concomitant of the Catholic conversion that followed Spanish conquest). The system of religious offices has been deemed central to Zinacanteco society. Pioneering ethnographic work in Zinacantan in the early 1960s suggested that "the degree and manner of a man's participation in the hierarchy is the major factor in determining his place in the community" (Cancian 1965, p. 2). The accepted analysis of the

91

relationship between religious office and one's "place in the community" views cargo performance as a device through which individual Zinacantecos exchange surplus wealth—which, if accumulated, would prove embarrassing, even dangerous—for prestige. Cargoholders spend large sums of money on ritual service, conceived to be beneficial to participants individually and to the community as a whole. Such community service enhances one's public reputation and at the same time ensures favor with ancestral and natural deities.

There remain, in this analysis, several unexplicated claims upon which gossip should shed some light. These concern the postulated relationship between public identity, prestige, and cargo performance, as well as the considerations said to motivate participation in the hierarchy. Gossip first reveals the conceptual apparatus (minimally, the words) through which participants perceive the hierarchy; gossip manipulates the relevant notions: hierarchy, progress, prestige. Second, gossip exposes the complex calculations by which people plan (or claim to plan) their own cargo careers and evaluate those of others. Gossip routinely penetrates beyond the formal structure of the hierarchy to include the relevant variables of (good and bad) performance in cargos. Third, gossip allows the observer (both native and foreign) to determine the place of religious service in a constellation of economic endeavor, civil office, and curing activity, given a life of shifting standards, changing opportunities for acquiring and employing wealth in Zinacantan.

In this chapter I describe in some detail the elements of a Zinacanteco's reputation that derive from participation in the cargo system. In particular, I outline the structure of the hierarchy to show how gossip rearranges and regularizes a complex schedule of offices to allow evaluation of individual performance. I reconsider the connection between prestige and cargoholding, and I examine the components of reputation on the evidence gossip provides.

The Hierarchy

It is not surprising, given the intricate calculations and strategic discussions about cargos that figure in conversation, that Tzotzil contains well-developed resources for describing the hierarchy, or that Zinacantecos deal routinely with what seems a complex set of rules governing progress through it.

Like other Meso-American systems of public office, the Zinacanteco cargo system comprises four hierarchical levels, with service at each level contingent upon successful completion of a cargo at the level immediately below. The relevant facts for the Zinacanteco system are the total repertoire of cargo offices, their places in the hierarchy of four levels, conceptual groupings of offices, and, most important for the traditional analysis, the relative prestige associated with each office. Cancian describes the hierarchy in the following terms:[1]

> The expressed purpose of the religious hierarchy is to guarantee performance of rituals for the saints in the local Catholic churches. Tradition dictates that these rituals be performed, and it is believed that harm will come to the community if they are not performed. When a man takes a cargo for a year he is responsible for part of the ritual, and is thus doing a service for the community. Most Zinacantecos believe that the saints will favor him if he performs his duties well, and punish him if he does not.
>
> Every year 55 Zinacantecos serve cargos in the religious hierarchy. The rights and duties of each cargo are set by tradition and do not vary with the incumbent from year to year. However, the rights and duties vary greatly between cargos. Each cargo has a distinct sphere of responsibility and a distinct name." [1965, p. 28]

The cargos are arranged into four hierarchical levels, so that a man passes in sequence a first cargo (typically called *martomo*), then after some years a second-level cargo (*ʔalperes*), then a third-level cargo as *rejirol*, and finally at the last level a cargo as *ʔalkalte*. The numbers have increased somewhat since the early 1960s: there are currently about forty first-level cargos, twelve second level cargos, five at the third level, and four at the terminal level (table 5 shows the entire list). A man who has been *ʔalkalte* has completed his formal service in the system and becomes a *pasaro* (Sp. *pasado*, "one who has passed"). Cancian (1965, p. 29) points out that incomplete careers are "the rule." "First service does not usually occur until the age of 35 or 40, and years of 'rest' between service periods are required to earn the money necessary to sponsor fiestas. Thus, many men who hope to compete for the limited number of offices on higher levels die before reaching their goal" (Cancian 1974, p. 165).

Formally each cargo pertains to a particular level of the hierarchy, although there is reason to believe that some cargo positions have changed level over time.[2] Similarly, the order of progression is ideally fixed: from first to second to third to fourth. The Tzotzil metaphor suggests passing upward from step to step.[3] A man begins with a first cargo, *sba yabtel* ("the front/beginning of his work"), after which he is able to pass a cargo at the second level, *xchaʔ-kojol yabtel* ("the second level of his work"), and so on. A man's last cargo, ideally, but for most people not actually at the fourth level, is *slajeb yabtel* ("the end point of his work")—the point at which he either completes or abandons his career.

Table 5   **Cargo Positions**

Location	Tzotzil Name	Spanish Name	Number
	First Level[c]		
Jteklum	martomoetik	Mayordomos	12[a]
	xanxevaxchan	San Sebastian	
	sanantonyo	San Antonio	
	jch'ulme?tik	Virgen del Rosario	
	santakrus	Santa Cruz	
	santorominko	Santo Domingo	
	sakramentu	Sacramento	
Jteklum (chapel of ?Iskipulas)	martomorey	Mayordomo rey	2[a]
	mexon	Mesonero	2[a]
?Atz'am	mayol	Mayor	1
	martomo jch'ulme?tik	Mayordomo de la Virgen del Rosario	1
Nabenchauk	martomo jch'ulme?tik	Mayordomo de la Virgen de Guadalupe	2[a]
?Apas	martomorey	Mayordomo rey	2[a]
	mexon	Mesonero	2[a]
Easter Season[b]	paxyon	Pasionero	2[a]
Fiesta of San Lorenzo[b]	kapitan	Capitan	2[a]
Cabildo	mayoletik	Mayores	2[a]
	Second Level		
Jteklum	?alperesetik	Alfereces	12[d]
	trinirat	Santisima Trinidad	
	sanjosep	San Jose	
	rosaryo	Virgen del Rosario	
	nativirat	Virgen de Natividad	
	xanxevaxchan bankilal	San Sebastian	
	santorenso	San Lorenzo	
	sorirat	Virgen de Soledad	
	sanantonyo	San Antonio	
	samparomartil	San Pedro Martir	
	sanjasinto	San Jacinto	
	santaroxa	Santa Rosa	
	xanxevaxchan ?itz'inal	San Sebastian	
	Third Level		
Jteklum	?alperes kajvaltik ryox	Alferez la Divina Cruz	1
	rejiroletik[f]	Regidores	4

Fourth Level

Jteklum	muk'ta ʔalkalteᶜ	Alcalde Viejo Primero	1
	bik'it ʔalkalteᶜ	Alcalde Viejo Segundo	1
	ʔalperes santorominkoᵍ	Alferez Santo Domingo	1
	ʔalkalte xuvesʰ	Alcalde Juez	1

a Most first-level cargos are arranged in senior/junior pairs. Hence, there are two *martomo* cargos bearing the same saint name: e.g.:

martomo sakramentu bankilal "senior mayordomo sacramento"

and

martomo sakramentu ʔitz'inal "junior mayordomo sacramento"

b The first level cargos of *paxyon* and *kapitan* have ritual duties only for parts of the year at certain fiestas.

c There are rumors of the creation of new first-level positions serving saints in the new churches, in Sek'emtik and Nachij.

d There are two additional cargos named *ʔalperes* (see third and fourth levels), but, although they perform ritual together with the other *alfereces*, they belong formally to higher levels of the hierarchy.

f The four *rejiroletik* and the two *ʔalkalteetik* perform ritual together and are known collectively as the *moletik* or 'elders.'

g *ʔAlperes santorominko* can be served either as a third- or fourth-level cargo.

h *Xuves* is a terminal cargo, ending one's service, but almost always taken by a man with only one previous cargo.

Again, the language is suggestive: the word *ʔabtel* ("work"), when used in a possessed form is always taken on first reading to mean cargo work, rather than, say, work in the cornfields or for wages. The grammar further suggests that a man's work or cargo career stretches through time from a definite beginning to an end.[4]

The hierarchy can be schematized as in figure 6. The decreasing number of positions at higher levels results in the pyramidal structure. I have labeled the three highest levels with a form of the cargo name that can refer to all individual cargos at that level. Thus, whereas a man can pass any one of a number of second-level *ʔalperes* cargos: e.g., he may perform the cargo of *ʔalperes santorenso* ("the alferez of San Lorenzo"), he may refer to this period of his life as the time he *ʔech'em ta ʔalperesal* ("was serving at the alferez level"); or he may reminisce about *yalperesal* ("his tenure as alferez"). The terms *ʔalkalteal* and *rejirolal* involve similar usage.[5]

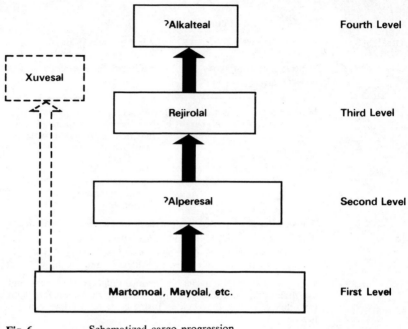

Fig. 6   Schematized cargo progression.
(Adapted from Cancian 1965,
p. 29)

Tzotzil provides evidence for some discontinuities in an otherwise orderly hierarchy. Certain *ʔalperes* cargos count at the *ʔalperes* level only in exceptional circumstances. For example, the office of *ʔalperes kajvaltik ryox*

> skwenta rejirol (mayol).
> "counts as (first) regidor."

Similarly, *ʔalperes santorominko*

> skwenta muk'ta ʔalkalte
> "counts as senior alcalde,"

or,   skwenta slajeb ʔabtel.
> "counts as one's final cargo."

These expressions display the notion of ideal progression, labeled as in figure 6; particular cargos in a career fit into this progression, but the fit is not simply congruent to cargo names.

Irregular careers are themselves held up against the ideal progression, so that observers can both evaluate them (mark them as exceptional, ambitious, disappointing, etc.) and come to understand the logic they display. Here gossip about nonstandard cases provides reliable evidence about the standards themselves. Consider the following discussion about a particular man's career:

"First he was *mayol* ['policeman']."
"Yes, he was a policeman."
"Then came his second-level cargo; then he was *mexon*."[6]
"Really? Was that for his *?alperes*-cargo [skwenta *?alperes*]?"
"Yes, for his second cargo he was *mexon*."
"Incredible!"
"No, no, that can't be right. He didn't count the *mayol* cargo toward his career. . . ."
"Oh, he only did that for respect, then. . . .?"
"Yes, he only did that for his own self-respect. First he spent a year as policeman; but he said that wasn't to count as cargo work. He said he didn't want to start his career that way."
"Ah."
"I myself did not see his year as *mayol*. I first knew him when he was *mexon*. He replaced our group—the year after I was *martomorey* he was *mexon*. After that he was *?alperes xanxevaxchan* as his second cargo. . . ."
"But isn't that all? He hasn't yet been *rejirol*?"
"But he will be next year. At New Year's he will become *?alperes kajvaltik ryox*."

This man appeared to have performed two first-level cargos, prompting the questions (precisely formulable in Tzotzil) whether the first-level *mexon* cargo can, in exceptional circumstances, "count as *?alperes*," that is, count as a second-level cargo. This man was himself unwilling to begin his cargo career as *mayol*[7] and went on to perform a more respectable first cargo, followed by a second-level office as *?alperes*. And next year he would serve as *rejirol* (i.e., in his third cargo) precisely by passing an office named *?alperes kajvaltik ryox*.

Cancian (1974, p. 170) argues that the prestige one garners from patterned social behavior—taking a cargo, for instance—depends on the assessment of that behavior by social alters. Gossip about behavior is presumably a crucial vehicle (and context) for such assessment.

Tzotzil clearly labels the levels of the hierarchy and provides means for talking about the underlying concepts. Certain cargos seem to fit flexibly into a rigid sequence of hierarchical levels to provide for individual needs. It may be that individual strategies in pursuing cargo careers require and may in fact have introduced such flexibility into the system. The choice between two cargos at the same level may involve considerations of cost, of time required (both in service and in waiting for a position to become available), and the nature of the concomitant ritual (see note 17).

Irregular or Short Cargo Careers

Two terminal cargos normally fall to men who have not completed three previous lower-level offices. Gossip suggests that both posts— ʔalkalte xuves and bik'it ʔalkalte—are viewed as acceptable, though lowly and in some sense laughable, ways out of a failing cargo career.[8]

Hence, a taunt to a man who pridefully complains of not being able to reserve a sufficiently prestigious cargo in the near future is:

"Why don't you just ask for xuvesal. . . . (Ha ha ha)?"

The implication is clear: "That cargo is certainly available; why not take that one if you are [as you imply] so anxious to finish your cargo career?" The same taunt, in different circumstances, can be based on one of the minor ʔalperes positions (e.g., xanxavaxchan ʔitz'inal) and, notably, also on the bik'it ʔalkalte.

Cancian cites the example of a man who served as bik'it ʔalkalte after only two previous cargos, but who had given considerable service in civil offices during his life: "Informants recognized the exception made in appointing him, but rationalized it by saying that because of his service in many capacities, he deserved to complete his cargos in an honorable fashion" (1965, p. 32). Gossip, however, does not in most cases bear out the inference that the junior ʔalkalte represents a completely "honorable" conclusion to a cargo career. On the contrary, most men who fill the post seem to be ineffectual, weak-willed, aged failures, frequently laughingstocks. Although there seems to be no principled reason why some exceptional individual might not manage to make more out of it, the cargo seems to be something like a booby prize, forced on the vulnerable (much as the mayol "errand-boy" cargo is forced on village troublemakers), even, pace Cancian, after only a single previous cargo. In fact, Who's Who lists show a man in Nachij who performed bik'it ʔalkalte as his only cargo.

Consider the following story of a particular bik'it ʔalkalte who resembles very little the hero of the above account.

Mol Manvel Komis had an unusual cargo career, passing only one cargo before becoming bik'it ʔalkalte.

"Long ago he was martomo sakramentu, for his first cargo. The next cargo he did was bik'it ʔalkalte; I was among those who accompanied him then [as a rejirol: another one of the six elders, or senior cargoholders]."

"But hadn't he asked to be ʔ*alperes santorenso?*"

"Yes, he had asked. That old man was *santorenso* many times. (Ha ha ha.)"

"But didn't he after all pass that ʔ*alperes* cargo?"

"No, never."

"But I remember hearing that he had already cut his firewood [in preparation for entering the ʔ*alperes* cargo]. . . ."

"Yes, but didn't he then run away just before he was to enter—it was about this time of year."

"That's right. . . ."

". . . but after all he must have done his cargo as *santorenso*. . . ."

"No, no, he never did. *I* know."

"But didn't his horse die . . . wasn't that when he fled?"

"Aaah, but his horse didn't die. He sold it; I think he sold it."

"So he never did an ʔ*alperes* cargo?"

"No. He was *sakramentu* long ago; I never saw that. . . ."

"No, he never did that cargo as *santorenso*. He asked for it several times. I used to see him at the fiesta of San Sebastian and he would always say to me—when I myself was in *my* cargo—'This time next year I will be San Lorenzo,' he would tell me. But it kept on that way year after year."

"That's how he got old. . . . (Ha ha ha.)"

"He kept putting it off every year. Later on—I've forgotten now exactly when it was—he did actually cut his firewood as you say. . . ."

"Yes, I know he cut firewood once. . . ."

"He went out to get helpers. He asked me: 'Please, let me borrow you for my cargo next year.' 'All right,' I told him. He also asked Old Palas Es from Nachij, his brother-in-law. We even drank two or three beers to seal the bargain. . . ."

"You drank with him?"

"Yes. Well, so his cargo grew closer. Let's see, I think it was about the fiesta of San Juan [in early June, about two months before the ʔ*alperes santorenso* takes office] when he fled; he ran off to Hot Country. He simply let the whole thing drop entirely."

"Aaah, he fled."

"I don't know who took the cargo instead; I can't remember. They just grabbed someone quickly as his replacement. Well, so after a time he returned, and that's when he was forced to take the cargo as junior ʔ*alkalte*. It happened at the *cabildo*. He went to return his paper [naming him to the ʔ*alperes* post] to the elders. His wife and son went with him. You see, the elders gave him liquor from their little bottles, right while he was supposed to be giving back the paper. In a moment, after a couple of minutes he started getting tipsy. '*Kere*, I can do the cargo after all; I'm a man; I know how to act here on Earth," he started to say. (Ha ha ha.)"

"Aha, *that's* how he returned the paper. . . . (Ha ha ha.)"

"That's what he was supposed to be doing. *Puta*, the old lady got angry too. 'Do you think we could survive the cargo after all?' she said. 'Look at the way you behave, look at the way your head is. What we decided at home was that we couldn't do the cargo; he isn't able to pass it; he owns nothing,' said the old lady."

"They had decided already that they didn't want it."

"Same with his son, he didn't want it either. But that old man, after he drank one shot or two shots got drunk right away."

"That's the way he is: he gets drunk in a moment."

" 'I can do it; I can do that cargo. Hah, don't worry about me,' he said again. Well in fact, he did enter his cargo, but when he entered he didn't after all give out any *atole*;[9] instead he was made the *bik'it mol* ['junior *alcalde*']."

"Yes, I accompanied him; he was *bik'it ʔalkalte* the year I was *rejirol*. . . ."

The *rule* for the *bik'it ʔalkalte*, as with the *ʔalkalte xuves* (which involves fewer expenses), seems to call for the position to be occupied by a man without enough resources or energy to complete his service in a more respectable way.[10] The positions are filled from the pool of men with undistinguished records who are unlikely ever to assume a more demanding cargo, but who can be pressured into taking this easy, though somewhat laughable, way out. Both cargos carry low prestige and are terminal.

At each level of service a man, by his choice of particular cargo position, can signal his ambition and energy and thereby his plans for continuing in the system (see fig. 7). Traditionally, high-ranking, high-prestige cargos at lower levels led to high-ranking cargos at higher levels and to an eventual complete career. Low-ranking cargos led to low-ranking terminal cargos (like *bik'it ʔalkalte* or *ʔalkalte xuves*) or simply to abandoned careers. It is notable that some men embark on high-ranking careers but because of age or economic setbacks never manage a fourth cargo. These men are often called *pasaro* (Sp. *pasado*, "one who has passed") after three cargos even without a fourth-level cargo; and no one expects such people to demean themselves by taking one of the low-ranking terminal cargos.[11]

When gossips encounter a cargo career structured in an unusual way they try to reconcile the facts with the peculiarities, disabilities, or bad luck of the individual. They explain, that is, why what happened was not exceptional, not surprising.

Manvel Komis did *bik'it mol* after only one previous cargo, but because of his own foolish boasting after failing to pass a regular second cargo, he got what he deserved by being forced to take that

Prestige Level

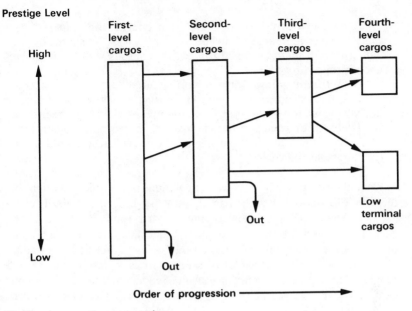

Fig. 7   Cargo strategies

laughable terminal cargo. As for the formal rule about successive levels of service—well, the elders can fill cargo positions as they see fit, if they have good reasons. After all, remember the case of Manvel Kasya, who did a *martomo* cargo and counted it at the second level.

This attention to past careers may point up a man's failure and disgrace. And equally it may celebrate a man's good fortune, skill, and cleverness at negotiating a difficult career or squeezing special merit out of what seemed undistinguished cargo positions, by "intelligent innovation" (Cancian 1974, p. 170).

One can, indeed, infer from gossip the principle that a man who passes a high-ranking cargo will, if he can, refuse a lower ranking cargo at succeeding levels.[12] One man who was considering whether or not to accept a moderately prestigious though low-ranking *ʔalperes* position, in a discussion with another man, cited his first cargo, which he considered to have been quite prestigious. He complained about not wanting to make a step down in his career.

"Yes, I want to be *ʔalperes*. But I want a cargo that is at least somewhat large, at least somewhat distinguished. One becomes accustomed to giving orders and having authority when one is *martomo sakramentu*."[13]

"Aaah, but this cargo you have been offered, this ʔ*alperes
sanantonyo* is in charge of all the other *alfereces*; he shares his
authority with *santorenso* and *trinirat*. He consults with the musicians
about proper procedure. . . ."

"Well, *trinirat*—now *that* is a worthy cargo!"

"Yes, but when *trinirat* doesn't know what to say, when he doesn't
know what is proper, then you—*sanantonyo*—would give the orders.
It all depends on what sort of man takes the cargo; some men are
weak, but others are forceful. Remember how last year old Chep
rose above his office."

Planning a cargo career involves calculations of prestige and often tor-
tured rationalizations. But the participant is not limited to a fixed schedule of offices and ranks. He has time to wait (and, indeed, the long
waiting lists often oblige him to) before he takes the plunge. He can
often pick his fellow officeholders, on the basis of what he knows about
them and the coming schedules of service, so as to insure that he will
stand out during his tenure in office. And of course he can pursue various
strategies in the choice of the cargo position itself. Gossip is a source
of information about these calculations, and hence about the principles
according to which participation in the cargo system of Zinacantan is
undertaken, understood, and evaluated.

Cargos and Reputation

Gossip propagates information about people's cargo histories and performance through a huge volume of conversation about cargos and
cargoholders. Complementing this conversation is correspondingly extensive knowledge about other people's cargo careers on the part of
almost every Zinacanteco man. Members of Who's Who panels had
remarkably full recollections of other people's careers—recollections
that extended far into the past and well beyond hamlet boundaries. In
fact, it seems likely that Zinacantecos actively collect cargo histories,
if for no other reason than that they can thus compare their own progress through the hierarchy with that of their fellows.

Ordinarily the most public aspect of a man's personal history will be
his cargo record. People from outlying hamlets, not otherwise familiar
to those outside their own areas, acquire instant names as holders of
such-and-such a cargo. A common identifying schema in conversation
is to give a man's name, then to pinpoint his identity by citing his most
recent cargo.

"Do you know Chep Vaskis?"

"Chep Vaskis? You mean the one living by the rock outcropping?"

"No, no, the son of Old Xap."

"Wait a minute. Is this Chep Vaskis the man who just passed *martomo jch'ulme?tik?*"

"That's right. . . ."

"Oh, that's who you mean! Certainly I know him; I went with him to Chamula to buy rum. So his name is Vaskis, is it?"

The identification of a man with his cargo position is a natural conse-quence of the ordinary channels of information within the community, which restrict (or do not promote) the circulation between hamlets of unremarkable bits of information. Cargo service brings otherwise un-distinguished individuals to public attention by bringing them to the ceremonial center.[14]

A person's cargo record is usually taken as an index of other aspects of his life and character. A distinguished cargo performance carries implications of other distinction; and failure in the religious hierarchy regularly is taken to attest to some personal deficiency. During Who's Who sessions, when members of the panel heard for the first time de-tailed gossip about people they knew only slightly, often from their cargo records alone, reactions to surprising disclosures bore out this expected connection between cargo service and reputation.

An old man, with a distinguished, now complete cargo career, is reputed to have made improper advances toward his daughters-in-law.

"He finished his cargo service long ago it seems, but nonetheless he still seems to have acted foolishly on occasion; they say he has been involved with his daughter-in-law. . . ."

"Actually, it was both daughters in-law. He was taken to the *cabildo.* . . ."

"But does he still know how to do that, such a 'distinguished gentleman'? . . ."

"Do you suppose he has forgotten, now that his cargo work is finished? (Ha ha ha.)"

"Yes, after all, doing a cargo is where one learns propriety. (Ha ha ha.) When we talk to him he seems an upright man, but perhaps he has little evil ways after all."

"He has given injections, but he is a well-behaved elder."

"He's a ritual adviser."

"He's a Holy Elder, but he gives injections. . . . (Ha ha ha.)"

Similarly, successful cargo service is evidence for other sorts of suc-cess. One Zinacanteco friend, whom I consulted about lending money to another old man I knew only slightly, mentioned the man's distin-guished cargo career as a comforting character reference. In the discussion of another lazy man who has neither corn nor money and who has fléd from two different cargos, one person remarked that the only work the man was known to perform was in his father's cornfields. When another man evinced surprise that the father of such a good-for-nothing could have large cornfields, another remarked, "But of course his father knows how to work: he has finished his cargo career!"

The connection here between success in the hierarchy and success as a corn farmer certainly rests on the fact that cargos are costly; that to complete four levels of service requires considerable wealth over a lifetime. It is also true that the idiom of cargo success is, in most conversation, synonymous with virtue, diligence, and worthiness. Gossip about cargoholders, fortunate and unfortunate, leads directly to the interrelated nations of wealth, prestige, luck, seniority, and success.

Prestige and Cost

The crux of the received analysis of cargo performance in Zinacantan is the proposition that "the cargoholder . . . receives a very special kind of prestige and respect, which is principally dependent on the amount of money he spends in the service of his cargo or cargos" (Cancian 1965, p. 27). According to this analysis, it is the quest for such prestige, and the accompanying standing in the community, that motivates Zinacantecos to perform cargos. Moreover, the system is flexible enough to permit ambitious men to excel: "From the point of view of the participant, the cargo system can be a clear way to communicate his abilities and his self-image to his fellows" (Cancian 1965, p. 80). The path for the energetic is clearly marked by the costly cargos at each level of the hierarchy.

Zinacantecos with sufficient resources are subject to a (socially and morally binding) expectation that they will participate in the cargo system. Cancian argued in fact that, traditionally, virtually all Zinacanteco men participated in the system; of those who did not "most . . . are very poor, usually because of sickness, injury, or bad luck" (Cancian 1965, p. 128). Wealthy men are subject to pressures to accept costly, prestigious cargos, whereas men of more moderate resources can appropriately settle for less ambitious careers. The direction of a man's eventual career may be clear from his economic success and interest in participation at an early age, so that "not only are all Zinacantecos included in the ranking system resulting from the hierarchy, but rough estimates of every man's ultimate standing can often be made by his fellows even before he has taken any cargo" (1965, p. 128).

The notion of "prestige" is central to this argument. Cancian admits that "prestige is an elusive quality, difficult to measure in any systematic way" (1965, p. 87). The idea of a scale of prestige for ranking cargos emerged naturally, he writes, out of "talking with dozens of Zinacantecos about cargos, and observing dozens of interactions between persons who had passed different cargos" (1965, p. 87). But Cancian remains uncomfortable with the result. "Though Zinacantecos constantly behave in ways that indicate that they defer to and respect their fellows according to the criteria [of cargo cost and authority], no informant was able to conceptualize the notion of prestige consistently enough to produce a prestige scale. Any direct attempt to ask about the relative prestige of cargos drew either a statement about the relative cost (which is public knowledge) or a retreat to the cultural ideal that all cargos are in service of the saints, and all service of the saints is equally virtuous" (1965, p. 92). Cancian makes use of informants' mistakes (which, not surprisingly, turn out to be patterned) in remembering other people's cargo careers to convince himself that "the prestige-ranking of cargos I had intuitively made coincided with the ranking made by Zinacantecos" (1965, p. 92). Yet the conclusion is limp: "I conclude that Zinacantecos, though they will not openly discuss it, actually do perceive cargos in terms of relative prestige, and are apt to remember the approximate prestige of an individual even when they have forgotten the particular cargo he passed in the process of achieving it" (1965, p. 96).

We are left with a somewhat cryptic claim about the prestige said to attach to particular cargos and to motivate individual performance. Do Zinacantecos think in terms of prestige but lack the concept (the ability to "conceptualize the notion of prestige")? Do they merely act in accordance with traditional rules of cargo service, with no particular thought to prestige and strategies? Were early Zinacanteco informants merely being intransigent or obtuse, refusing to discuss "openly" a well-understood scale of prestige, and mouthing instead an empty "cultural ideal"? Is "prestige" anything more than the analyst's metaphor for differential participation, which in turn is an artifact of differential economic success and the expectation that Zinacantecos participate according to their means?

Gossip about cargos gives content to the notions of prestige and respect in a way that a mechanical and idealized prestige scale of offices cannot. On the one hand, in gossip Zinacantecos are not at all reticent about success and failure, prestige and scorn. And on the other, gossips demonstrate that the particular office one serves is only one indicator of the sort of reputation one will derive. I shall consider both points in order.

Gossip suggests that Zinacantecos are skilled at manipulating notions of prestige, success, and respect (and their opposites) and are capable of making and expressing in Tzotzil complex calculations of rank. Indeed, it would be hard to argue that cargo prestige is central to an understanding of the religious hierarchy, much less the entire social structure, were Zinacantecos unable to make sense of the ideas involved. There are Tzotzil expressions which constitute a vocabulary of prestige and respect.

The man who refused to count service as a "policeman" toward cargo advancement was said to have made that choice "for respect." The Tzotzil expression—*p'is ta vinik* ("to measure as a man")—figures frequently in conversation about respect, for elders, for senior cargoholders, and so forth. The calculations of the man who wanted a cargo that was "somewhat large" (*muk'muk'tik jset'*) clearly involve a notion of prestige/rank that relates to relative authority. The metaphor of size recurs in this context.

> One man was suddenly advanced from fourth to second *rejirol* by the fortuitous death of the incumbent.

> "He would have been the runt, the smallest (*sk'oxil*). But he ended up in second position, when one man died and the other fled his cargo."

Zinacantecos are proud of their cargo records, and boast of their successes. A man who takes no cargo, whatever his success in other areas of life, whatever his wealth, must walk about sheepishly at fiesta time, when men are mocked for avoiding the service of the saints.

> "The story about Mikel Komis is that he asked for a cargo long ago. But Mikel didn't check that his name was on the waiting lists year after year. Then the elders removed his name, seeing that Mikel just hid himself every year when he should have been checking the lists. Perhaps, when he asked for the cargo, he thought he could do it; he didn't know how costly it would be. But then he heard how much money others spent on their cargos, and he gave it up. He isn't a very good worker, and anyway he has fought with his father—he is rather ill-tempered—and had to go elsewhere to live with his wife. He kept moving from one borrowed house to another. The elders said: 'How are you going to do a cargo with all this houseborrowing?'

> "Anyway, this past year Mikel, who was the musician for *martomo Santa Krus*, dressed up as *mamal*[15] as the replacement for his *martomo*, who was missing several finger joints and could not dance and frolic properly. But all the people knew that Mikel had lost his cargo and should have been ashamed to perform at the fiesta. They all said, '*Kere*, is Mikel now doing his *second* cargo? Does he have so much money that he can be *martomo* twice?'

"So Mikel was told to his face that he had done two cargos. People mocked him right in his own ears: 'You're such a man, you're so rich!' they said. He was much embarrassed as a man who had done no cargo, but still standing in for a *martomo*."

The shame of nonparticipation is particularly acute at the fiesta of San Sebastian, when special ritual entertainers carry small furry animals, who are given the names of failed or truncated cargoholders and mocked publicly throughout the fiesta (Bricker 1968, p. 271; Vogt 1969, p. 542). Such shame may even prick at one's relatives.

"Weren't you there when old Xulubte? was standing in for the entertainers at San Sebastian when he got so angry? His son was named."
"Yes, I heard about that."
"You see, Xun, the old man's son, was supposed to be *martomorey* that year. And the Blackmen were supposed to say his name, to mock him for fleeing the cargo. But old Xulubte? himself was also standing in as the Jaguar. He was also an entertainer.
"So the Blackmen said, 'Look here, look here. This is Xunka? Xantis. Look how thick her pubic hair is! Look how her pubic hair stands on end! We can hardly squeeze in. Ha ha ha!
"That is how they talk."
"But then they said Xun Xulubte?'s name, too. 'Look, this is Xun Xulubte?. He has finished his *martomorey* cargo. He is now an entertainer himself,' they yelled.
" 'Damn, don't say that,' said old Xulubte?. 'You bastards, that is my son you're talking about,' he said.
" 'We don't care if he's your son,' they replied. 'You should be mocking him, too.' (Ha ha ha.)"

Cargoholders also expect deference and respect for their accomplishments. A *compadre* of mine was once greeted on the path by another, apparently older man, who addressed my *compadre* as *totik* ("father, sir"). When I asked why the other had used a form of address reserved for men older than the speaker, my *compadre* replied: "We are actually about the same age; but because of my cargo (as *martomorey*) he accords me more respect." But gossip shows that deference is often ironic, backhanded, a mask for secret ridicule. The idioms of respect are often metonymic references to cargoholders' dress.

Antun Saklum had a secret affair while he was the ritual adviser to a cargoholder.

"He once went to be the ritual adviser of the *martomorey*. He tied his head up in a red kerchief;[16] we were all there—the *martomorey* was leaving office. We were all seated around a table, facing each other, including the ritual advisers.

"But Old Antun wasn't interested in talking just among the men. All the women were sitting there, too, to one side. He turned his chair slightly to one side and kept looking, glancing sideways at the wife of one of the helpers.

"We were sitting behind him, watching him, laughing. Even when he was saying a long prayer, kissing the others' rosaries, his heart wasn't in it. He was watching the woman. But then he heard us laughing at him. . . ."

"Aha, his ears were alert. . . ."

"Yes, yes. We spoke to him outside the church. We went outside to urinate. The drummers were standing around, and when he went to urinate, they said to him, 'Is that just piss that's coming out, Father?' (Ha, ha ha.)

" 'Hey, be quiet there, boy,' he said. 'I don't know what you're accusing me of. I am an elder now. Can't you see that my head is [wrapped in] red?' He was angry.

" 'Your head may be red, but who knows if perhaps your pants are, too,' he was told."

"Ha ha ha."

Gossip supports the proposition that a cargo is what one makes of it. A costly senior cargo will bring more shame than fame if bungled. Conversely, sterling performance in a lesser post will not go unnoticed. One man recounted how he had arranged to take a second cargo of only medium rank rather quickly after his first cargo. He did not disguise his ambition, and revealed that his choice had been influenced by the fact that the senior man with whom he would serve (*alfereces* are arranged in junior/senior pairs) was well known to be rather weak-willed, not well-spoken, and given to intoxication. He boasted often of the fact that he had dominated the *alfereces* during his year in office, that he had been much beloved by the musicians for his joking—signs that he felt himself to have risen above the actual cargo position he occuped.[17]

Conversation about cargo careers and performance suggests that the idea that cargos can be ranked "in terms of the prestige they bring to the person who passes them" (Cancian 1965, p. 96) misses an essential part of the process by which prestige is assigned and reputation gained. Gossip reminds us that people fail, that careers go wrong, that following the rules is not the rule. Earlier excerpts from Zinacanteco gossip attest to the multiple ways that cargos and the cargo system can bring more embarrassment than prestige. Consider these further stories about men whose performance in high-ranking cargos[18] is tarnished.

A friend delivered the following long monologue to me about a recently retired *martomorey*.

"Well, as for Marian, there was gossip about him recently in this past cargo of his. You see, he couldn't borrow enough for his expenses. So he didn't give his helpers or the sacristans anything to eat. At every fiesta the sacristans must be fed. No one asks first whether you've got the money or not. Everyone takes his turn at feeding the sacristans. Well Marian took them home to feed them once, but he gave them rabbit to eat. He is always hunting rabbits, anyway, since he doesn't have any chickens. Why, he didn't even give any liquor each time the rosary was counted at his house. He gave only poured-off liquor,[19] and it was very weak. They say it wasn't even drinkable. The sacristans put up with it, though, because Marian was so ill-tempered they didn't want to cause trouble. So that is the gossip that has come out about Marian. Also they say that when the New Year came he barely had a few cups of corn left over, because he hadn't very much to begin with. And also he didn't have a house, he just borrowed a house; just as if he came from the outlying hamlets and didn't live in the Center."

People may embark on ambitious careers by entering "prestigious" first-level cargos, but prove unsuccessful in the hierarchy because of some deficiency of performance.

"Old Aguilar was senior *martomorey*. It was Sunday and his helpers had gone there, for they take the rosary out early on Sunday. One of the helpers had a daughter and she had gone along to help. So the girl went outside. Aguilar was just sitting there outside. . . ."

"Wasn't that Paxku? Komis?"

"Yes. Paxku? Komis again. Well, anyway, they started to embrace one another, old Aguilar and the girl. He started to stick his fingers in her, right there standing up. Just then a musician came out, and he found them there like that.

" 'Shit, what are you doing?' said the musician.

"Aguilar ran off right away. He went inside. A little later the musician came in.

" '*Martomorey*, have you washed well? Are you now going to touch the rosary of Our Lord, after what you were handling outside?' That's what the musician said as he came in. Everyone heard— Aguilar's wife, the musicians, the helpers. He didn't say anything. I guess he had already had trouble before; he had already been to the

cabildo to settle with his wife. He would have married his lover
if it had not been for his cargo."

"Ah, but he was ruined because of that. He was ruined. He became
a pauper, from touching another woman. . . ."

"Yes, he still has debts to this very day. . . ."

"He has debts, yes. He finished that *martomorey* cargo; he sold off
all his land; he sold off his mules. Did he get it back? No; he never
recovered. He has stayed poor. He touched another woman during
his *martomorey* cargo. Ever since then that has been his story."

"Gossip about him will never cease, because you see he still can't
repay his debts. . . ."

"No, he can't pay them. 'Go touch Paxku? Komis' they used to say
to him, those who knew the story. . . ."

Stories about misdeeds by cargoholders are common, though nonetheless shocking. Gossip moralizes easily about correct and proper performance of cargo duties; transgressions are grounds for public ridicule, institutionalized in the joking of ritual entertainers at the fiesta of San
Sebastian (Bricker 1937a), and add negative footnotes to the reputation
one derives from cargo performance. The man who gets through a fairly
prestigious cargo only by stealing and reselling flowers from the church
may be treated, deferentially to his face but scorned in conversation.
A man whose continual drunkenness often lands him in jail and allows
him to be cuckolded by his own brother-in-law will derive little prestige
from a patchy year in a high cargo office. Even a long career can go
wrong.

"They say he was a truncated *martomorey*. He just did six months."

"Yes, just half a year. Old Xun K'obyox went to Hot Country
at the fiesta of San Juan [in June]. . . ."

"Ah, was he still alive then. . .?"

". . . and there he became ill. He returned home only to die. That's
when Antun Tzu entered; he replaced old Xun."

"Yes, Antun Tzu only did six months as *martomorey*. Then later
he was *Alferez Trinirat*. Then he was third *rejirol* with me. . . ."

"But Antun gets drunk all the time."

"*Puta*, he gets terribly drunk. But he has finished three cargo
levels. . . ."

"But he didn't pay attention to his duties even as *rejirol*, did he?"

"He drank too much; his body started to swell up [from cirrhosis].
'*Puta*, don't drink so much, man,' I told him. His younger brother
got angry with him. 'Why do you drink so much? You're always
drunk. You'll die, forget it. Go ahead . . . ,' he would say. But he
wouldn't listen. He tried to get cured. . . ."

"He was jailed, too. . . ."

"That's right, he was jailed. He just wouldn't take care of himself."

These examples are intended to show that prestige, as allocated by gossip at least, accompanies cargo *performance* rather than following mechanically on incumbency in particular offices. (Perhaps this is one reason Cancian's informants resisted a relative prestige scale in the abstract.) It is clearly true that what is known of a Zinacanteco, and what is said of him (roughly, that is, his reputation), will centrally include his cargo record, if any. But a prestige scale that shows only a systematic connection between prestige and particular offices seems empty beside the sophisticated evaluative procedures gossips employ.

Gossip makes heaviest use of notions of prestige in a negative way: gossips are forever running down the performance of others. Talk is littered with failed careers, frustrated ambition, the pitiable and the laughable; and gossips never hesitate to announce why men have bungled their cargos, to discriminate new ways to fault performance. A picture emerges of cargos and the people who perform them that revolves around the same central concepts earlier ethnographers have employed. But bankruptcy and poverty are more tangible than wealth and success; shame and ridicule predominate, prestige and respect seeming dismayingly infrequent concomitants of cargo work.

A frequent theme is the truncated career, set aside by misfortune or misdeed.

"Old Muchik had already been made *muk'ta ʔalkalte*; he would have been in office right now. He had already accepted the paper naming him to office. His scribe was ready, and they got together at the fiesta—it was just about this time of year. . . ."

"You mean for the fiesta of San Lorenzo?"

"Yes. Well, they say lots of people who wanted to request cargos went directly to his house. He accepted their bottles himself; the scribes didn't hear about it. . . ."[20]

"Ah, he took the bottles in secret. . . ."

"Yes, he took their bottles in secret. 'You now have a cargo,' he would say. Even if someone else had signed up for a cargo, he would give it to another. . . ."

"They say he also took money at his house. . . ."

"Yes. Well, it became known that people had been asking him for cargos. The other elders didn't know about it; the scribes hadn't heard. Just Old Muchik himself was planning to make all the decisions. 'Well, let him stay behind,' said the others. So Muchik didn't ever actually enter as *muk'ta ʔalkalte*. . . ."

"Ha ha ha. . . ."

"He was left off the path; that's why he never became *muk'ta ʔalkalte*. Now he is left behind."

"Well first Xun Nuj had asked to be *martomo jch'ul-meʔtik*.[21] The senior one, I think."

"Is this the Xun Nuj who lives with Katal Te?tik?"

"That's right. Well, who knows what crime he committed—perhaps he beat her—but he separated from his wife. He was always beating her up.

" 'Well, how are we going to get you to behave?' said the presidente. Immediately he appointed him a *mayol*, a policeman."

"Ha ha ha. He became an errand-boy and he lost his chance to be *martomo jch'ul-me?tik!*"

"That's right. He had his cargo taken away from him when he cut his wife's head with a knife."

"What was his first cargo?"

"*Santorominko*. Then, for his alferez cargo he was *Trinirat*. He was going to pass one more level, but he never reached it. . . ."

"Oh. He ran off?"

"No, that was when his wife died. He was going to be second *rejirol*. But he never did it. . . ."

"If his wife were alive, she would be making tortillas for the elders right now."

Gossip demonstrates that as a device for acquiring prestige the cargo system is often treacherous: people delay, default, flee, and fail, turning the elusive prestige that might have accompanied successful cargo performance into a liability which must be overcome in some other way: into a reputation for drunkenness, stupidity, or dishonesty. And here is the main defect in the more mechanical view of the relationship between cargos and "social status" that anthropologists have urged: though the relationship exists potentially (one might say: structurally), it remains for Zinacantecos to exploit it, to bring off a cargo and to squeeze out of it what they can, or to avoid cargo service and somehow to avoid the consequences. While ethnographers may content themselves with stating the relationship between cargo and prestige as a rule, the gossip need not be so hasty. Certainly a man may pass an extremely expensive cargo; but, after all, he got his money from the sweat of his neighbors, by lending money at interest. True, a certain man may have fled his cargo; but he had been tormented by a series of illnesses which had consumed his corn and left him destitute. And of course, it may be that another man performed a rather unworthy cargo; but we must admit that he rose above it, that he talked reasonably and led his fellows to perform correctly.

Gossip does, in fact, mock the man who performs no cargos and who distinguishes himself *in no way* during his life. Of such a one it may be said:

Solel imolib ta yech.
He simply grew old for nothing.

But gossip tells us the bare facts—that Petul X passed cargo Y—and a good deal more besides: Manvel fled from his cargo; Xun had requested a cargo twenty years from now; Maryan would have served a third cargo, but his wife left him; and so on. Gossip reveals, that is, the extenuating circumstances, the special facts, the misfortunes, the character traits that bear on the evaluation of a man's cargo career, and accordingly on the reputation he derives.

Cargos and Public Identity

To establish a relationship between cargo careers and "social position" we need to find independent criteria of the latter while looking more closely at the range of variation in the former. A survey of the Who's Who lists of cargo participation yields a crude tripartite division of the men in each hamlet into (*a*) the nonparticipants, (*b*) the average participants whose records approximate the average number of cargo years in each age group, and (*c*) the superstars, whose records are much higher than average and who mostly are already old men. Complicating the classification by adding the variable of the prestige level of individual cargos would improve its efficiency (with respect to providing a unique rank for each man in the community). But the resulting ranking might, I claim, still fail to provide a useful guide to social standing— especially since, as I have shown, taking a high-prestige cargo does not guarantee a man success in achieving the desired respect.

Gossip, however, not only can distinguish participation from nonparticipation, but can uncover the differential commitment of individuals —or entire hamlets—to cargo performance. Calling all participation simply "participation" obscures what is, for gossip, the crucial distinction between, say, the ambitious young *ʔalperes* and the aged, tired *ʔalperes*; or, again, between (*a*) the hapless, failed farmer with no land and, hence, no cargo, (*b*) the wealthy truck owner who disdains cargos, and (*c*) the civil official, versed in Spanish, who hobnobs with cargoholders in official capacities but himself never participates. It is unrevealing to view all men who have progressed to the same *ʔalperes* cargo as enjoying the same "social standing" or to consider all three types of nonparticipants equally "nonmembers of the community," at the bottom of the social ladder. The cargo system interacts with Zinacanteco social structure (however that is to be delineated) in a more elaborate way.

First, notice that a man who has never had a cargo, or served in any way in the community, may still have a reputation of sorts.

"He is not known to people."

"That one hasn't served in any post at all. . . ."

"He's just a hidden person; we never see him leave his house."

"But why is that? Why do you think he remains hidden?"

"As far as I'm concerned, you don't ask him anything, and you don't tell him anything."

"Even when everyone gets together for a meeting, he doesn't show his face."

"No, no, when people gather in the open for a meeting, when there are matters to discuss, he doesn't come out. He just stays there hidden, like some girl. . . ."

"But then you might say he's just a leftover. . . ."

"But he's a good man. . . ."

"Hah, you can't say he's a good-for-nothing. He is a good man. He won't let himself be seen on purpose. He just hides himself away on purpose. . . ."

"Because, perhaps, he doesn't want to be given anything [i.e., any cargo or civil office]. . . ."

"Then he doesn't want to serve for anything. . . ."

"You might say he considers himself just worthless; a good man doesn't act that way. . . ."

"But he is rich. He's a rich man."

If we look at other indexes of social standing, based on characterizations, both positively and negatively evaluated, occurring in Who's Who gossip, the relationship to cargo service seems far from straightforward. Figure 8 presents graphically the Who's Who characterizations of men of different ages in Nabenchauk with respect to six different indexes of reputation. Cargoholders are distinguished from nonparticipants. The first three categories in figure 8 include men known as curers, civil officials at either the municipal or hamlet level, and men known as frequent auxiliary personnel for cargo ritual: musicians, helpers. Men listed in the next two categories are (a) those known for wealth, for special skills or professions (distillers, hat weavers), or for owning trucks, stores, or corn mills; and (b) men known for frequent participation in political disputes or troublemaking. Finally, the last category includes men judged to be deficient in some way: poor, stupid, or criminal. These are rough, intuitive categories and are only crude marks of social position. It seems clear from the results, however, that cargoholders have no monopoly on success in other areas of Zinacanteco life; moreover, cargoholders are not themselves immune from the defects and character faults of their nonparticipant fellows. Though the numbers are too small to be significant, certain regularities emerge: curers who take cargos seem to outnumber those who do not, while the opposite is true for

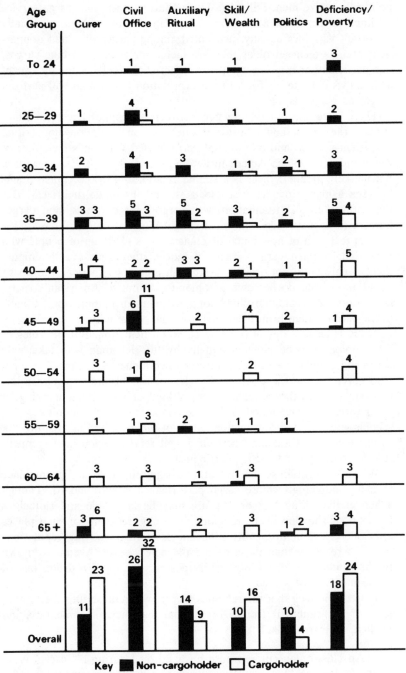

Fig. 8   Who's Who categories for
Nabenchauk

politically active men. Still, the Who's Who suggests that cargo service is simply a feature of advancing age in Zinacantan, with other socially important variables equally distributed among participants and nonparticipants. As men get older they are increasingly likely to take cargos; but participation may arguably not affect their social standing except as it allows them to conform to the expectation that a man will perform cargos as befits his age.

There is certainly a relationship between economic success in Zinacantan, the extent and efficacy of one's personal relationships (ritual kin, friends, etc.), and one's cargo performance. Cancian's metaphor of Zinacanteco cargos as American automobiles (1965, p. 90) suggests a not unlikely parallel: there is a similar relationship in the United States between a man's income, his associates, and the make of his car. But the anthropological fascination with cargos, cargo rituals, and cargo-holders (who have been the most sought-after informants) has dulled our appreciation of how much of Zinacantan is made up of people who have bungled their cargo careers, if indeed, they have ever attempted them. Analysts do not ordinarily (though much of American life does) define those who do not own automobiles as out of American society; neither does Zinacantan exclude nonparticipants or marginal participants in the cargo system from membership in the community.

There is an ideology advocating cargo participation. But the rules of this ideology can be violated equally by the rich man who takes one cargo and thereafter steadfastly refuses to continue and by the poor man who never tries or the truck driver who weasels his way out of service. Conversation, furthermore, indicates a kind of conceptual merging of other sorts of service noted in figure 8: on hamlet-level committees (for schools, *ejido* land, electrification, etc.), at the town hall as civil official, as curer, as ritual auxiliary personnel—all service which may compensate to some extent for an undistinguished cargo career.

Who's Who gossip seems, in fact, to assign reputation and prominence to many individuals whose cargo performance is substandard. Though a hamlet like ʔElan Voʔ or ʔAtz'am may be laughable and ridiculous for its poor showing in the religious hierarchy, residents of such places are nonetheless unmistakably Zinacantecos, often enjoying reputations more far-reaching than those gained through cargos: ʔAtz'am is known for its witches; an ʔElan Voʔ family possesss the *t'ent'en* drum, one of Zinacantan's most sacred objects.

Indeed, the idea that the religious hierarchy circumscribes the boundaries of Zinacantan is troublesome. Note that there is some rare, but explicit, anticargo talk.

An old woman curer, whose husband died during his cargo, is known for speaking against cargos during drunken moments.

"That's what the old woman says. She doesn't want to dance; she doesn't want to enjoy herself there beneath the feet of Our Lord. She says that the saints are eaters of men, that that is why her husband died so young."

"Yes, that's what the old woman is likely to say when she is drunk."

Lol, a wealthy man (who has, incidentally, taken a local Nabenchauk cargo and is a curer), scolds cargoholders who want to borrow money.

"But Lol's head is bad anyway, if you ask to borrow money from him. Old Telex, when he was about to enter his cargo as ?*alperes santorominko*, went to borrow money from him. He had a hard time getting to talk to Lol, but he finally found him.

" 'Well, all right, you can have the money,' he said. 'You can have the money; but why have you asked for a cargo if you don't have any money of your own?' "

"Yes, they say he got angry right away."

" 'People take cargos, but they only use up the money they have borrowed from others; they take pride in doing cargos, but on other people's money,' he says."

" 'What does God want? What does San Lorenzo want? The saints just stand there silently. They just stand there silent on their long legs, with their eyes closed,' he says. Lol doesn't want to aid cargoholders."

" 'Our Lord doesn't know how to drink liquor; He doesn't go asking people for money. It is *you* who squander the money. It is to *your* companions that you give liquor. For them you measure out the rum, you give meals, not for Our Lord,' Lol says to cargoholders. (Ha ha ha.)"

Similarly, some men reverse the normal pattern of avoiding civil service —considered an impediment to a cargo career—by taking civil office or employing other ruses to avoid cargos. Sometimes their motives are perceived to be personal.

Antun refused a cargo in order, the story goes, to pursue his womanizing.

"He used to have a lot of mistresses and that is why he has become poor."

"Well, Antun used to sell flowers and he made lots of money. But when it was seen that he had money, they sent him the candles [signifying selection] for *martomo santorominko*. But Antun wouldn't accept them. He returned them to the elders, saying he had no money, that he was poor. But what was in his heart then was all his mistresses.

"Well, the elders were unwilling to take back the candles; Antun only managed to get off with great difficulty. Then Antun was elated because he was free from the cargo. Well, he still didn't abandon his mistresses; he kept going to visit them, and eventually he lost his money from it. He ended up poor.

"Now it may be seen that he didn't accept his *martomo* cargo. Now it is clear that Our Lord gave punishment, and thus Antun lost all his money."

"The story about old Xap is that he never did a cargo. He just got old here on earth, never wanted a cargo."

"Yes, but that was because he was the money-collector for the *ejido* committee. That's why he never asked for a cargo, he said he wasn't free, he didn't have time, since he had been elected to the office. And now he has given up because he is too old."

"But other people say that he just offered himself on purpose for the money-collecting job, so that he wouldn't have to do a cargo."

Cancian's hypothesis about this deviation from the normal cargo ideology is stronger. "The nonparticipants who are *not* held back by economic limitations or the demands of other roles in public life are very few. They are men whose loyalty is divided between Zinacantan and the Ladino world outside. (Note: An undetermined number of Zinacantecos disappear completely into the Ladino world each year, losing all contact with their relatives.)" (1965, pp. 128–29). This view rests on what is at present an untenable dichotomy between what is in and what is out of Zinacantan. It is not necessary to postulate the existence of a faceless mass of disappeared Indians: there are many Zinacantecos with whom I am acquainted who have left Zinacantan in one way or another without having to "lose all contact with their relatives." Indeed, many politically active Zinacantecos themselves returned to the community after some period in the "ladino world" and now occupy important positions. One wealthy cargoholder in Nabenchauk has sent two sons away to school in the lowland city of Tuxtla Gutierrez; Zinacantecos travel, work, and—in at least one new lowland colony—live outside the *municipio* in ladino environments. It is thus a distortion to insist on the central role of the cargo system in defining the limits of the community, when many young Zinacantecos avoid cargos, and when the boundaries of the community are themselves under attack. Cancian, in a recent paper describing changes in cargo participation from the early to the late 1960s, makes this same point: "Population growth was producing many more adult men than could be accommodated in the cargo system, while economic prosperity was producing a great over-demand for the most expensive and prestigious cargos" (1974, p. 167).

One result, with wide community ramifications, was that "the cargo system was becoming unable to provide a controlled mode of expression that would commit men to the community by exchanging their money for prestige good only in Zinacantan" (1974, p. 167). Zinacantecos have discovered, and have been peddled, new ways to spend their money, from wider Mexican and world society. Cancian concludes that "while the cargo system served Zinacanteco identity, it was never equivalent to it" (1974, p. 172).

Notice, also, that gossip shows how cargo service, from an individual standpoint, may represent something other than a commitment "to the Indian way of life" (Cancian 1965, p. 133). Zinacantecos employ cargos in their personal life strategies in manifold ways: for showing off and self-aggrandizement, to stave off criticism and envy, to salvage otherwise failed lives. I cannot avoid the feeling that some Zinacantecos take cargos or involve themselves with ritual simply because they enjoy it. They are part of the core of ritualists who surround the hierarchy year after year—much as some devoted alumni return for homecoming year after year. Similarly, some men, like Lol in the story above, perform cargos but still criticize the tradition, call it into question, ridicule others for participating.

Again, though cargo service may provide for "socially controlled . . . display" by stipulating "rules under which a man may enhance his public image" (Cancian 1965, p. 135), gossip reveals that it is also possible for overzealous pursuit of cargo glory to backfire. Men can overuse or twist the rules. A man progressing too rapidly will offend his elders. One Zinacanteco, trying to decide whether to accept a chance to take a second cargo at a relatively young age, went to his father for advice. The older man, who had completed only one cargo, flew into a rage and accused his son of disrespect for trying to surpass his own father in the hierarchy. Similarly, I recall the remarks of a young man unwilling, though technically qualified, to serve as ritual adviser, in which position he would have been senior to men much older than he. Hubris and ambition are rarely appreciated.

Public opinion may accord only grudging admiration to even the most ostentatious cargoholder when gossip grumbles about the sources of his wealth: he got money from the Earth Lord, from charging interest to his fellows, from selling his daughters' weaving, from gringo anthropologists. Furthermore the argument that the good man is rewarded by wealth and cargo success is hardly convincing, still less satisfying, to the poor Zinacanteco who can never afford a cargo. Zinacantecos are no more receptive than we are to the argument that they have never gotten ahead because they don't deserve success. Conversation does make use of an idiom of fate and luck, and no one hesitates to run down the lazy good-for-nothing. But gossip is two-faced: occasionally it is willing to pity the unfortunate and excoriate the wicked rich.

I suggested in chapter 1 that gossip provides members of a community with a map of their social environment. Individuals in Zinacantan and elsewhere know (perhaps with varying certainty, in ever-widening, more diluted concentric circles) the identities of their neighbors. More than this, they know a good deal *about* their neighbors: Some of the information they possess may have direct practical importance; a man's community map will mark not only, say, the best spots for gathering firewood or for planting a particular variety of bean, but also the most likely lenders and the most powerful curers. Some of the information they possess about their neighbors may also feed speculation of a less instrumental sort; it may enable evaluation and moral calculation which influence how a man *feels* about his fellows—whom he counts as friends or enemies, allies or rivals. I may portray this social map as a collection, thoroughly cross-indexed but uneven, of dossiers on salient individual neighbors (whose dossiers might, for example, be considered to include information about less salient individuals peripheral to them—for example, adolescent sons and daughters).

My survey in chapter 5 of frequent gossip themes, along with the list of Who's Who categories, constitutes an index of sorts to the set of possible dossier entries. Gossip provides, on this analysis, a common source of input to the ongoing reputations people acquire, and the short characterizations which figure in Who's Who eliciting sessions represent a kind of distillate of gossip items, on their way to becoming reputation—that is, entries in individual dossiers.

In this chapter I have concentrated on a central component of reputation (an especially important entry for Zinacanteco dossiers)—one's cargo career. It should be clear that a cargo career, to extend the metaphor, opens new pages in one's dossier. Cargo performance enables and provides data for speculation about ambition and self-esteem. Moreover, the fact that a man embarks on a cargo career implies that his performance will be carefully scrutinized, and various facets even of his private life (his success at corn farming, his proper relations with his wife and kinsmen) will suddenly become relevant to calculations of his success (or probable success) in office and the esteem he will merit as a result.

A person's dossier will be pieced together from bits of information gathered in varying circumstances, crucially including gossip. And it is precisely by attention to gossip that we can tease apart, within a person's reputation, several interacting components (see fig. 9). In a society like Zinacantan we can distinguish certain culturally given possibilities: roles or identities which individuals can occupy (in various clusterings, and with all the familiar sorts of complexity). But when gossips deal with

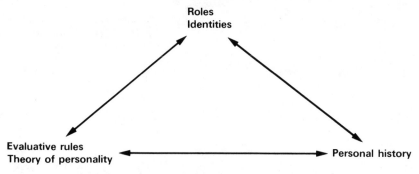

Fig. 9   Components of reputation

real individuals, not mere analytical abstractions, they play off idealized identities against their protagonist's personal history—a history that can be widened to include all mishaps, strokes of luck, favorable marriages, unforseen illnesses, grand inheritances, and so forth, that are deemed relevant to the issues. The gossip strains all this through a conceptual apparatus that contains evaluative words, theories of personality or motivation, and logical mechanisms by which actions are interpreted and evaluated, opinions formed, agreement solicited, and conclusions promulgated. What emerges from this process is an item of gossip that can be entered in a person's dossier. An aggregate of such bits is his reputation—a record of his personal history, filtered and evaluated.

Notice that the process of compiling dossiers on one's neighbors may lead one to expect certain *interdependencies*, whose status is inductive and empirical (based on a collection of individual cases) but which acquire a logical, analytic character. Thus, many people known as *jsaʔ-k'opetik* ("troublemakers")—men and women who frequent the town hall and the San Cristóbal courts in one intrigue after another—are also renowned as competent Spanish-speakers. Similarly, to name someone as a powerful curer is automatically to wonder whether he is also a witch. Thus, too, are the lazy man, the poor man, and the thief linked. It is for such reasons that the man with a distinguished cargo record, in theory a paragon of propriety and high-minded public generosity, is the same man whose illicit sexual exploits and shady financial dealings (or, worse, alleged connections with the Earth Lord or wealth gained by selling souls) make such juicy news. Discussion tends to follow these conceptual interdependencies, which thereby become gossip formulas as well.

Cargos are, then, a major input to reputation, as they are realized in an individual's personal history. And as a man's performance survives the scrutiny of the gossip's evaluative apparatus, it will yield something we may as well call prestige; just as, when it does not survive such scrutiny, a career may result in notoriety, scandal, and shame.

Gossip Words

Mu xlam sk'oplal; mu xa xich' k'op rason.

"Stories about him will not be eased; he no longer listens to reason."

7

At the level of figure 1 in chapter 4, gossip consists of words and phrases: it is text. Gossips depend on their skill with words to draw morals from (apply rules to) the events they describe and to elicit the desired responses from their audiences. Words with evaluative power, or words that invite speculation and evaluation, occur frequently in gossip. If there were moral philosophers in Zinacantan (and there may be), they might look at gossip to understand the primary verbal tools of moral argument.

Anthropologists have long recognized that a basic and unique resource in learning (whatever it is that one learns) about an alien society is language. The earliest empirical ethnography began with lists of kin *words* and the systematic study of the semantic structure of lexical sets. Whether or not formally elicited taxonomies take the ethnographer very far, they certainly take him somewhere. Taxonomies belong among the resources natives have for construing their lives and the world.

In gossip, though, we see not simply the resources, but the *process* of construal. To look at the vocabulary that occurs in Zinacanteco gossip is to discover what words facilitate evaluation and transform mere narrative into gossip. Words are the gossip's primary *tools*. When people argue on moral questions (or when they gossip), does the argument hinge on word meanings, on the facts of a situation, on a (moral) rule, or on the conditions for the application of a rule? Often, perhaps, all these will be at stake. In a vacuum it may be possible to assign a word

122

its referent (as we can state a rule baldly, out of context). But gossip bends the already tenuous relationship between words (and, for example, the verbal propositions that embody rules) and reality—that is, the facts. The gossip uses words for particular purposes; thus in gossip one has an unimpeachable example of how verbal tools *can* be used.

A study of gossip vocabulary reveals first the semantic resources available to the gossip; further, these same resources are at once objects of study and sources of insight for the ethnographer as well. In this chapter I make some tentative efforts at describing the use of certain words in Zinacanteco gossip, samples of the verbal tools native Zinacantecos manipulate and apply in negotiating their lives.

Many crucial active words in gossip will typically be polysemic; but their use involves a complexity and evident indeterminacy that goes beyond multiple meanings. Words describing personality traits, dispositions, and so forth, refer only to elusive entities, if they refer at all.[1] Words with evaluative implications draw communicative power from their positions in sense systems (Lyons 1963; Haviland 1970*b*)—that is, in relation to other words—as well as from metaphor. A narrator *may* base his claim that "Xun has a bad head" (i.e., an evil temper) on certain objective characteristics Xun possesses; but we understand what he means insofar as we appreciate the existence of other words the narrator could have chosen to describe Xun's temperament differently. We stand most in need of a semantic theory when we try to describe the behavior of such words and expressions.

From transcribed gossip conversations I selected what seemed interesting occurrences of words and phrases.[2] By a mechanical procedure I kept track of certain stems which occur typically in explicit or implied evaluations, as they appeared throughout the corpus. The gossip context provides natural examples of usage. I was thus relieved of the necessity to work from translations or definitions.[3] I extract semantic facts from such natural examples—material essentially like that available to native language-learners.

I was most interested in words of the following sorts:

a. Words frequently used to mark approval, disapproval, agreement, disagreement, pleasure, displeasure, and so forth. For example, a common expression meaning "that won't do" is *mu stak'* ("it isn't possible"; lit., "it doesn't answer"). Such words are part of a metalanguage for cultural evaluation.

b. Key words in the implied rules underlying questions of fact in gossip discussions. I showed in chapter 4 how the dialogue between narrator and interlocutor often concerns key aspects of the protagonists' behavior: in a courtship, did the parents of the bride *tak'av* ("answer favorably")? Did one man *p'is ta vinik* ("respect") another properly? Gossip focuses on the key clauses of underlying rules (propositions expressing rules) through the medium of words.

c. Words about what I have called unobservables: personal propensities and traits of character, motives, emotions, desires, and so on. Buried in this segment of vocabulary is a native theory of personality, a native psychology which figures freely in gossip sessions.

d. Words which evoke hypothetical outcomes, alternative courses of action, or contrary-to-fact possibilities. Much of the evaluative portion of a gossip session may be devoted to speculation about how things should have been done, how they could have turned out otherwise.

Underlying these verbal investigations is the Wittgensteinian premise that words and the phenomena with which they are associated are inseparable. We learn about the world (or about a particular world) as we learn a language. I may again invoke Austin: "When we examine what we should say when, what words we should use in what situations, we are looking again not *merely* at words (or 'meanings,' whatever they may be) but also at the realities we use the words to talk about: we are using a sharpened awareness of words to sharpen our perception of, though not as the final arbiter of, the phenomena" (1961, p. 130). As ethnographers we must at least in part be interested in seeing how the elements of the cultural universe, the conventions and rules of a culture, are mirrored in its vocabulary; and how words themselves are objects for speculation and manipulation. That the resources of a language may lead us to speak of moral dilemmas in a certain way must certainly affect the nature of the dilemmas themselves, as they are perceived by the protagonists. What we cannot talk about is irrelevant, or at least unavailable for scrutiny. For the outsider, it is talk that leads directly to what is relevant, on the native theory.

In this chapter I present several groups of words and expressions from Zinacanteco gossip, arranged somewhat haphazardly by notional and superficial grammatical criteria. Thus, I have distinguished surface "adjectives" from surface "nouns," and so on.[4] Within a particular superficial "part of speech" I have separated subclasses by distributional and intuitive criteria: adjectives which modify human nouns are distinguished from those which modify verbs; within the former class one can distinguish roots which describe physical characteristics from those dealing with personality, propensity, and "mental" states.

Once I had arrived at a set of terms I asked a Zinacanteco to perform a special sorting task, to produce the groupings shown in what follows. I asked him to arrange the expressions (written on cards) in piles, not on the basis of "semantic similarity" (whatever that means; see Berlin 1968, p. 28), but by virtue of their "going together well"[5] in the sense that the expressions could occur together as descriptions of a certain situation, or in a coherent story. These groupings of words do not represent some ultimately small semantic domains; rather they exemplify the ordinary use to which words are put in practical situations (like gossiping): words evoke culturally salient images—types of people, frequent social situations, and so forth. We learn the code (the language) not only by understanding its units (the meanings of words) but by being familiar with frequent messages (typical ways the language is employed).

Adjectives

Tzotzil contains a large number of adjectives which are used frequently to refer to human beings. Of these, the adjectives which most clearly reveal the evaluative power of gossip are those with a normative component, which imply some trait of character, usually negatively evaluated. Here are some examples, listed alphabetically, of roots of this class which figure prominently in Zinacanteco gossip. For each entry I give a gloss, examples from the gossip, and occasionally distributional or derivational information. Glosses preceded by a dollar sign ($) may be found in Laughlin (1975).[6]

ʔabol -ba	$"be suffering"; "be abject, poor"
1.	Batz'i ʔabol abaik, yiluk yil, laj xa koʔon.
	"You are *suffering* so; never mind, I am no longer angry." [A parent addressing his previously estranged daughter]
bol	"stupid"
	Has noun form -*bolil* "stupidity"; and intransitive verb -*bolib*, "become stupid."
2.	Mi ta jnaʔ k'u xʔelan sbolil?
	"How should I know about his *stupidity*?"
3.	Yaʔyoj sbolil.
	"People have heard of his foolishness."
4.	Miʔn chavak'be ta ʔora ta jtz'ikbe sbolil?
	"If you give her immediately then I will put up with her *transgressions*." [A suitor trying to bargain for a wife whose reputation has been compromised]
5.	Ibolibtasat.
	"He was made *foolish*." [A man given a potion who became feebleminded]
chich	$"extremely loquacious, saying everything that occurs to one"; "foolish, befuddled"

6.   Ibolib i*chich*ub xa.
"He has now become stupid, become *foolish.*"

chopol   "bad"

7.   Leklek ʔantzon xitun, muʔnuk *chop*likon, jnaʔ xiʔabtej.
"I am a *good* woman, not bad; I know how to work."

8.   Toj *chopol* sjol tajmek chyakub.
"He gets a very *bad* head when drunk." [I.e., he is an ugly drunk]

chuvaj   "crazy, mad"; $"silly"

9.   Ivovi ʔo, ipas ʔo ta *chuvaj.*
"He went crazy and became *mad* because of it."

10.   Iʔech' ta *chuvaj*il.
"He had a period of *madness.*"

ch'aj   "lazy"

11.   Xulem xutik yuʔun toj *ch'aj.*
"They call him 'Buzzard' because he's so *lazy.*"

ch'inin $"itchy"; "promiscuous, licentious"

lek   "good"

12.   Maʔuk *lek*il vinik ta melel.
"You're right, he's not a *good* man."

13.   Mu jnaʔ mi *lek*il krixchano leʔe, mu jnaʔ mi chvovi nan.
"I don't know if he's a *sane* person or if perhaps he is going mad."

14.   *Lek* yoʔon.
"He has a *good* heart." [I.e., he is good-natured]

15.   Mi k'un to lapukujib ti *lek*ot toʔoxe?
"Did you only gradually become evil? For you used to be *all right.*"

loko $"provocative, oversexed, boy-crazy"

16.   Yuʔnox ʔunen *loko*tik tajmek ch'iem taj tzebe.
"That girl just grew up to be somewhat *wild.*"

manya   "mischievous, wicked, underhanded"

17.   Kavron, toj *manya* molot!
"Damn! You are such a *dirty* old man."

18.   ʔAn ch'anuk, mu jnaʔ k'usitik *manya*on anaʔoj, voʔone molon.
"Shut up! I don't know what *wickedness* you are attributing to me; I am an elder." [Man rebuking those who made lewd insinuations]

me'on   "poor"
        This is most probably a noun root meaning "orphan."
19.   *Me'on*, naka chon-si' tzpas
        "He is so *poor* he lives by selling firewood."

mol   "old, elder, large."
20.   K'usi amulil, pero *mol*ot xa, mi xana' xasa' k'op to?
        "What crime have you committed? But you are an *old
        man*. Do you still get into trouble?"

mu $"delicious, fragrant, disgusting"
21.   Yan x'elan li *mu* jvabajome.
        "That *awful* musician is disgusting."

22.   Li *mu* paj-ni' vinik 'une, listzakik noxtok.
        "That *disgusting* droop-nosed man raped me."

pentejo $"stupid or awful"
23.   Mu xa *pentejo*ikon xkik' akechel.
        "I'm not so *stupid* as to take your leftovers [i.e., a
        cast-off lover]."

24.   Kavron, pero ma'uk vinik li *pentejo*.
        "Damn! That *stupid fellow* isn't a man."

pim   "stubborn, thick"

porkirya   "disgusting"
        Use of this word is usually restricted to women.
25.   Mu xa much'u xchi'inon, *porkirya* mol sbon sba ta pukuj.
        "No one will now accompany the old *disgusting* man,
        since he has painted himself up with evil." [Woman
        complaining of her husband, who has contracted
        venereal disease]

povre   "poor, unfortunate"
26.   Svov xa la iyuch' i *povre*.
        "The *poor* fellow drank it right down, they say."

27.   Ikom 'o ta *povre*.
        "He became *poverty-stricken*."

28.   *Povre* me'el jun yo'on batem, pero yochel ta skobbel
        smuk.
        "The *poor* old lady went off without a care; but they
        had already begun to fuck her sister."

pukuj $"dangerous, devilish, evil"; "ill-tempered"
29.   Xa'i sba batz'i *pukuj*.
        "He thinks himself to be quite *tough*."

30.   *Pukuj* ilok', mu sk'an mantal, mu sk'an xchi?in stot.
               "He has turned out to be *unpleasant*; he won't obey; he
               won't live with his father."

31.   Ta sk'opohel no?ox xvinaj ti toj *pukuj*.
               "From his speech alone it is evident that he is terribly
               ill-tempered."

32.   Toj *pukuj* tajmek k'al xyakube, ?i skotol sa? smul.
               "He is very *ugly* when drunk, and he gets into all kinds
               of trouble."

p'ij $"clever, smart, intelligent"; "deceitful"
               The verb *p'ijubtas* means "to instruct," especially to
               instruct in deceitfulness.

33.   Sonso pukuj, *p'ij* yilel pero batz'i sonso.
               "He is foolishly ill-tempered; he seems *smart* but he's
               really dumb."

34   Taj x?elan s*p'ij*ubtas ti ?o spoxil.
               "That is how he *informed* him about the existence of a
               potion [an aphrodisiac]."

35.   Ja? nan x*p'ij*ubtasvan li vinik ?une.
               "Probably the man *told* [her] *how to act* [to deceive a
               supernatural being]."

sonso   "stupid, ordinary, ingenuous"
               See example (33) above.

36.   ?Unen *sonso*tik nan chk vo?one.
               "He's just a *stupid ordinary* person like me."

37.   Mu k'u bal ?o, batz'i *sonso*, mu xul tzjol k'u tzpas.
               "He is good for nothing, just *stupid*; he can't think
               what to do."

38.   Yu?nox *sonso*, mu sna? kastiya.
               "He's just *stupid*: he doesn't know Spanish."

39.   Mu sna? mi cho?el komo *sonso* xch'ulel.
               "He didn't know he was being tricked, because he has
               a *simple* soul." [I.e., he has no curing powers]

sovra   "leftover, worthless"
40.   Muk' bu tun ta jmoj, komuk ta *sovra*.
               "He hasn't served at all [i.e., in cargo positions]; he's
               just *worthless*."

tuk' $"honest, upright, conscientious"
               The intransitive verb *-tuk'ib* means "become *tuk'*,"
               "straighten out." The transitive verb *-tuk'ulan* means
               "notice, pay attention, take care of."

41. *Tuk'*il j'ilol.
     "He's a *straight* curer." [I.e., he's not a witch]
42. *Tuk'* inupun.
     "He got married *in the correct way.*"
43. *Tuk'*an no'ox me, k'an me chtal li Maryane.
     Straighten out! Maryan might come! (Woman trying
     to discourage the advances of her lover in the face
     of husband's arrival.)
44. Batz'i mu x*tuk'*ulanat yu'un stot sme'.
     He just wasn't *cared for* by his parents.
45. Is*tuk'*ulan nan ta batz'i yech mu yechuk.
     Perhaps he *took care of* it, but carelessly.

tutz   "homosexual, coward"
              Laughlin (1975, p. 347) lists the root as deriving from
              a positional meaning $"stubby, stunted."
46. Ta la ssok 'o li 'antze, mu xa la x'alaj, timi xchi'in li
     tutze.
     "A woman will be ruined, they say—she will no longer
     bear children—if she sleeps with a *homosexual.*"
47. *Tutz* chalbeik 'o li ch'abal xch'amal.
     "They call him '*sissy*' because he has no children."

xilim   "blabbermouth, wild talker"; $"imprudent"
48. Batz'i toj *xilim* chk'opoj.
     "He talks *tactlessly, without thinking.*"
49. *Xilim*tik xa'i sba.
     "He acts *imprudently*, with a devil-may-care attitude."

vaxal $"quiet, calm, gentle, tame"; "faultless, upright, good"
              This is evidently a positional root having to do with quiet
              and calm; when applied to people it denotes lack of
              evil tendencies.
50. Mu no'ox yu'un sna' ti *vaxal* jset'.
     "He doesn't know how to *behave properly.*"
51. *Vaxl*an kavron!
     "*Behave yourself*, you bastard!"

vov   "mad"
              This root has only a few adjectival properties.
52. Solel *vov*iem yilel ta jmoj.
     "He seems to have gone completely *mad.*"
53. A*vov*il xa.
     "What you are doing is *madness!*"
     Cf. example (13) above.

yan	"different, unpleasant, disgusting"
54.	*Yan* tzpas, kapem.
	"He acts *unpleasantly*: he is angry."
55.	*Yan* sba avoʔon.
	"Your heart is *unhappy*."
56.	*Yan* xʔelan xchak svex.
	"The seat of his pants is *revolting*."
57.	*Yan* tzpas ti jjole.
	"My head is *misbehaving* [I am having wild thoughts, mad inclinations, etc.]"
yij	$"thick, ripe, old"; "disgusting"
	Within a single noun phrase the adjective *yijil* often means "disgusting" rather than "old," etc.
58.	Mas *yij*ot.
	"You are *old*er."
59.	K'u ʔonox sjol li *yij*il ch'aj krem yaʔel?
	"What's the matter with that *disgusting* lazy boy, anyway?"
60.	ʔAnimal *yij* s(*yih-*)il ʔat.
	"His *disgusting* penis was terribly *thick*!"
yo	$"miserable, wretched, humble, lowly"; "less severe"
61.	Pukuj ʔonox pero mas *yo* jset'.
	"He is evil-tempered, too, but somewhat *less so*."
62.	Mas *yo* jtz'uj, jaʔ mas xaʔi k'op.
	"He is a bit *less* [unapproachable]; he is more amenable to talk."
63.	*Yo* chopol vinik.
	"He is a *miserable* bad man."

The sorting procedure when applied to this set of words produced the following clusters, each justified as indicated.[7]

a.	sovra	"leftover, worthless"
	sonso	"stupid"
	chopol	"bad, defective"
	bol	"stupid"
	chich	"stupid, foolish"
Exegesis	"Such a person has served for nothing. He just is totally useless."	

b.	xilim	"imprudent, wild-talking"
	vov	"mad"
	loko	"crazy, oversexed"
	chuvaj	"mad, insane"

| | Exegesis | "Such a person will just say or do anything. He also is totally useless." |

c.

bal	"satisfactory, adequate"
ch'ul	"holy"
vaxal	"good, quiet"
tuk'	"straight, honest, upright"
lek	"good"

Exegesis   "Such a person is good; he acts the way a good man does, and he serves cargos. He knows the proper way to do things. He is harmless when drunk."

d.

| p'ij | "smart" |
| bivo | "quick, lively, clever" |

Exegesis   "This person is good; he talks wisely. He knows where he is going, what he is talking about, how he should conduct himself."

e.

| yan (yan xʔelan) | "disgusting, different" |
| mu | "disgusting, stinky" |

Exegesis   "Such a person is bad, good for nothing. He is just disgusting and unpleasant."

f.

tutz	"homosexual"
yo	"wretched, lowly"
povre	"poor, unfortunate"
meʔon	"poverty-stricken, orphaned"
ch'aj	"lazy"
ʔabol -ba	"unfortunate, suffering"

Exegesis   "This sort of person is probably just worthless. He doesn't pass cargos; he is just there, doing nothing. He might be homosexual, or lazy, or just a wretched poor man."

g.

| pukuj | "evil-tempered" |
| yijil | "disgusting" |

Exegesis   S(yih)il pukujil noʔox: "It's just a matter of this person's disgusting evilness."

h.

pim	"stubborn"
porkirya	"disgusting"
manya	"wicked, mischievous"
pentejo	"stupid, awful"

Exegesis   "This person is awful. He won't do what he is told, but what he does is wicked; perhaps he lies all the time, or steals."

i.   ch'inin   "itchy, promiscuous"
            puta   "whorish, licentious"
    Exegesis   "This is for sex-crazed women."

These clusters suggest a highly tentative diagram which opposes nega-tive to positive characteristics (see table 6). Predictably, more common words in gossip deal with negatively evaluated character traits than with positively evaluated ones.[8]

Table 6   Personal Propensity Marked by Tzotzil Adjectives Often Used in Gossip

	Negative	Positive	
b	Imprudent	Wise	
	Stupid	Clever	d
a	Useless	Serves *cargos*	
g	Evil-tempered	Good-tempered	c
f	Poor	(Wealthy)	
	Perverted		
e	Disgusting		
h	Wicked	(Obedient)	
		(Law-abiding)	
	Perverse		
i	Sexually improper	(Modest, proper)	

NOTE   Marginal letters correspond to lettered lexical clusters explained in the text.

Another important class of adjectives contains "adverbial" words which modify the main verbs of Tzotzil sentences. Several of the words in the previous section function this way; for example, we may say

64.   Pukuj xloʔilaj.
            "He talks in an *unfriendly, unpleasant* way."

Similarly, sentences (42) and (48) show *tuk'* and *xilim* used adverbially. Aside from such uses of otherwise semantically loaded words, there are

adverbials which seem primarily to be intensifiers, or semantically neutral pointers. The following list contains the most frequent of such words
in Tzotzil conversation.

ʔanimal $"lots of, very much"
               Used to modify nouns, verbs, and adjectives.
65.   ʔAnimal saʔ smul.
               "He gets into trouble *all the time.*
66.   Toj ʔanimal la pukuj xʔilin tajmek li meʔele.
               "They say the old lady is *terribly* shrewish, always
               getting angry."
67.   ʔAnimal smanya ʔuk.
               "He, too, has *lots of* evil tendencies."

batz'i   "very, real"
               With adjectives and verbs this word is ordinarily an
               intensifier.[9]
68.   *Batz'i* ixiʔ.
               "He was *really* afraid."
69.   Yech s*batz'i*-nop.
               "He was *completely* lying."

ben   "good, very"
70.   Batz'i *ben* ch'ajot.
               "You are just *awfully* lazy."
71.   *Ben* xa vinik yilel pero stak'in la ʔantz.
               "He now seems to be a *good* man, but it is, they say, all
               because of a woman's money."

ʔentero   "very, real, exactly, completely"
72.   Mu ʔonox batz'i ʔ*entero* tajmek sk'opon sbaik.
               "They still don't *really* get along."
73.   Lek ʔ*entero* vinik.
               "He is a *real* man."

labal   "completely, continuously, simply, constantly"
               This word most frequently modifies de-verbal nouns.
74.   Taʔlo li *labal* k'abtael.
               "I've had enough of being pissed on *all the time.*" [Wife
               complaining about aging husband]
75.   *Labal* ʔelek' tzpas.
               "He just steals *constantly.*"
76.   Mu jk'antikotik k'u s*labal*-ʔal tajmek.
               "We don't like the things he *keeps* saying."

lek   "well, successfully, excessively"
               As I show above, when used with nouns, *lek* means

simply "good"; with verbs it means "be good at. . .";
with verbs referring to bad activities, it means "do to
excess." With adjectives, the word is an intensifier.

77.   *Lek* xa spasoj k'op.
"They are *deeply* involved in the dispute."

78.   *Lek* iyich' ʔarsyal.
"She was *well* whipped."

79.   *Lek* jyakubel vinik.
"He is *quite* a drunkard."

80.   *Lek* me bosol yuʔun tajmek.
"It [pubic area] really bulges *nicely* on her."

naka $"just, only, completely, nothing but, simply, hardly"

81.   *Naka* ʔonox pistola snaʔ ʔonox li j'aʔyele.
"That guy *always* has the custom of carrying a pistol."

82.   *Naka* xa tzvokol xchiʔiltak isk'anbe sjol li tak'ine.
"When he lends at interest, he *just* lives on the labor of
his comrades."

83.   *Naka* me yak'bel, *naka* me taluk krixchano.
"*Just hurry up* and give it to her [fuck her]; people *might*
come along."

solel $"just, simply"

84.   *Solel* yiluk yil li kajnile, *solel* batuk ta jmoj.
"I'll *simply* forget about my wife; let her *just* go for
good."

85.   Mu k'u chismanbe, *solel* yech noʔox tajmek.
"He doesn't buy me anything; he's *just* a good-for-
nothing."

toj   "so much, too much, very, just"
This word occurs frequently in conversation; in gossip it
signals a quality that a person displays to excess.

86.   Mu snaʔ ta yoʔon yech, *toj* pukuj, mu stak' k'oponel.
"He isn't well disposed to that; instead he is *terribly*
nasty. One can't talk to him."

87.   *Toj* palta sjol.
"His head is *too* faulty." [I.e., he misbehaves]

88.   *Toj* mas chilbajin parajel.
"He has mismanaged the hamlet affairs *too much*."

toyol   "very, highly, often"
Toyol literally means "high" or "tall"; its shortened form
tol occurs as an intensifier.

89.   Batz'i *tol* chk'elvan, *tol* sokanbe sjol viniketik.
"She *always* looks at people; she *often* seduces men."

90.   *Tol* stij yak' chamel.
             "He is *always* threatening witchcraft."

yalal   "on purpose"
             Laughlin (1975, p. 382) lists this word as a particle; it,
             like other words in this list, modifies main verbs. It
             implies intent, and thus it parcels out the blame.

91.   Mu *yalaluk* isk'opone.
             "He didn't speak to her *on purpose*."

92.   *Yalal* saʔbil yuʔun.
             "He *asked for it* [some sort of trouble]."

yech $"like that, in that way, just nothing"
             Yech appears in many idiomatic constructions. With
             verbs it often means "do for nothing, for no reason." In
             the subjunctive, *ti yechuke*, "if it were thus," often
             implies "this is how it should have been, or would have
             been had something not occurred." *Yech* also means
             "true."

93.   Solel *yech* xkapet.
             "He's just irritable *for no reason*."

94.   Muk' bu xkil ti *yech* chispasbe.
             "I have never seen him treat me *that way*."

95.   *Yech* tal avak' avokol.
             "You took the trouble to come *all for nothing*."

96.   Pujbeik smoton ti *yech*uke.
             "They *should have* hit him with a little gift [i.e., a
             punch]."

97.   ʔAti tuk'uk batuke yuʔvan ʔu k'usi smul ti *yech*uke.
             "If he had gone directly, you can't mean to suggest that
             he *would have* been at fault?"

In sorting these words my informant made only two groups. The first
contained the words *lek*, *ʔentero*, and *ben*. He explained:

"This is a good man. He is *lek vinik* ['a good man'], *ben vinik* ['a
fine man'], *ʔentero vinik* ['a real man']."

The second group contained all the other intensifiers and particles. My
informant urged:

"Think of a drunkard. One could say all these things about a man
who drinks:"

Yech jyakubel skotol k'ak'al.
"He's *just* drunk all the time."

Tol xyakub.
"He gets drunk *a lot*."
Toj ʔuch'el yuʔun.
"He drinks *too much*."
Solel jyakubel.
"He's *simply* a drunk."
Naka yakubel tzpas.
"*All* he does is get drunk."
Mero jyakubel.
"He's a *real* drunk."
Labal yakubel tzpas.
"He is *continually* drunk."

This sorting tends to confirm my suspicion that in gossip, intensifiers occur mostly as markers which point to negatively evaluated behavior or propensities. Such words in Tzotzil punctuate and emphasize the spoken word.

Nouns

The largest class of roots in Tzotzil, and perhaps the only open class, is that of nouns. The most interesting uses of nouns in gossip involve: (*a*) characterizations of individuals by nouns naming identities, roles, social positions, and so forth; (*b*) talk about emotions, motives, and personal capabilities through "metaphorical" use of body-part nouns; and (*c*) descriptions of disputes and evaluations of particular settlements.

From the most commonly occurring nouns from transcribed gossip, my informant produced the following clusters, which suggest types of people, roles, or identities.

a.	muchacho	"boy, helper"
	ʔuloʔ	"friend, visitor" [reciprocal term of address between Zinacantecos and Chamulas]
	ʔintyo	"Indian" [impolite]
Exegesis	"These people are Indians; they work as helpers, as hired hands—especially Chamulas."	
98.	Spas ta s*muchacho* yajval balamil.	
	"He became a *servant* of the Earth Lord."	
99.	Srason *ʔintyo*etik.	
	"That is the way *Indians* do it."	
100.	Toj mas jʔoʔlol *ʔintyo*etik liʔ toe.	
	"Some of the *Indians* around here are too much."	

b.   chujil   "runt; fool, feeble-minded"
            Mat   "Mateo" [name of the
                                          town fool in Naben-
                                          chauk]
            palta   "fault, defect, failure"

    Exegesis   "Such a man has a defective head; he is feeble-minded
               [like Mat in Nabenchauk]."

101.   Toj *palta* sjol.
            "He has a *faulty* head." [I.e., he is a fool]

102.   Ta byernexetik mu stak' mas jpastik *palta.*
            "During Lent we must not *fail* in our duty."

103.   *Xchujil* no²ox.
            "He's just a *moron.*"

c.   j²elek'   "thief"
            ²elav   "diversion"
            patil   "back, backside"

    Exegesis   "This man offers a diversion, because he is a thief. He
               comes from behind and steals; he sneaks around behind
               people's backs."

104.   Chispak'ta ta *²elek'* jchi²uk kajnil.
            "She falsely accuses my wife and me of being thieves."

105.   Ta *patil* chut sbaik.
            "They scolded each other in *secret, where we couldn't
            see them.*"

d.   totil   "father; senior"
            ²ajvalil   "lord, master, capable
                                          person, owner"
            rason   "reason, wisdom, reason-
                                          ableness"
            balamil   "land, property"

    Exegesis   "This is a senior man who is wise; he is owner of much
               land."

106.   *Totil* jk'ulej.
            "He is one of the *rich*est men."

107.   Batz'i *totil* j²ak'-chamel ta ²alele.
            "He is supposed to be one of the *most dangerous*
            witches."

108.   Yu²nox y*ajval*il ta jmoj, ²oy smarchante.
            "She's a complete *professional* [whore]; she has her
            steady customers."

109.   Tol la ²ep ²ochem *yajval.*
            "They say she has had many *lovers.*"

110.   *Yajval yajval* much'u sna? sk'oponel.
               "*Only a few* know how to talk."

111.   Chapal xa?ox *yajval.*
               "His *murderer* was already ready."

112.   Mu sna? *rason* jset' li mole.
               "That old man is not at all *reasonable.*"

113.   Mu xa k'u sta ta *balamil.*
               "He know longer manages to get anything on *earth.*"
               [He is a total failure]

e.   kavron   "cuckold, bastard"
           tyavlo   "devil, bastard"
           xulem   "buzzard, lazy person"

Exegesis   "These are bad words that would be said of a lazy man, a man who is not respected."

114.   K'u akwenta xatik' aba *kavron* mol?
               "Why are you butting in, you old *bastard?*"

115.   Sme?el *tyavlo*, mi chapoj ?uke?
               "You old lady *devil*, will you try to defend her, too?"

f.   j?ilol   "curer, shaman"
           ch'ulel   "soul"

Exegesis   "He has a clever soul; he knows how to cure."

116.   *J?ilol* ?ox ti vo?ne.
               "He was going to become a *curer.*"

117.   Mu?nuk ta ryoxetik ta jk'an ?o *kilolal.*
               "I didn't gain my *curing ability* from asking talking saints for it."

118.   Te nan x*ch'ulel* jset' li jkobel tzeb.
               "That fucking girl has something of a *soul.*" [I.e., she has some sense]

119.   Vo?one, ijvaychin xa, li?ay me ta j*ch'ulel.*
               "As for me, I have dreamed about it; my *soul* was there."

There are certainly identities and types of people not characterized by word clusters on this list. The limited class of nouns from the gossip corpus suggested to my informant various types of undesirable person —peons, fools, thieves, lazy buzzardlike louts—and only two neutral or positively evaluated types: the rich landowner associated with the wise man, and the spiritually potent curer. The sample sentences show that such associations correspond closely to the senses of the words as they occur in gossip. Note that even in the positively evaluated clusters (*d*) and (*f*) individual words occur in negative contexts in actual speech. *Totil* applies not only to wise and respected elders, but also to master witches and incurable troublemakers. And in cluster (*f*) talk about a person's *ch'ulel* may point as much to soul weakness and lack of discipline as to soul strength and potency. The verbal associations into which each word enters make it possible for the native speaker to create conceptual clusters and to illustrate each with hypothetical representatives of some common type of person. (Presumably some similar conceptual lumping allows gossips to attribute unobserved and unreported qualities to real people on the basis of limited or rumored bits of information.)

Certain body part nouns in Tzotzil carry heavy metaphorical weight. They often describe emotions, motives, character traits, and other mental phenomena. The two roots with the heaviest burdens of this sort are *-jol* ("head") and *-oʔon* ("heart"). In the following lists I consider various concatenations of verbs and adjectives with these roots. For each construction I show the word with which the body-part noun occurs, give a gloss for it, and then show the meaning of the compound expression, often with examples. Thus, under the adjective + *jol* construction, one adjective that can occur is *bik'it* ("small"); the resultant expression, as in, e.g., *bik'it ajol* (lit., "your head is small"), means "have weak head for liquor"; hence, here, "you can't hold your liquor."

a. Adjective + *jol* ("head")   *Compound meaning*

bik'it	"small"	"low tolerance for liquor"
chopol	"bad"	"unpleasant, uncooperative, unfriendly"
palta	"faulty"	"imprudent, unwise, foolish"
koʔol	"equal"	"in agreement"
parejo	"similar"	"in agreement, friendly with"
jp'ej -jol *xchiʔuk*	"one head with. . ."	"in agreement with, together with, friendly with"
jchop ʔo -jol	"different head"	"strange, queer, evil, odd"
-jololal yech	"——'s head thus"	"the way one is by nature"

120.   *Koʔol sjolik* ti batz'i naka vinik ta saʔike.
           "They have *similar proclivities* in that they are always
           chasing after men."

b. Adjective + *-oʔon* ("heart")

jun	"one"	"content, happy"
lek	"good"	"happy"
chopol	"bad"	"unhappy, anxious, worried, ill-tempered, grief-stricken, mean"

yan sba	"disgusting, odd"	"worried, anxious, sick"
pukuj	"evil"	"ill-tempered"
tzotz	"strong"	"brave, courageous, strong, uncomplaining"
bik'it	"small"	"weak, fearful, sensitive, quick to anger"

121. Batz'i mas xa *pukuj* yo²on li yajval balamil.
      "The Earth Lord is now terribly *ill-tempered*."

122. S*lek*il nan yo²on.
      "It was, perhaps, from the *goodness* of his *heart*."

123. S*jun*ul xa²ox ko²on ta xkik'.
      "With *all* my *heart* I was going to marry her."

124. Mi ²o jset'uk abankilale, yu²un *tzotz* ²o avo²on bu
      xaxanav.
      "If you have a bit of your older brother, then you will
      be *brave* wherever you go." [Proverb about *moy*,
      native tobacco]

c. Verb + *-jol* (subject)
    We assume sentences of the form
            Verb _Subject_ [Possessor + *jol*]

lik	"arise"	"decide to do something, be provoked, have an idea, have mischievous or wicked thought"
kap	"become angry"	"lose temper"
xi²	"be afraid"	"become afraid"
ch'ay	"lose, be lost"	"forget, be befuddled"
vovi	"go mad"	"go mad"
yan -pas	"do bad or disgusting thing"	"have crazy or wicked thoughts"
sok	"break, be broken"	"be provoked, become wicked"

d. Verb + *-o²on* (subject)

²ech'	"pass"	"be satisfied with, try as hard as one can, do until one is tired of something"
laj	"finish, be finished"	"stop being angry, be reconciled, be placated"
ch'ay	"lose, be lost"	"be distracted, unaware"
sok	"break, be broken"	"be unhappy, distraught, worried"

lok'	"exit, leave"	"do one's best, be sated"
lik	"arise"	"have pain in chest, be excited"
vaxi	"become calm"	"lose anxiety, lose evil proclivities"
k'upij	"long for, desire"	"have longing"
k'an	"want"	"desire, want"

125. *Ch'ay sjolik*, mu sna? bu chbatik.
"They were *dazed*; they didn't know where to go [after committing murder]."

126. Te ista *ch'ay*bel yo?on.
"He was *distracted* there.

127. Sk'an *sok*anbeik s*jol* kremotik.
"She wants to *provoke* [and *seduce*] boys."

128. Mu xa*sok*be yo?on abankile ta ?i?onel.
"Don't make your brother *unhappy* with your babbling."

129. *Yo?on* la x*lik* tajmek.
"They say his *heart* would *pound*." [Man with heart condition]

130. I*lik* ?o s*jol*ik iyuch'ik mas trago.
"As a result [of drinking] they *decided* to drink more rum."

131. *Yan* tz*pas* ti j*jol*e, mu jna? mi ?ipon.
"My *head* is *crazy*; I don't know if I'm sick."
[Man with a secret desire to frighten people at night]

132. Batz'i mu x*vaxi* li ko?on*tike, mu x*vaxi* li j*jol*tike.
"Our *hearts* won't *behave*, our *heads* won't be *obedient*." [Man who admits being a witch]

133. Muk' ?onox i*laj* yo?on yech komo te sbik'oj sk'ak'al li mole.
"He wasn't *placated* in that way, for the old man swallowed his anger."

e.   Verb + *-jol* (object)

-il	"see"	"know a person's bad tendencies"
-lo?lo	"deceive, trick"	"maliciously mislead or trick someone"

134. Kilojbe s*jol* taj ?une.
"I've *seen the way* that one *thinks*."

135. Yalal ilo?lobat s*jol*.
"She was purposefully *deceived*."

f. Verb + *-oʔon* (object)

-kux	"rest"	"enjoy oneself"
-at	"count"	"worry, be anxious"
-pat	"mold, form"	"gratify, mollify, decide"
-il	"see"	"be acquainted with person's character"
-nop	"think, think about"	"want, decide to"
pich'	"make into lump, set"	"long for, be tantalized by"

136. ʔEp ʔojtikinbil, ʔi*l*bil k'u xʔelan *yoʔon*.
"He is known by many; people have *see*n what *his heart is like*."

137. Jaʔ to ba s*pat*be *yoʔon* taj yajnile.
"Only then did he go to *mollify* his wife."

138. Jaʔ noʔox s*pat*oj ʔo yoʔon li yilolale.
"He must *content himself* with his curing powers alone."
[I.e., he is not a witch, too]

139. Jaʔ yech xʔelan y*at*el ko*ʔon* chk liʔe.
"This is what is *troubling* me."

140. Kere, i*pich'* la yo*ʔon* sbaik noxtok.
"Boy, they must have *longed for* each other again."

g. Verb + *ta* ("at, on, to, in") + *jol* ("head")
For example:

141. Xaʔuk nan lekuk ti k'u chaʔal y*ul*em *ta* s*jol*.
"He perhaps thought what had *occurred to him* was good."

-yul	"arrive"	"remember, occur to one"
-joy	"encircle, surround, be surrounded"	"think up, have thoughts"
-nop	"think, think about"	"decide, think up"

142. Batz'i x*joy ta* s*jol* k'usi xal.
"He just *dreams up* out of nowhere what he says."

h. Verb + *ta* + *-oʔon*

-ak'	"give, offer, put"	"harbor grudge, take to heart, be offended"
-naʔ	"know, long for, miss"	"be concerned about, take pity on, be sympathetic"
-k'ux	"be painful, have pain"	"be unhappy, be desolate"

143. Mu s*naʔ ta* yo*ʔon* yech, toj pukuj, mu stak' k'oponel.
"He *has* no *pity*; he is ill-tempered and can't be reasoned with."

144.   Yiluk yil miʔn av*ak' ta* avoʔon.
            "Forget it, if you are *offended* by it."
145.   K'*ux ta* koʔon voʔon yech.
            "That sort of thing would make me *unhappy*."

i. Idioms with freely occurring -*jol* or -*oʔon*

146.   Batz'i yuʔun s*jol*olal yuʔun yech.
            "That's just *the way he is*."
147.   K'u ʔonox s*jol* li yijil ch'aj krem.
            "What's *the matter with* that lazy awful boy?"
148.   Yoʔon*u*k skob li sniʔ meʔele ta ʔalele.
            "He supposedly *wanted* to fuck his mother-in-law."
149.   Yil xa noʔox yil, mu xtal avak'bon sk'ak'al koʔon.
            "Let's forget it; don't come here and make me *angry*."

Idioms occurring with these two roots in natural conversation seem to show a fairly clear dichotomy between thinking, personality, and intellectual capacities which are associated with *jol* ("head"), and emotions, attention, desire, and well-being, which are expressed in terms of –*oʔon* ("heart"). Much of the power of Tzotzil to deal with internal mental processes and states stems from metaphorical use of these two words. And, on the basis of gossip, we may posit some implicit contrast between things of the heart and things of the head (not unlike a similar contrast in English).[10] The wider domain covered by these idioms is itself explicitly represented in a ritual couplet:

150.   Ti sjole ti yoʔone.
            "His head, his heart." [I.e., his thoughts and his feelings]

Related formal couplets occur elsewwhere, as for example in sentence (132) above.

Listening to gossip brings to one's awareness such semantic and expressive facts of a language—facts which seem to imply native theories about the world (or, at least, about the human body), statable in no simpler way than by giving examples.

Nouns dealing with disputes and settlement of arguments are also prominent in gossip; and this set of nouns is similarly revealing. Jane Collier (1973, chap. 4) writes about "Zinacanteco legal concepts" through the medium of certain Tzotzil expressions having to do with bringing up, searching for a settlement to, and reaching an end of disputes. Of the clusters of nouns produced by sorting prominent gossip nouns, several evoke conflict situations.

a.   *perton*   "pardon, forgiveness"
            pasensya   "patience"

Exegesis   Chʔakʼvan ta pertonal, ʔoy spasensya.
            He pardons people; he has patience."

151.   Mukʼ s*perton*, mu xaʔi kʼop.
        "He has no *mercy*; he won't listen to reason."

b.   moton   "gift"
            limete   "bottle" [fifth-size, for
                                      liquor]

Exegesis   ʔOy smoton, iʔakʼbat slimete.
            "He has a gift; he is given a bottle."
            [Refers to the fact that a man who settles a dispute is
            always given a bottle of liquor by the disputants.]

152.   Ta *limete* ilaj ʔo kʼop.
        "The dispute was settled *with a bottle* [i.e., with one
        party asking pardon of the other, and presenting a bottle
        which was accepted]."

153.   Islokʼesbe li s*limete*al jaʔ xa islajes ʔo smul.
        "He pulled out his *bottle* [to give to the other] and
        thereby apologized."

c.   ʔakwerto   "in agreement, agreement"
            ʔamiko   "friend"

Exegesis   Koʔol skʼopik, ta ʔakwerto, komo ʔamiko yaʔel.
            "They have the same words; they agree, because they
            are friends."

154.   Spas tal sba ta *ʔakwerto*.
        They came to an *agreement*.

155.   Lek y*amiko* sbaik ta xloʔilajik.
        They are good *friends* to judge from how they talk
        together.
        Cf. sentence (31) in chapter 3.

d.   tajimol   "games, foolishness,
                                   frivolity"
            melol   "proper or traditional way"

Exegesis   Mu snaʔbe smelol, tajimol chkʼopoj.
            "He doesn't know the correct way to handle the matter;
            he talks as if it were a game."

156.   Ti yechuke tukʼ noʔox tal avalbe s*melol*.
        "You should have come straight here to explain *the facts*
        of the situation."

157.   Muk' bu *tajimol* li k'op lavie.
                     "This affair now is no *game*."

e.   *ʔil pletu*   "quarreling"
          kavilto   "town hall, *cabildo*"
          koj   "fault of ———"
          mulil   "guilt, sin, fault, misdeed"
          multa   "fine, bribe, assessment"
          kronta   "enemy"
          k'op   "dispute, argument,
                                       affair"
          ʔixtol   "toy, plaything"
          k'ob   "hand"
          pus   "sweatbath" [euphemism
                                       for "jail"]

Exegesis   My informant offered the following hypothetical story:
           ʔIl pletu xchiʔuk yajnil.
           "He *quarrels* with his wife."
           Tol chk'ot ta *kavilto*.
           "He's always going to the *town hall*."
           S*koj* s*mul* chak' *multa*.
           "As a *result* of his *misdeeds* he pays a *fine*."
           S*kronta* sbaik xchiʔuk yajnil.
           "He is an *enemy* of his wife."
           Tol saʔ *k'op*.
           "He's always making *trouble*."
           Tol x*ʔixtol*-k'opoj.
           "He always talks *irresponsibly*."
           Tztzak *k'ob*ol ʔun, chʔoch ta *pus*.
           "They seize his *hands*, and he enters *jail*."

Some sample sentences from conversation:

158.   Batz'i meʔ *pletu*.
                     "She's a *troublesome* old lady."
159.   ʔO s*kavilto*al, ʔo x*chuke*lal.
                     "For such behavior there is a *town hall* and a *jail*."
160.   S*koj* chuvaj.
                     "It's the *fault* of his madness."
161.   S*koj* stzak-ʔantzile.
                     "It's the *fault* of his propensity for raping women."
162.   Isyakubtas xa sba mas yoʔ mu k'usi s*mul* ʔo.
                     "He made himself drunker so that he would appear
                     *blame*less." [Zinacantecos believe that drunkenness is an

extenuating circumstance in committing crimes (see
J. Collier 1973, p. 159).]

163.   Stzinanbe sbaik *multa.*
        "They strapped each other with *fines.*"

164.   Chba sjelik ta tak'in li skrontaik.
        "They went to exchange their *enemies* for money [by
        selling their souls to the Earth Lord as his laborers]."

165.   Solel iy*ixtala*n tak'in sa²–*k'op* spas tajmek.
        "He just *frittered* away his money by making *trouble*
        all the time."

166.   Ko²olko²ol sk'upinik *pus.*
        "They equally enjoyed the sweatbath [i.e., the jail]."

Jane Collier (1973, pp. 91ff.) concentrates on what she calls "legal
concepts" that underlie the use of particular Tzotzil expressions based
on the roots *mul* ("sin, crime") and *k'op* ("dispute"). She suggests that
"Zinacantecos have cultural explanations for the reasons people do
wrong, for the consequences of a wrong, and for the nature of an appropriate settlement. These ideas are part of a native theory that relates
man to god and god to man. But in explaining Zinacanteco cosmology
my aim is not to suggest that ideology determines behavior, but rather
to point out that ideology provides a language for justifying behavior,
for explaining behavior, and for directing future behavior" (1973, p.
91). Collier argues that the legal concepts involved underlie (and can
be inferred from) Tzotzil terminological usage. "In exploring the meanings of Tzotzil terms used in legal proceedings, I have concentrated on
the consequences implied by their use. I have defined words not in terms
of the attributes of the objects they refer to, but in terms of the assumptions that must underlie their use. For example, I have defined the word
mulil as 'an act that displeases the gods' instead of making a list of all
the actions that could be called a mulil and proceeding to extract the
semantic features shared by these actions. I have looked at terms in
relation to their implicit assumptions, to explore their implications for
future action. People rarely call an act a mulil for purposes of neutral
observation, but rather to imply that something must be done about it.
The gods must be placated. Mulil is a loaded term and its use spurs
people into action" (1973, p. 92). Gossip offers glimpses of contexts
of the use of such "loaded" terms, contexts in which the prods to action
are somewhat less formal (and obligatory) than those which arise in
litigation.

Informal speech often alludes to aspects of a formal legal theory of
the sort Collier details. For example, sentence (162) suggests a relation-

ship between drunkenness and one's liability to *mul* ("guilt"). In a less obvious way, the vocabulary of gossip leads to an implicit understanding of the origins of disputes and the mechanisms of their settlement. One need not resort to formal interviews to understand from clusters (*a*) and (*b*) that settling a dispute is sometimes a matter of begging pardon or offering a bottle. Furthermore, the metaphor of "words" (*k'op*) pervades Zinacanteco talk about conflict, as if fighting were a matter of not listening (see sentence [151]), as if a rash, irresponsible talker gets himself into more trouble (see the examples based on *tajimol* ["game"] and *?ixtol* ["toy"]), and as if the end of a dispute is the end of talk (sentence [152]) or a matter of bringing stories into agreement (see cluster [*c*]).

The town hall is the most fertile source for gossip, and gossip sessions are accordingly rife with accounts of disputes and the accompanying verbal duels. Thus it is not surprising that nouns culled from gossip should suggest to an informant situations or personalities related to conflict, the *cabildo*, drinking in settlement of disputes. In cluster (*e*) my informant was able to create a whole imaginary court case from the semantic prods contained in a list of nouns. Words are suggestive objects in a speaker's universe.

I could continue with other root classes: intransitive verb roots include a large class of words having to do with emotional states; positional roots govern idioms of emotion, and of human quality based on metaphors of shape and size; transitive verb roots occurring in gossip are easily sorted into classes of evil and negatively evaluated acts. I leave to another place further exposition of the semantic facts involved. Here I have tried to show, first, how one can present interesting and culturally salient semantic facts of a language through examples from actual speech—lacking, as we do, a theory of semantics which might provide a more formal (and less voluminous) descriptive mechanism. Second, I hope to have thrown some light on Zinacanteco culture as one perceives it through a gradually acquired understanding of the language. I believe that as one begins to be able to talk and to understand what people say about their doings one's appreciation of those doings changes in quality; the challenge to the fieldworker is to convey some of the insight one gains from learning a native language without having to teach the whole language. The appeal of gossip lies in its full use of the resources of the language to talk about a wide range of cultural phenomena.

Rules in Gossip

Mu xa k'u stak' spasik, mu xa stak' xbak'ik.
"They can no longer do anything; they can no longer act up."

8

I have suggested that gossip is implicitly *about* rules; that it involves the interpretation of behavior through rules. I have located in the mouths of gossips seemingly absolute rulelike propositions linking certain actions to certain consequences, extracting morals from events. Rules are slippery things—in anthropological, philosophical, and legal discourse as well as in our everyday lives. Much of the history of social anthropology revolves around a debate over the nature of cultural rules (particularly marriage rules), over criteria for saying that a rule "governs" behavior or that behavior "conforms to" or "invokes" a rule, over the possibility of coming to understand a society partly through coming to appreciate the rationale of its rules of conduct and classification. Similarly, many of the central problems of moral and legal philosophy rest on the notion of rules and their intimate connection with human institutions. A related issue lies at the very heart of the philosophy of social science: namely, How are explanations of human action to relate to social institutions and the rules with which they are interwoven? (A common, perhaps misguided, way of formulating this issue asks the following question: Will the natural science notions of regularity and cause elucidate human action [including rule-following], or is a distinct conceptual framework appropriate?)

Ethnography, at least in recent years, has involved the search for cultural rules: rules which characterize appropriate behavior in particular societies. In our anthropological lives we confront (and are accustomed to speak of) a multiplicity of such rules: so-called statistical rules, normative rules, moral rules, jural rules, rules of procedure, rules of thumb, practical rules (maxims), rules of etiquette (which, as human ethnographers in the field, we must live by as well as describe), and so on. The beginning fieldworker, trying to understand what is going on around him, observes certain regularities (which leap to even the uninitiated eye): people do things in similar fashion, have similar routines, treat each other in patterned ways, and are generally predictable. As he begins to understand more of what he sees and hears, the fieldworker becomes aware that people have definite opinions about other peoples' behavior and the state of the world in general: they condemn or condone, justify or disapprove, cite custom, and point out innovation. A subtle terminological shift occurs: the ethnographer begins to talk of rules underlying patterned behavior, and of rules embodied by native opinion and value—in short, of the rules of a culture.

We notice right away a fundamental ambiguity in the word "rule" that should alert us to its dangers. The hypothetical ethnographer has found rules here to apply to distinct phenomena: regularities and norms or standards.[1] The two notions here are related to Rawls's (1955) "summary view of rules" and "practice conception of rules." I shall consider various senses of the word "rule" shortly.

The ethnographic preoccupation with rules is especially appropriate if, as some have argued, the notion of a rule is central to the idea of human action and institutions.[2] Peter Winch argues that "all specifically human behavior" is *meaningful* behavior and, paraphrasing Wittgenstein,[3] suggests that "the notion of a principle (or maxim) of conduct and the notion of meaningful action are *interwoven*" (1958, p. 63). Indeed, it is possible to argue that the very notion of a regularity in behavior itself derives from the application of a rule (about what is to count as the same sort of behavior in one case and another). And the application of a rule, in this case as in others, is itself a practice, a particular human institution, which can be learned and taught.

> It is not possible that there should have been only one occasion on which someone obeyed a rule. It is not possible that there should have been only one occasion on which a report was made, an order given or understood; and so on. —To obey a rule, to make a report, to give an order, to play a game of chess, are customs [uses, institutions]. [Wittgenstein 1953, sec. 199]

The gossip's preoccupation with rules is still easier to comprehend, on this account. The gossip will be concerned first with saying ("describing") *what* some particular protagonist did—a procedure which in various ways itself calls upon rules, as I argued in chapter 4.[4] (To take a special example that anticipates a later point, an observer could not describe an action by saying "He put his opponent in check with his knight" except with reference to the rules of chess.) But the gossip commonly goes on to comment on the behavior he has described. He may offer a particular sort of explanation for it, by speculating about the *reasons* or *motivations* of the protagonist that might have produced his action. He may interpret the behavior as intending to accomplish this or that goal. He may justify, or more often condemn, what has been done. And all of these activities, in various senses to be described, involve appeals to rules: to render action *intelligible* and to decide how to evaluate it.

Consider first several types of rules that have been distinguished by philosophers and other theorists.[5] John Rawls (1955) distinguishes two conceptions of rules as part of an attempted defense of utilitarianism. The first is what Rawls calls the "summary view."

> It regards rules in the following way: one supposes that each person decides what he shall do in particular cases by applying the utilitarian principle; one supposes further that different people will decide the same particular case in the same way and that there will be a recurrence of cases similar to those previously decided. Thus it will happen that in cases of certain kinds the same decision will be made either by the same person at different times or by different persons at the same time. If a case occurs frequently enough one supposes that a rule is formulated to cover that sort of case. I have called this conception the summary view because rules are pictured as summaries of past decisions arrived at by the *direct* application of the utilitarian principle to particular cases. Rules are regarded as reports that cases of a certain sort have been found on *other* grounds to be properly decided in a certain way (although, of course, they do not *say* this). [P. 321 in Care and Landesman 1968; page references to Rawls's article are to this reprinting]

It is questionable (as Rawls himself notes)[6] whether such reports or summaries could be rules at all: to treat a rule as a mere summary is certainly a confusion. And yet we may recognize in this conception the common ethnographic attempt to formulate rules on the basis of summarizing people's like behavior in like cases. Traditional formulations of "residence rules" (fraught with the well-known difficulties) have this form: "Sons live with their fathers after marriage," with the usual hedge "in most cases." Similarly, there are clearly rules ("rules of thumb") which natives employ and ethnographers observe based on the principle: if it worked in the past it will work now. Hence, Zinacantecos decide how many kernels of corn to plant in each mound for a particular piece of land on the basis of past experience.

Rawls's second notion of rules is called the "practice conception."

> On this view rules are pictured as defining a practice. . . . It is the
> mark of a practice that being taught how to engage in it involves
> being instructed in the rules which define it, and that appeal is made
> to those rules to correct the behavior of those engaged in it. Those
> engaged in a practice recognize the rules as defining it. The rules
> cannot be taken as simply describing how those engaged in the
> practice in fact behave: it is not simply that they act as if they were
> obeying the rules. Thus it is essential to the notion of a practice
> that the rules are publicly known and understood as definitive; and it
> is essential also that the rules of a practice can be taught and can
> be acted upon to yield a coherent practice. [P. 324]

There are difficulties with this account,[7] but the "practice conception"
of rules successfully draws our attention to certain more or less codified
activities ("practices"), only within the context of which can certain
actions be said to occur. Thus, my earlier example—when a person is
said to have "put his opponent in check with his knight"—depends upon
the practice of playing chess, in turn defined by the rules of chess. The
rules define what it is for a knight to put the king in check (and, indeed,
what knights and kings are); if I have moved improperly or the conditions are not met, I have not, say, "put him in check poorly," but have
not done so at all. Ethnographers typically investigate practices, in
Rawls's sense; and such investigation implies that the ethnographer will
try to formulate the rules of the practice.

Related to this "practice conception of rules" is H. L. A. Hart's discussion of what he calls the "internal aspect" of rules (1961, p. 82).

> Where rules exist, deviations from them are not merely grounds for
> a prediction that hostile reactions will follow or that a court will
> apply sanctions to those who break them, but are also a reason or
> justification for such a reaction and for applying the sanctions.

Rules that *define* the standard of behavior (of action within a practice)
are literally definitive; behavior which deviates from the standard is
ruled out of the practice. Not surprisingly, this point is clearest in the
context of games. Zeno Vendler points out that while deviations from
so-called laws of human behavior remain nonetheless instances of human behavior,

> if . . . I play chess and suddenly start moving a pawn backward,
> then I am to be blamed for violating the rule and not the rule for
> failing to account for my move. For, after all, my move was not
> really a move; it is the rule that determines what counts as a
> move. [1967, p. 14]

Rules conceived as summaries of past regularities could not have this character.

B. J. Diggs (1964) elaborates Rawls's practice conception by distinguishing different sorts of "practices" which may be said to be defined by rules. Diggs proposes two characteristics of certain rules, upon which to base a classification:

(1) The rules prescribe action which is thought to contribute to the attainment of a goal. This is the "design" of such rules, at least in the sense that if the prescribed action does not effectively contribute to the attainment of the goal, for the most part, then the rule itself is subject to criticism. (2) The rules are "laid down" or "legislated" or "made the rule" by a party which has power or authority of some kind; one cannot learn "what the rules are" simply by determining what general procedures most effectively promote the goal. [1964, p. 33]

The first characteristic distinguishes what Diggs calls "instrumental rules," which have a goal, from, say, the rules of competitive games, which do not. (Games may have an "object," but the point of the game will itself be a product of the rules, logically dependent on them.[8]) The second characteristic is meant to distinguish, say, practical maxims from a more complex sort of job- or role-defining rules. Diggs characterizes these two types as follows:

The simplest of [the instrumental rules] is the "practical maxim" which one ordinarily follows at his own pleasure, such as "Be sure the surface to be painted is thoroughly dry" or "Do not plant tomatoes until after the last frost." [1964, p. 32]

Instrumental rules [of the job- or role-defining kind] unlike practical maxims, have a social dimension: It *makes sense* to ask whether a jobholder (or role-taker) is *obligated* to follow a particular rule, or whether this is one of his *duties*, and the penalty attaching to a breach of the rules does not consist simply in his not "getting the job done." [Ibid.]

And Diggs goes on to clarify the force of the second characteristic.

It is clear enough that an employer, for example, who "informs" his employee of the rules, is not simply "giving information." Moreover, this act or performance is very different from one's "adopting" a maxim or making a rule "a rule for himself." Note that in the case of a maxim the adoption of the rule is "incomplete" so long as one simply resolves to follow it. Rules of the present kind, however, are normally made for others to follow: To make their adoption complete, one must get at least some of these others "to agree," in some sense, to follow the rules. [1964, p. 34]

All three types of rules thus delimited—rules of games, practical maxims, and job- or role-defining rules—are associated with definite practices: games (and the playing of games), practical activity that is informal or uncodified in some sense, and various kinds of organized institutions,[9] respectively. Yet the practices have very different characters, and appeals to rules will have different forces within the context of their respective practices.

The various sorts of rules that the theorists I have considered distinguish all fall broadly into the category of what H. L. A. Hart calls "primary rules"—rules of human conduct. He distinguishes "secondary rules" which in various ways govern the use and scope of primary rules.

> Under rules of one type, which may well be considered the basic or primary type, human beings are required to do or abstain from certain actions, whether they wish to or not. Rules of the other type are in a sense parasitic upon or secondary to the first; for they provide that human beings may by doing or saying certain things introduce new rules of the primary type, extinguish or modify old ones, or in various ways determine their incidence or control their operation. Rules of the first type impose duties; rules of the second type confer powers, public or private. Rules of the first type concern actions involving physical movements or changes; rules of the second type provide for operations which lead not merely to physical movement or change, but to the creation or variation of duties or obligations. [1961, pp. 78–79]

Secondary rules are metarules, in precisely the way that, for example, an ordering of rules (in a grammar) is a metarule specifying the order in which rules are to apply.[10] An ethnographer, as he sets out to learn the rules of conduct in a society where he works, will also learn the criteria by which rules are said to apply to particular cases, by which they may be sidestepped, ranked, neutralized, and so forth.

In these preliminary remarks I have intended to show that a disastrously confusing range of phenomena falls within the notion of rule. Diggs gives an admittedly partial list for moral rules:

> moral rules can be (and thus tend to be) conceived as summaries, reports, practical maxims, rules designed to promote a goal, rules which define institutions, rules which protect institutions, and as particular forms of the fundamental principle of justice. [1964, p. 44]

Before the ethnographer out to discover "the rules of a culture," can find out what the rules are, he must delineate what phenomena he is seeking to describe: what counts as a rule; what counts as following a rule; what counts as (what are the circumstances of) invoking or applying a rule.

Alice, the intrepid participant-observer in *Through the Looking Glass*, faces precisely this dilemma:

> "She's *my* prisoner, you know!" the Red Knight said at last.
> "Yes, but then *I* came and rescued her!" the White Knight replied.
> "Well, we must fight for her, then," said the Red Knight, as he took up his helmet (which hung from the saddle, and was something the shape of a horse's head) and put it on.
> "You will observe the Rules of Battle, of course?" the White Knight remarked, putting on his helmet too.
> "I always do," said the Red Knight, and they began banging away at each other with such fury that Alice got behind a tree to be out of the way of the blows.
> "I wonder, now, what the Rules of Battle are," she said to herself, as she watched the fight, timidly peeping out from her hiding-place. "One Rule seems to be, that if one Knight hits the other, he knocks him off his horse; and, if he misses, he tumbles off himself— and another Rule seems to be that they hold their clubs with their arms, as if they were Punch and Judy—What a noise they make when they tumble! Just like a whole set of fire-irons falling into the fender! And how quiet the horses are! They let them get on and off them just as if they were tables!"
> Another Rule of Battle, that Alice had not noticed, seemed to be that they always fell on their heads; and the battle ended with their both falling off in this way, side by side. When they got up again, they shook hands, and then the Red Knight mounted and galloped off.
> "It was a glorious victory, wasn't it?" said the White Knight, as he came up panting. [Carroll 1960, pp. 294–96]

Alice tries to extract Rules of Battle (having been forewarned by her informants that such rules are to be observed) just as ethnographers (forewarned only by their theories of ethnographic description) try to extract Rules of Culture from the goings-on they observe.

Let me survey the sorts of rules they might find in Zinacantan.[11]

1. Rules which summarize (and are supposed to underlie) actual observed behavior, at various levels of abstraction:

The more expensive the religious office the more prestige accrues to its holder.

A person will inherit part of an estate only if he contributes to the burial expense of the deceased.

The youngest son lives with his parents after marriage.

Successful courtship costs about 3,000 pesos.

2. Rules which amount to definitions:

Ritual dress consists of a black full-length wool tunic, head wrapped in a scarf . . .

The godfather at a wedding wears ritual dress.

To make a proper "bow" is to do this [demonstration]; to "release" a bow is to do this [demonstration].

When corn is cooked with lime it is *panin*, but when cooked without lime it is *hux*.

3. Noninstrumental rules of practices (rules of propriety, not relating directly to a goal):

The violin player is the most senior-ranking musician, regardless of age.

The most senior person is served [liquor] first and marches last in procession.

The curer carries his baston of office.

4. Instrumental rules of practices—job- or role-defining rules:

Martomo Sakramentu supervises the duties of all the other *martomo* cargoholders.

The violin player leads the songs.

The godfather at a wedding instructs the bride and groom in proper marriage behavior.

5. Practical maxims (relating to particular goals, and widely observed):

In hoeing, hold the hoe this way [demonstration].

Plant three or four kernels in each hole, on this land . . .

Hold your corn crop to sell in July for highest return.

Avoid getting mixed up with ladino legal institutions.

Turn a tortilla the second time when the edges just begin to shrivel up.[12]

The examples of these (often overlapping) types of rules all might be drawn from ethnographic accounts of Zinacantan. They include most of the types discussed by the philosophers whose work I have treated above; and they are the sorts of rules that an ethnographer might formulate—Alicelike—from observing what people do. Strikingly missing here, however, are the sorts of rules which, at least in gossip, seem most likely to be openly formulated and expressed by Zinacantecos. I may distinguish three further kinds which are often mouthed by Zinacanteco gossips.

6. Rules of strategy (relating to particular goals, or within certain practices, but not necessarily of wide currency):

A quick way to make money is to plant lots of beans in October.

To acquire a high-prestige cargo, one should first request a low-prestige cargo (which is easy to get) and later change to a higher post as openings occur.

7. Rules of interpretation, lending sense to the action; (these often take the form "If he does . . . , then it must mean that . . ."; or "He wouldn't do that unless . . .").

When two men shake hands they are showing [expressing] their equal rank.

People who build houses of brick [rather than adobe] are showing off their wealth.

People seek as godparents for their children men from whom they can borrow money.

8. Rules which embody openly stated norms and standards; moral rules:

Children should respect their parents.

The youngest son ought to remain with his parents to care for them and inherit their house.

A cargoholder must refrain from sexual activity during certain fiestas.

The magistrate should properly listen impartially to both sides of a dispute.

This categorization is not exhaustive,[13] and the categories themselves are doubtless muddled and ill-defined. Why are such different sorts of propositions all *rules* at all? In what sense do such propositions enable us to describe action as underlain by rules? I suggest that the study of gossip affords a new perspective on the nature and use of rules in ordinary discourse.

Let me consider first what seem fairly straightforward rules: those governing the settlement of legal disputes. Individuals find themselves in conflict for a wide variety of reasons and in quite different situations.[14] By the time they seek a legal solution to a conflict, disputants have phrased the dispute and the attendant facts in ways that call legal rules into play. Jane Collier makes this argument in a study of Zinacanteco law.

> Cases do not emerge directly from social trouble spots. They begin
> as a series of events that are given descriptive labels by litigants
> and are finally taken to a legal procedure selected on the basis of
> personal desires. [1973, p. 252]

In phrasing disputes, disputants clearly make use of what I call "rules of interpretation," by which they can judge the consequences of labeling an action in a particular way. This is what Collier has in mind when she remarks that "Zinacanteco couples . . . employ a set of actions that convey easily understood messages" (p. 183). By failing to prepare his food on a particular occasion, a wife can show her husband that she is angry with him without taking a more drastic step (such as returning to her parents' home) which would precipitate a more difficult reconciliation or which might activate more formal legal procedures.

Rules may pattern disputes and their outcomes, according to this view, in the particular sense that

> the legal language through which claims must be advanced and decisions justified constrains both the types of claims and the range of possible outcomes. [1973, p. 244]

Both this legal language and the rules themselves are used selectively, providing a conceptual framework in terms of which disputants can frame their arguments.

> Legal concepts do not have a direct effect on behavior; they provide a way of talking about behavior. In ordinary experience, legal concepts appear to structure observable social regularities, because behavior falling on the fringes may be assimilated into the norm through classification, and because individuals consciously planning to act think in terms of the labels that can be applied to their behavior. [Ibid., p. 259]

Collier's argument suggests that legal rules, in fact, exist only as they are used: invoked, applied, cited, and so forth. Such rules constrain largely after the fact: when someone chooses to find fault with another person, he phrases his complaint in such a way that the other may be considered to have violated a rule.

Moreover, rules—as propositions framed in words—can be freely manipulated as people attach varying meanings to the active clauses. Zinacantecos are familiar, as are we, with the glib lawyer who can convince the magistrate that a rule applies and who then goes on to draw the desired conclusions. In the rest of this chapter I extend this line of argument to rules outside the realm of law. I remarked above that it is plausible to think of gossip as "about rules." More precisely, if we conceive of Zinacanteco culture as statable in terms of some complex set of propositions about behavior, then gossip is an activity through which actual behavior is verbally bent into a form amenable to the application of rules. As people gossip they fit their culture (propositions about the world) to the world itself.[15] How then are we to understand the relationship between rules and action?

What is the nature of rule-bound activity? Here again it may be help-
ful to refer to Peter Winch's argument relating rules to the idea of
"meaningful behavior." The argument has two parts. First Winch links
the idea of "following a rule" to the possibility (in some circumstances)
of "making a mistake" or *evaluating* behavior so characterized.

> The notion of following a rule is logically inseparable from the notion
> of *making a mistake*. If it is possible to say of someone that he is
> following a rule that means that one can ask whether he is doing
> what he does correctly or not. Otherwise there is no foothold in
> his behavior in which the notion of a rule can take a grip; there is
> then no *sense* in describing his behavior that way, since everything he
> does is as good as anything else he might do, whereas the point
> of the concept of a rule is that it should enable us to *evaluate* what
> is being done. [1958, p. 32]

This account directs our attention to the typical case in which people appeal to rules: to decide whether certain behavior accords with the rules
or defies them—to evaluate behavior in terms of rule-set standards.[16]
Rules display their peculiar *force* in this sort of evaluative discourse,
when people consult them or apply them as part of justifying or condemning behavior. The language of rules includes a bundle of words
like "obligation" and "duty" whose use is to draw particular behavior
under a rule. (Words like "mistake," "crime," "sin," "misbehavior," and
"faux pas" belong, too, in this language.)

H. L. A. Hart distinguishes two points of view regarding rules of
special significance to the ethnographer and the gossip.

> When a social group has certain rules of conduct this fact affords an
> opportunity for many closely related yet different kinds off asser-
> tion; for it is possible to be concerned with the rules, either merely
> as an observer who does not himself accept them, or as a member of
> the group which accepts and uses them as guides to conduct. We
> may call these respectively the "external" and the "internal points of
> view.". . . [W]e can if we choose occupy the position of an observer
> . . . content merely to record the regularities of observable behavior
> in which conformity with the rules partly consists and those further
> regularities, in the form of the hostile reaction, reproofs, or punish-
> ments, with which deviations from the rules are met. [1961,
> pp. 86–87]

This option, I suppose, is open to the ethnographer, but it is decidedly
impossible for the gossip. The gossip—whether he espouses the rules of
his society or desires to bring them down, in this case or in general—
must comment on (interpret) behavior in terms of its compliance or
noncompliance with rules in force. (He may also comment on the rules

themselves.) This is the nature of justification, criticism, or condemnation.

Moreover, this is also part of rendering behavior *intelligible*, as the second part of Winch's argument shows. Following Weber's discussion of the subjective sense (*Sinn*) of behavior, Winch associates the idea of "meaningful behavior" with the ideas of "motive" or "reason" for behavior (1958, pp. 45ff.). He goes on to suggest that even when someone can be said to have acted without a particular reason or motive, his action can still be said to have a *sense* by virtue of its place in a set of social institutions of which the actor is conscious.

> Let us return to N's exercise of his vote: its possibility rests on two presuppositions. In the first place, N must live in a society which has certain specific political institutions. . . . Secondly, N must himself have a certain familiarity with those institutions. His act must be a participation in the political life of the country, which presupposes that he must be aware of the symbolic relation between what he is doing now and the government which comes into power after the election. [1958, p. 51]

When a gossip interprets what other people are doing and why, he speaks of their making choices, having reasons, intending or responding to this or that, being "guided by considerations"—all notions which, according to Winch, depend on the idea of a rule, or represent appeals to rules:[17] "One can act 'from considerations' only where there are accepted standards of what is appropriate to appeal to" (1958, p. 82).

As we ask, then, when and why people appeal to rules we confront the centrality of rules to ethnographic description: appeals to rules are part of the language by which behavior is made intelligible and is justified, criticized, or condemned. Hence rules are basic parts of the gossip's tool kit.

Are some rules conscious and others unconscious? This is dangerous ground. Even when our action conforms to a rule (this is already a careless way to talk; I mean to say, when no violation is detected in what we do), we are not necessarily conscious of the rule (aware of it as we act). We do not appeal to rules of grammar as we talk; often, in fact, we cannot even formulate them. Rules for dividing fractions or computing square roots, on the other hand, seem to guide our pencils as we calculate, especially when we have only lately learned how. Consider some further cases. Rules of the road surface only in unusual circumstances—for example, when we appeal to them ruefully after the accident to determine who was at fault. Parliamentary rules may guide our action, but we need experts to keep track of them. Sometimes we can't perform at all without a rule: rules of thumb (how to convert farenheit to centigrade) define the answer. And some rules (college conduct rules, most laws) are of more concern to the authorities who enforce them than to those affected. The extent to which we are bound by rules, or conscious of rules, as we act depends on the sort of thing we are doing.

To be available to gossip a rule need not hover in the minds of actors who observe or break it; nor need it be explicitly formulable in most contexts. In gossip, ordinarily it is nonstandard behavior that activates rules; the oddness of a man's behavior stimulates gossip about what is odd in it.

> Xun has only very old, ragged clothes. He has an old, torn leather
> bag, with its pocket torn off, that is almost completely black. He
> probably bought it back when he was courting his wife and hasn't
> bought another since.

> Lol used to buy liquor near *k'onlum*, and while there would stay in
> the house of an old woman who was perhaps fifty-five years old.
> He screwed her several times and then married her. She has given him
> no children (and probably has sapped his potency) because she
> is too old. When they walk around together you might think to look
> at her that she is his mother.

> Mikel, the youngest son of an elderly man, decided to move away
> from his paternal home and leave his older brother behind. He has
> accused his father of witchcraft, and one day, when they went on a
> long trip in the same truck, Mikel addressed not one word to his
> father.

These facts are noteworthy enough to gossip about because of the departures from expected, normal behavior implied by (1) not buying new clothes, (2) marrying someone who is mismatched in age (something Zinacantecos believe can cause a severe, ultimately fatal illness), and (3) not respecting (and, hence, not talking politely to) one's father. The rules in question here are automatic, unconscious, and usually unimportant. One pays minimal attention to dress until there is some striking omission or defect. Similarly, one ordinarily takes no note of married couples appropriately matched in age, or of the everyday cordiality between father and son. Gossip, when it detects something queer, tries to pinpoint the source of the queerness; the rules of a culture single out not normality but departures from normality.

I am talking about more than a conversational fact here; in an earlier chapter I suggested that conversations tend to dwell on unusual behavior and transgressions rather than on unmarked, unobtrusive normality. Here I suggest that bringing up a rule, appealing to a standard, reminding oneself (or one's interlocutor) of a value is appropriate precisely to discussions of some exceptional (hence exceptionable) behavior. Gossip is a *typical* context for talk about rules. There is a parallel here with talk about "motives" and "intentions." We typically speculate about someone's motives or intentions when we are puzzled about why he did what he did; we may volunteer information about our intentions to forestall some suspicion about how our actions may go wrong ("My intentions are honorable").[18]

> There is no contradiction in saying that someone who never before manifested any signs of a jealous disposition has, on a given occasion, acted from jealousy; indeed, it is precisely when someone *acts unexpectedly* that the need for a motive explanation is particularly apparent. [Winch 1958, p. 80]

It would be absurd for a gossip to retell the story of a son who behaved only with proper respect for his father, appealing to "rules" for such filial respect (except, perhaps, if he were commenting on the abnormality of such a relationship—say, in a world where such ways of treating one's parents were on the wane—or if, trying to exemplify the "rule" to an inquisitive ethnographer or other cultural novice, he cited the case as an object lesson).

Gossip deals as well with questions of *propriety*, over and above normality and convention. Zinacantecos would willingly state rules for proper courtship, proper ritual performance (indeed, there are specialists who supervise ritual), or for appropriate domestic division of labor. These same rules are promulgated (and often reformulated) in gossip about improper behavior, as well as in court cases.

Again, behavior within social institutions has striking analogies with playing games. Certain moves are legitimate (in accord with the rules); moreover, certain moves force certain other moves (allow one to expect conventional responses). Departures from normality may take the form of moves outside the rules (which cease to be moves at all—they do not belong in the game), or of unconventional (senseless, unbelievable, stupid, self-defeating, unfathomable) moves. When in ordinary life our expectations fail we are stopped short; we gossip about what has gone wrong.

There is a certain nonsense to the notion that there can be a gulf between rules and behavior (see Keesing 1971). The ethnoscientist's search for rules of behavior cannot end with a set of principles which tell us little or nothing about what behavior to anticipate. After giving a list of various principles that operate in Zinacanteco inheritance claims, for example, Jane Collier notes:

The fact is that these principles do not govern Zinacanteco inheritance, but only serve as justifications for a claim to property. The
actual distribution of inheritance is determined by a compromise
between competing claims advanced at the time the land is being
divided. [1973, p. 179]

But "compromise" here amounts to throwing up one's hands. Since
native actors only rarely surprise each other by their actions, there must
be mechanisms by which one man can anticipate the behavior of another. Similarly, since legal settlements are rarely incomprehensible,
native actors must understand the procedures through which settlement
is made. Hence, it may be that the rules of inheritance conflict, and that
rules serve primarily as justifications for claims. Or it may be that, for
ordinary action, there are conflicting alternatives—Shall I wear shoes
or sandals? Do I call him "Joe" or "Professor X"? Shall I have my ham
and swiss on white or rye? Shall I shake his hand or punch him?—
between which one chooses on the basis of the standard (i.e., rule-
bound) implications and consequences of each alternative. Yet there is
presumably more to the resolution of conflicts than compromise. Rules
are clearly not on an equal footing with each other, and thus some
compromises are easier to come by than others. Keesing's (1970) work
on Kwaio sharing of bride-wealth shows that it is possible to untangle
the competing claims of relatives and to anticipate eventual outcomes
by paying precise attention to anomalous cases. The rights and obligations which ordinarily coincide in single individuals are split among
several in the case of adoption or changing residence. The outcomes of
cases in which several people have claims to goods ordinarily reserved
for one person show in greater detail the rules which govern bride-
wealth distribution. Individuals in conflict have the freedom to appeal
as they like to rules; but it may often be that conflicts between rules
once invoked are themselves resolved by rules—rather than by something as nebulous as compromise.

There is, unfortunately, the disturbing possibility that the natives'
ability to anticipate the outcomes of disputes and the actions of individuals amounts to little more than the ability to give post factum rationalizations for eventual outcomes. The ethnoscientist may be able to
produce a model of residence that gives a perfect match with the residence patterns observed during a field stay. But there is nothing more
remarkable in this than in the villagers' ability to justify or at least to
come to understand another villager's decision about where to live—
after he has built his house and moved in. The ethnographer and the
gossip perform similar operations: they observe behavior and use rules
to understand its implications or the motives behind it. In fact, the ethnoscientist can *make up* rules to justify the behavior he sees. We need not

be satisfied with a "compromise" between rules or a "gulf" between
rules and behavior; the gossip and the ethnographer have a stake in
reconciling rules with behavior. The power of rules as determinants of
action stems from the fact that each time we construe a particular
sequence of behavior in accordance with rules, we strengthen the presumption that future behavior will also accord with the rules. Natives
base their ability to anticipate on such presumptions.[19]

Note that the gossip has an advantage over the ethnographer in that
he can reject certain behavior outright as deviant, antisocial, wicked,
reprehensible, nonsensical, incomprehensible, ill-conceived, or generally
out of line with (some) rules. The ethnographer has a harder time
establishing some criterion for calling a particular residence choice "deviant," even when the natives are willing to agree among themselves
that it is wrong, bad, unmanly, queer, or fishy. The ethnographer, building his model, is obliged to say, "The man must have had his reasons."
The natives, gossiping, may counter, "They were bad ones." Gossip
trades on rules and "should" statements, urging certain behavior by
praising it, and throwing out other behavior by condemning it. The
ethnographer makes do with only the brute facts of observed regularities.

Consider the moralizing and the conflicting values—stated often in
categorical, rulelike propositions—that figure in the following gossip
sequence about a rich man made poor by excessive lending.

"*Kere*, he has a lot of money, indeed!"
"I hear that he has just scattered it all over."
"But he isn't repaid; he himself has had to go into debt now."
"*Puta*, that's bad. . . ."
"The old man has lost his wealth now; I don't know why. Perhaps
he can't get his money back now because he spread it so widely
around."
"It's just as if he gave it away."
"He treated his money as if he could just pick it off a tree, as if
he could manufacture it; that's why he distributed it among so
many different men."
"But the poor old man is extremely good-hearted. When my son
Chep made his house he told me, 'I'll give you the money.' He just
offered it by himself."
"But he always lent so much; he didn't just lend a few hundred
at a time. Instead he would lend ten thousand to just one single man."
"Well, he should have made some sort of deal. He didn't take
care to lend only to those who would probably pay him back, to
those who seemed to be good men. Instead if anyone at all went to
ask him for money, 'Here, take it' he would say. He didn't wait
to see from their faces if they were good men."

"Well, they say that at first he was always repaid the money he had lent. People would keep asking him for some amount—people are very crafty—and after a year they would return it. So, you see: the old man was elated since he got his money back. But then the next time—well, he never saw his money again. Old Xun Inas died, for example, and the whole deal was ended."

"Son of a bitch, he lost five thousand on that!"

"So the poor old man had thought to lend out of the goodness of his heart. But now he isn't given even a penny. It's awful. He wanders around asking for it, but no one gives it back. None at all. He says his children are getting angry.

" 'My sons are angry,' he says. '*Kavron*, the way you lend the money, it seems that you just like to drink beer.' they say. 'But I don't care about drinking beer,' he says."

"Well, his sons are the ones who do the work; the old man no longer works."

"*Kere*, I think that's terrible".

"Well, the old man has patience; he has compassion for others."

"Ah, he is forgiving. He has a good heart."

"He doesn't believe in stealing peoples' sheep by charging interest the way Lukax does."

"No, he doesn't drag out of people what he could by asking for interest on his loans."

Several clear, though obliquely stated, normative propositions are implicit in this conversation. Here are some of them:

1. A rich man, if he is good-hearted, will lend money.
2. A good-hearted, reasonable moneylender will not charge interest.
3. A man lending money should be sure that the recipient is likely to be able to pay him back.
4. A man should never lend a lot of money to just one person.
5. One should be careful of one's money, since it doesn't grow on trees but is the product of work.

Gossiping about this one unfortunate old man allows the participants to agree on these principles and to apply them to (derive them from?) a concrete situation. They can decide together what to think about the man himself, and—more pragmatically—they can assess the causes for his misfortune and guide their future actions accordingly.

The process is related to that described by Schutz:

Only in particular situations, and then only fragmentarily, can I experience the other's motives, goals, etc.—briefly, the subjective meanings they bestow upon their actions, in their uniqueness. I can,

however, experience them in their typicality. In order to do so, I
construct typical patterns of the actors' motives and ends, even of
their attitudes and personalities, of which their actual conduct is
just an instance or example. These typified patterns of others'
behavior become, in turn, motives for my own action, and this leads
to the phenomenon of self-typification. [1962, p. 60]

Applying a rule, or extracting a rule from a gossip story, is much like
"typification." And here it is not so much that the behavior was bound
by the rules; gossips *find* the rules *in* the behavior (which may be to
reconstruct the behavior around the rules—if only in their violation).

In most situations individuals have a wide range of alternatives. Individuals construe the circumstances and choose between alternatives on
the basis of many different constraints (some of which may be what I
have called above rules of strategy). Strategies are not random; nor are
they morally neutral. Native actors are able to fathom the import of
peoples' actions partly with the help of their knowledge of different
rules of strategy. Consider the following synopsis, from various gossip
sources:

About a month before the scheduled wedding, an engaged girl
disappeared from her home and was missing for one night. The girl's
family tried to keep her disappearance hidden, but the groom's
family discovered that she had run away. After a day's searching the
girl was found at her grandmother's house. All concerned assembled
at the *agencia* to decide what had happened and what was to be
done. The girl's family claimed that she had been beaten by her
fiancé and one of her brothers and had run away, in fright, hiding
with her grandmother. The groom's party suggested that perhaps one
of the girl's kinsmen, who did not favor the match, had prompted
her to run away and hide to avoid marriage. The groom himself
hinted that he harbored suspicions that the girl might have run off
with a lover. The options were to break off the courtship—with
the girl's family repaying the considerable courtship expenses the
boy had incurred—or to have the two get married immediately, with
the church ceremony to follow at the scheduled time. The girl's
mother eventually bowed to pressure from her kinsmen (who did
not want to have to repay the bride-price) and allowed the girl
and the boy to start living together, with the strong stipulation that
the wedding ceremony and fiesta still take place.

The parties to this dispute were concerned to interpret the actions of
the girl in running away. What did she mean to be doing? Had she a
lover? Did she want to call off the marriage? Both sides tried to cast
the events in such a light that rules could be brought into play to govern

the outcome. Thus rules enter into the proceedings at both ends: they help shape peoples' impressions and interpretations of what the problem is, what the behavior entails; and they then specify an outcome, given agreement on the situation.

Rules of interpretation allow one to understand the implications of action. If a girl fails to greet her suitor, refuses to feed him when he visits, or—worst of all—runs away unaccountably, he understands her to be refusing his suit, by virtue of the "rule" that states that a girl should treat her suitor well. If a girl's parents suddenly refuse gifts proffered by their daughter's suitor, the boy receives a clear message about the status of his supposed marriage contract. Receiving the gifts of a suitor energizes the rules governing agreement to a marriage proposal; continuing to receive the gifts throughout the courtship binds the girl's family further.

In gossip rules are laid gridlike over the continuum of behavior, to allow participants to interpret the events they are discussing. During the events recounted above various stories circulated in gossip. One account had it that the girl had run off with another lover to elope; another claimed that the suitor had beaten the girl severely, and that she had run off as a result. A third version maintained that one of the girl's uncles, an enemy of the groom and his friends, had persuaded the girl to hide in his house to avoid the wedding. Each story represents an interpretation of the facts—that the girl was missing from home one night—in a form that suggests certain consequences.

Rules of interpretation are symbolic statements of relationships between categories of behavior. "Accepting a gift of liquor" is tantamount to "agreeing to a request." "Being absent from home" is equivalent to "running away." And so on. Rules of this sort allow people to formulate expectations on the basis of past behavior—expectations which have more force (even if less reliability) than those based on statistical regularities alone.

Rules allow actors to communicate through action. In Zinacantan, putting on ritual dress implies certain contexts and is inappropriate in everyday life. Shaking hands in greeting rather than bowing implies a certain sort of equality derived, in the purest cases, from age, but often reflecting an equality of ritual status instead.

Here is a limitation of the analogy of the game. Rules of chess define proper moves ("A knight moves like this . . ."); rules of strategy point to favorable lines of play ("When attacked in this way, a solid defense is as follows . . . ; these moves, on the other hand, are weak . . ."). Cultural grammars have analogous rules. But a game of chess leads to a single end; moves in the game may have meaning with respect to that end, that is, winning or losing. ("His gambit with the queen showed his desperation." "When he threw his king across the room it meant he was resigning.") But ordinarily, to move a knight according to the rules is not to say anything in particular (mean anything in particular), whereas to shake a Zinacanteco's hand in greeting is to do more than simply abide by the rules; it is to imply something definite about status.[20]

Here I return to the central point. Though rules may not be causal determinants of behavior (whatever that might mean), they figure in *explanations* of behavior. Part of the answer to the question "Why do people act as they do?" or, more commonly, "Why did he do that then?" will be an appeal to cultural rules ("That's how it's done . . ."; "He meant to . . . , and so he . . ."). While a native actor may not be able to predict, from his knowledge of his own culture, what another will do, or what people will say about it in gossip, he will nonetheless be an appreciative audience: he will recognize the appropriateness of another's remarks.

Gossip can lead to contradictory conclusions, from the same premises and with equally legitimate reasoning. Consider the contrast between the following two accounts of adultery, both offered by the same man on different occasions. When he told me the first version, my informant was having a fight with Maryan and his brothers, and was inclined to ridicule.

Version 1   Maryan has recently been dragged to jail in Jteklum
                   over a long-standing fight with his ex-wife and her father.
                   His ex-wife had, by a previous marriage, a daughter
                   with whom Maryan began having sexual relations. The
                   girl became pregnant, and Maryan's wife moved out in
                   anger. Now the ex-wife and her father are demanding
                   bride-payment for the girl, who is herself unsure
                   whether to stay with Maryan. He has been jailed for not
                   paying and for his foolish lack of sexual restraint.
                   Why does he need two women in his bed?

Later my informant was asked to help get Maryan off. Returning from Zinacantan Center after the court case he offered the following account:

Version 2   Maryan got into trouble because of his stepdaughter.
                   His wife left them alone together often, and he even-
                   tually got her pregnant. When questioned, the girl
                   claimed that she had never felt a thing. She said she
                   didn't know how she could possibly have gotten
                   pregnant. (We know how, ha ha ha.) Maryan's wife
                   ran home in anger to her father, leaving her daughter to

take care of Maryan. Maryan was willing to divorce
his wife and offered to marry the girl, but his
ex–father-in-law (the girl's grandfather) demanded
1,000 pesos in bride-price. That amount seemed high,
considering that as the girl's stepfather Maryan had
contributed most of the money toward raising the girl in
the first place. At the *cabildo* I argued that no harm
had been done; that the girl wouldn't die from having
her stepfather's baby.

Clearly both versions of this story are possible; both, that is, can be
framed in language appropriate to Zinacanteco gossip. Either account
would be appreciated by an audience of Zinacanteco men. The behavioral rules which underlie such cases are compatible with the biases
in either account, and dictate in favor of neither Maryan nor his ex-wife.
A convincing moral argument can be made for either side.

What is more, this apparent open texture of rules is not an aberration.
After observing receptionists "applying" relatively precise rules to a
particular concrete situation, Don H. Zimmerman remarks:

It would seem that the notion of action-in-accord-with-a-rule is a
matter not of compliance or non-compliance per se but of the various
ways in which persons *satisfy* themselves and others concerning
what is or is not "reasonable" compliance in particular situations.
Reference to rules might then be seen as a common-sense method
of accounting for or making available for talk the orderly features
of everyday activities, thereby *making out* these activities as orderly
in some fashion. [1970, p. 233]

To ignore the flexibility of the process by which behavior is fitted to and
accounted for by rules, a process which we all employ continually and
which is paramount in gossip,

invites the treatment of rules as idealizations, processing stable
operational meanings invariant to the exigencies of actual situations
of use, and distinct from the practical interests, perspective, and
interpretive practices of the rule user. [Ibid., p. 223]

Gossip draws our attention to the characteristic use of rules in justification and explanation.

Does the "open texture" of rules lead inevitably to the conclusion
that rules are vague, incomplete, indeterminate? There are two observations to be made. First, the notion of a vague or indeterminate rule
confuses a false ideal precision with the actual use of a rule.

A rule stands there like a sign-post.—Does the sign-post leave no
doubt open about the way I have to go? Does it shew which direction

I am to take when I have passed it; whether along the road or the footpath or cross-country? But where is it said which way I am to follow it; whether in the direction of its finger or (e.g.) in the opposite one?—And if there were, not a single sign-post, but a chain of adjacent ones or of chalk marks on the ground—is there only *one* way of interpreting them?—So I can say, the sign-post does after all leave no room for doubt, or rather: it sometimes leaves room for doubt and sometimes not. And now this is no longer a philosophical proposition, but an empirical one. [Wittgenstein 1963, sec. 85]

This is to say, as Wittgenstein does, that "The sign-post is in order—if, under normal circumstances, it fulfills its purpose" (sec. 87). Similarly, we do not demand of a rule ever more and more exactness;[21] we ourselves apply the rule when necessary.

The second observation is that our knowing how to apply rules in ordinary circumstances is part of the whole activity (partly, of describing and evaluating action) to which the discourse of rules belongs.

"Then can whatever I do be brought into accord with the rule?"—Let me ask this: what has the expression of a rule—say a sign-post—got to do with my actions? What sort of connexion is there here?—Well, perhaps this one: I have been trained to react to this sign in a particular way, and now I do so react to it.

But that is only to give a causal connexion; to tell how it has come about that we now go by the sign-post, not what this going-by-the-sign really consists in. On the contrary; I have further indicated that a person goes by the sign-post only in so far as there exists a regular use of sign-posts, a custom. [Ibid., sec. 198]

The gossip and his interlocutors are in a clear sense negotiating the scope and import of the rules, the range of behavior that requires explanation; but they begin with (a background of) a common perspective. If we reach outside this activity, outside the normal realms of discourse, we may well be puzzled about rules and their role as determinants of behavior. But I take it to be an axiom of anthropology that the ordinary realm of discourse need not be discarded when we enter other human societies. We may have a good deal to learn, but some constraints we must take for granted:

Following a rule is analogous to obeying an order. We are trained to do so; we react to an order in a particular way. But what if one person reacts in one way and another in another to the order and the training? Which one is right?

Suppose you came as explorer into an unknown country with a language quite strange to you. In what circumstances would you say that the people there gave orders, understood them, obeyed them, rebelled against them, and so on?

> The common behavior of mankind is the system of reference by
> means of which we interpret an unknown language. [Wittgenstein
> 1953, sec. 206]

I am trying to suggest that the notion of "action in accord with a rule"
itself depends on the social institutions in which action is located. One
learns how to "follow rules" (when to say a rule has been followed),
and consequently how to talk about behavior and associated rules (as
in gossip), as part of learning how to act, how to "live as a social
being."[22]

It should now be clear that gossip is a powerful instrument for manipulating cultural rules. Gossip is a primary metacultural tool, an
activity through which people examine and discuss the rules they espouse. Through gossip people not only interpret the behavior of others,
but also discover other people's interpretations; they can thus learn
cultural rules at a distance. Through dialogue, gossip allows rules to
change: it redefines the conditions of application for rules, thus keeping
them up to date. Finally, gossip exploits the interpretive potential of
rules to advance particular (personal, factional) ends. One talks, in
gossip, as if the rule of culture were absolute, whereas cultural rules
actually legitimize disparate and often contradictory modes of action.
By catching someone's ear in a gossip session, one can introduce a particular assessment of the facts and cloak it with the garb of absolute
morality and unflinching truth.

Cultural Competence: Gossip and a Theory of Ethnography

Ilaj no?ox lo?ilajkotik che?e.
"Our gossiping together has, then, come to an end."

9

Studying gossip, in Zinacantan and elsewhere, reflects what I take to be the obvious fact that one can gossip only in a culture one is competent in. What precise parameters of competence operate here can be seen, in part, from my earlier discussion of the knowledge, general and particular, of rules and of facts, that gossips draw upon. The converse proposition—that competence in a culture presupposes at least the ability to *understand* gossip, if not to gossip—is more contentious but certainly arguable. But if these propositions hold, they have important consequences for the theory of ethnography, at least in the special but widely accepted sense of "ethnography" understood as the characterization of "cultural competence." In these concluding arguments I focus on some ramifications of the notion that an adequate account of cultural competence must encompass the native's ability to gossip.

First let me make plain what I do *not* mean to argue. It may be the case, as a matter of practical method, that attention to gossip in a community will elucidate or bring to early attention phenomena otherwise relatively obscure or inaccessible. (I have in mind matters of belief, native theories of personality and motivation, etc.) But it will doubtless be equally true that much will elude the ethnographer who has eyes and ears only for gossip. Other sorts of research which totally ignore gossip as a natural forum for native speculation may well be equally probing. Nor do I claim that we can know nothing useful about a society until we have learned to gossip in it—a

171

fatuous and self-congratulatory position that would deny most social science. Certainly the fact that most any Zinacanteco can participate, admittedly with varying skill and involvement, in gossip is something that an ethnography of Zinacantan must be able to account for; the skills required of a gossip are part of a wider range of skills that ethnography seeks to describe, whether or not ethnographers master them. But again there are familiar levels of analysis that go well beyond the ordinary understandings a native has of his world—levels of analysis that attention to gossip will inform but not exhaust.

It may be thought that the gossip's skills are relatively arcane, subtle, and possibly irrelevant—certainly not central concerns of an anthropology fascinated by social structures and kinship, power and politics, symbols and subsistence. On the contrary, I hope to have demonstrated that gossips dwell on precisely the issues that concern them and their fellows most: the familiar world of neighbors and kin, dissected into relevant bits and marked more often as petty successes or mishaps than as, say, triumphs, tragedies, or revelations. Roger Keesing has suggested recently that "it may be precisely in exploring the phenomenological world of the familiar and immediate, the everyday and mundane, that we stand to gain the most crucial knowledge of how humans perceive, understand, and act" (1974a, p. 93). Moreover, looking at gossip demonstrates that this phenomenological world—familiar and immediate though it may be—generates a formidable and complex set of routines, by which the gossip disassembles, evaluates, and reconstitutes its parts. Indeed, the routines are of a nature that raises doubts about the "cultural competence" said to be (at least in part) the object of ethnographic description. The skills of the gossip, I suggest, provide us with a somewhat different set of ethnographic goals.

Early notions of what an ethnographic description might look like were based loosely on an analogy with linguistic grammars.[1] When Chomsky wrote of "discovering a mental reality underlying actual behavior" (1965, p. 4), he might have been describing the task of uncovering either Language (Saussure's *langue*) or Culture (as represented in Goodenough's writings [1957, p. 167; 1961, p. 522] or in Kay [1966, p. 106]). Two sorts of definitional idealizations are involved here: first a decision must be made about what classes of "actual behavior" are to be considered—a grammar is concerned, presumably, with "linguistic behavior" somehow delimited and ethnography with "cultural behavior" (which might, for example, exclude the ravings of a brain-damaged person but include, perhaps, the actions of a schizophrenic). And second, only certain features of the selected class of behavior must be singled out for analysis; the relationship between the behavior and the "reality" that "underlies" it must be made precise.[2] Just as an early generative grammar could be thought of as a finite device for characterizing the (infinite) class of all and only grammatical sentences of a language, ethnographic descriptions were envisaged that would characterize the class of appropriate behavior in a culture—or, somewhat more ambitiously, would "succinctly state what one must know in order to generate culturally acceptable acts and utterances appropriate to a given socioecological context" (Frake 1962, p. 39). Bits of such ethnographies include descriptions of routines for greeting, for taking a drink, for choosing a place to live or dividing an inheritance, and so forth.

We can speak about the rules of a language and the abilities that derive from mastery of those rules (for example, the ability to detect ungrammatical utterances, to produce an endless string of grammatical ones, to disambiguate, paraphrase, and otherwise transform sentences) regardless of the fact that many people who have mastered the rules make slips of the tongue, speak elliptically, or differ from one another in some aspect of their speech. The distinction between competence and performance in linguistics has survived the battering of suggestions that irregularity and variation (even in the speech of monolinguals) must be accounted for in an adequate grammar: Lakoff 1965; Labov 1972. By analogy, we can talk about the bounds of appropriate behavior in wider behavioral domains without, it seems, worrying that many people at many times *mis*behave, falter, act improperly or outrageously, or simply baffle one another. Keesing argues that the notion of cultural competence can be usefully salvaged:

Culture, conceived as a system of competence shared in its broad design and deeper principles, and varying between individuals in its specifications, is then not all of what an individual knows and thinks and feels about his world. It is his *theory of what his fellows know, believe, and mean*, and his theory of the code being followed, the game being played, in the society into which he was born. It is this theory to which a native actor *refers* in interpreting the unfamiliar or the ambiguous, in interacting with strangers (or supernaturals), and in other settings peripheral to the familiarity of mundane everyday life space; and with which he creates the stage on which the games of life are played. We can account for the individual actor's perception of his culture as external (and as potentially constraining and frustrating); and we can account for the way individuals then can consciously use, manipulate, violate, and try to change what they conceive to be the rules of the game. But note that the actor's "theory" of his culture, like his theory of his language, may be in large measure unconscious. Actors follow rules of which they are not consciously aware, and assume a world to be "out there" that they have in fact created with culturally shaped and shaded patterns of mind. [1974a, p. 89]

Keesing urges that such a view of cultural competence must be coupled with a concern with wider "sociocultural performance."

Difficulties remain even in this enlightened account. In the previous chapter I discussed some uncertainties in the notion of cultural "rule," which plague any account which holds Culture to consist of codes, rules, and routines, with actual behavior considered only an approximation. It is furthermore unclear how much variation a system of shared competence can tolerate and what depth of behavioral complexity it must encode. The gossip's knowledge of his cultural world stands in revealing counterpoint to this hypothetical cultural theory, in ways I shall examine in the remainder of this chapter.

How much of what a native knows belongs to his theory of the world? In what unfamiliar circumstances will he refer to the theory? How will he actually behave? Such questions arise directly when anthropologists try to catalog favorite facts. What, for example, is an appropriate residence choice? The answer is muddled by a seemingly endless string of contingencies. I live with my father after marriage; except that, if he is dead, I may live with my father's brother; except that, if he is too young, I may live with my mother; except that, if she has moved back to her father's house, I may move in with my wife's family; and so on.

Ethnographers may truncate this list of "except" clauses at some arbitrary point—when, say, the informant runs out of breath, or when his imagination fails him—hoping that the resulting characterization (in the above case, say, a rule of patrilocal residence) will not run afoul of too many everyday contingencies. Practitioners of an expanded "ethnoscience" have tried to untangle from consciously formulable rules and lexically labeled analytic units—shorthand formulas that people may use more for describing than for justifying the ordinary, unproblematic flow of everyday events—"deeper" underlying units (e.g., bundles of separable rights and obligations, unitary "roles" which ordinarily but not always rest with single individuals; Keesing 1970) which surface, typically, in unusual or exceptional circumstances. Young men in a village may generally live with their fathers after marriage; but what will happen to Xun, who is an orphan? or to Mikel who has quarreled with his father and been disinherited? Presumably the "system of shared competence" will include mechanisms necessary to account for such unusual events, to accommodate extenuating circumstances.

Here I can distinguish two sorts of *accounting for*. It may happen that people are baffled about what to do; they may need to *figure out*, say, how to divide up bride-wealth when the normal recipients are not around. But it may also happen, I should think much more commonly, that exceptional circumstances have already generated a solution (resulted in an outcome) by the time people have noticed that something is amiss; and in this sort of case people figure out not what to do, but how to interpret what has happened, how to understand or justify it, and usually how to feel about it. Since people rarely behave in ways that strike their neighbors as outlandish, there are presumably ways to figure out what to do, how to respond, what to think, when ordinary precepts fail. And, inversely, when people act surprisingly in what seem ordinary circumstances, there must be ways to figure out (or try to figure out) what is going wrong. I emphasize that all these are matters to *figure out*; it is a mistake to suppose that culture provides ready-made answers to all problems. There can be no infinite list of contingency rules.

Note that the ethnographer's task can now be seen to resemble closely the gossip's métier, with the crucial difference that the naive ethnographer, unlike the old-hand gossip, has trouble distinguishing the exceptional from the ordinary. Still, neither ethnographer nor gossip confronts "raw behavior"; instead, both interpret what they see and often label it in a way that presumes antecedents and suggests consequences and sequels. ("I can tell from the way he slammed the door that he fought with his wife and is now probably going out to get drunk.") Geertz has suggested that the characteristic and proper job of the ethnographer is to *inscribe* and *interpret* microscopic bits of action:

> Doing ethnography is like trying to read (in the sense of "construct of reading of") a manuscript—foreign, faded, full of ellipses, incoherencies, suspicious emendations, and tendentious commentaries, but written not in conventionalized graphs of sound but in transient examples of shaped behavior. [1973, p. 10]

Gossips spend their time reading, in this sense, their neighbors' behavior; they may do it well or badly, but ethnographers presumably have much to learn from them in either case.

Is the notion that culture is a shared, systematic theory of the world well defined? How much of the world does the theory of the world allow us to model? Keesing argues that the ideational system is not to be confused with the behavior "on the ground."

> A competence model of Trobriand culture would tell us what classes of things, people, and events there are and what kind of a world they are situated in, and it would give rules for how to garden, trace descent, exchange, and reside. But it would tell us nothing about residence patterns, descent groups, agricultural production, or the flow of exchange—or even how many Trobrianders there are and where they live. [1974a, p. 90]

Still, recent ethnoscientists (see Kay 1970) allege the possibility of reconciling the native's cultural competence with observed statistical facts. Consider the suggestion that a particular model of decision routines by which natives decide where to live on a particular island will, given· the appropriate input (i.e., a census and other relevant demographic information), generate a pattern of residence that very nearly corresponds to the facts—a pattern that is, say, 90 percent correct in its "predictions" of the number of patrilocal, matrilocal, . . . residence choices. If the model is simple (i.e., not unreasonably elaborate or ad hoc), it may reasonably be supposed to isolate the important considerations that bear on any individual's choice of where to live.

But is this "prediction"?[3] Since we already have the facts (the statistical facts) when we start, what is to prevent us—if we are ingenious enough—from building a model that is 100 percent correct: that generates every single residence case? What is to prevent a linguist from writing a "grammar" of twenty-five sentences of a language? It may be a good one or a bad one—how do we know? It would be a neater (and far more difficult) task to say something about residence patterns in, say, the same village in ten years, or in several villages on the basis of fieldwork in just one village. But in the latter case we should not be inclined to suppose that we could "model" every single residence choice.

The question remains, How much of what goes on in the world is part of people's theory of the world (knowledge of the world)? What limits, other than practical limits of size (we may compile a census of eight hundred people more easily than a census of three billion), are generated by the formal properties of our models?

I can clarify matters with a different example. Imagine that we set out to account for (write a "cultural grammar" of?) the behavior of motorists at traffic intersections—a favorite example for beginning anthropology students aimed at demonstrating the complexity of their own cultural knowledge. This can be made to look like a good ethnographic problem by listing some of the elements of the situation. We should presumably need to describe and analyze the "semantic structure" of sets of salient objects: traffic signs, distinguished by shape and function; equivalence classes (traffic signs, stoplights, traffic cops, etc.). What forms might a solution take?

1. We might state the traffic laws, which are presumably precise and finite (though possibly complex). We could then declare behavior in conflict with the laws not only "illegal" but "culturally inappropriate." Few would find this solution adequate.

2. We might interview a few drivers and enumerate principles according to which people claim they act at intersections. (We might serve as our own informants.) Such principles might form a list, ordered in terms of importance or precedence. For example, consider the following list:

a.	Stop for a red light, stop sign, or yield sign;
b.	except, in the last case, when the intersection is empty.
c.	Go with a green light or an unmarked intersection;
d.	except, in the latter case, when the intersection has other traffic;
e.	except when there is a traffic policeman; in which case stop if he says stop, and go if he says go;
f.	except, in the latter case, when there is traffic in the intersection;
g.	and, except when the traffic light seems to be broken, after an appropriate wait, go when an opening appears;
h.	and except, when it is late at night with no one around, ignore all signs and go;
i.	and except, when it is an emergency (see rules for emergency—"on the way to a fire," "having a baby," etc.), in which case . . .

There is no clear criterion that tells us when to stop; we can embellish the situation indefinitely. It is no help to the ignorant ethnographer to say: "Well, the rules are quite simple, other things being equal . . ." or ". . . in the absence of special circumstances."[4]

3. We might film traffic at a representative sample of intersections, hoping for a wide variety of contingencies. We could undoubtedly produce from the resulting "corpus" of traffic crossings a model to encompass whatever percentage of the cases we liked. H. L. A. Hart proposes a similar example to show that such a procedure, from an "austere" external point of view that encompasses only the raw observable facts, "cannot be in terms of rules at all" but only "in terms of observable regularities of conduct, predictions, probabilities, and signs" (1961, p. 87). And to describe how people operate at intersections in such terms is to "miss out a whole dimension of the social life of those" people— in particular, the fact that people judge behavior as right or wrong. Thus, we might want to exclude certain navigations of the intersection recorded on film as defective or inappropriate: we might discard confrontations that resulted in crashes, cases in which pedestrians were mowed down, close shaves, hit-and-runs, and so forth. Indeed, the entire enterprise might benefit from assembling a panel of experts to rule on individual cases—which would be to change the nature of the solution.

4. Following the insight of similar studies of pedestrians who manage to walk the sidewalks (usually) without jostling, treading on, or decking others,[5] we might imagine that each motorist abides by a set of rules and conventions, and that motorists *interact* with one another, exchanging signals, adjusting to each other's communicated or intuited inten-

tions. Why else, indeed, do motorists employ conventionalized hand and directional light signals?

> Voluntary coordination of action is achieved in which each of two parties has a conception of how matters ought to be handled between them, the two conceptions agree, each party believes this agreement exists, and each appreciates that this knowledge about agreement is possessed by the other. [Goffman 1971, p. 39]

Thus the "rules" which delimit how one navigates the sidewalk or the intersection are not merely elaborated for contingencies; more than that, they provide for interaction and intercommunication between this rule follower and other individuals, also conceived as rule followers. And, as each of us knows, the presumption that others whom we meet at intersections are following the same rules occasionally fails, and we screech to a halt, swerve and swear, or crack up—all fates that await us in other social situations as well.

Notice, here, that the notion of interacting sets of actors, each bearing some (overlapping, one hopes) segments of the system of rules and understandings that are supposed to "underlie" behavior—rules some of which themselves relate to the interaction between actors—severely tests the formal devices which ethnographers have developed to codify "cultural grammars." A linear ordering of routines which make binary (or, perhaps, *n*-ary) choices will hardly do justice to this admittedly trivial traffic situation. And as we add to the wrinkles and complications, we may justly start to wonder (along with the hapless motorist) when patterned decision-making comes to an end and (not necessarily random) temporizing begins.

Something seems to crumble in the notion of the native actor's competence.

A reasonably good driver decides in a flash what to do as he approaches an intersection; and he may change his mind several times equally quickly. Even a swift computer with an elegant program devised to simulate the situation (or more ambitiously, designed to pilot a remote automobile equipped with sensors that simulate the driver's perceptions)[6] would seem dull-witted by comparison. And, as life goes, this is a trivial problem. The object of the rules is to get a driver through the intersection; his best strategy is to do it as quickly as possible, avoiding a confrontation with the law or with someone else's car. There is room for alternative modes of action; some drivers stick to the letter of the law. (Of course we know from the frenzied anger such drivers inspire in us that they are deviant.) But we are disinclined to call what happens "compromise between alternatives." There is no compromise between a red light and a policeman waving you on; or between a green light, a car honking behind you, and a ten-ton truck running the light in the other direction.

The problem is not that we cannot explain every contingency, but rather that we do not know what limits to set. How much of a native actor's ability to make decisions belongs in ethnography, is part of cultural competence?

B. J. Diggs suggests that certain rules, like these traffic laws, have a *point*—they are designed to lead to a certain instrumental goal—and thus there need be no endless list of contingency rules.

> No statement of a rule includes reference to all conditions pertinent to its application; one would not wish to so encumber it, even if every contingency could be foreseen. This implies that every rule follower is expected to know "what he is doing" in a sense larger than "following the rules"; and if the rules are instrumental he is often expected to know the goal to which his rule-directed action supposedly contributes—to know "what he is doing" in this sense. Not always, to be sure, but often he could not make a sound ¡judgment of when and how to apply the rule without this knowledge. [1964, p. 36]

How much, then, of this calculus of *points* and *goals*, of knowing what one is doing (and, in a larger sense, *what there is to do*) is part of the shared theory of the world that is the object of ethnographic description? And how do we as ethnographers characterize these goals?

Here again the gossip is in an advantageous position. It is precisely by formulating an account of what the protagonists of a gossip story "are doing" that the gossip puts himself in a position to pronounce on the rules involved, the degree to which they have been satisfied or disregarded, and the sense or senselessness of the outcome. This is, once more, a matter of (motivated and justifiable) interpretation, of Geertz's "thick description"; and again the ethnographer can learn from the gossip.

Let me start again from the beginning, to reconsider what an individual, a Zinacanteco, for example, "knows about his world"—what skills he or she must possess. What belongs in an ethnography? A Zinacanteco first must be able to accomplish certain tasks. A man must know how to hoe corn, how to accept a drink, how to enter a house politely. A woman must master tortilla-making techniques; she must know how to tie up her hair and her skirt. Within the Zinacanteco universe it makes little sense to talk about rules governing these skills. Departures from standard behavior no longer constitute behavior at all. Nonnormal action conveys no messages (except the ultimate message: "I am no longer a Zinacanteco [or a human being]"). Only when there are alternatives can behaving a certain way have meaning. These basic skills are unremarkable[7] and are certainly unlikely to be remarked upon in gossip. (Compulsive ethnographers will, of course, record skirt-tying and hoe-holding techniques to demonstrate the thoroughness of their observations.)

Such invariant skills range into more complex abilities as one enters realms of activity where there are principled alternatives. Zinacantecos choose between goals; they know what modes of action are appropriate to what ends (or are likely or unlikely to achieve them). They have mastered decision schemes and strategies which enable them to pursue their purposes. They have learned to produce coherent and largely unsurprising behavior in the face of infinitely varied circumstances. But no one's plans succeed without a hitch. Zinacantecos also know how to gossip; and gossip arises precisely when people do apparently surprising things; when order gives way to confusion and incoherence. Gossips reconcile aberrant action with the current standard.

So far my argument can be taken to suggest an extension of the notion of "cultural grammar" which has a clear parallel in linguistics. George Lakoff (1965) argues that an adequate grammar must generate certain ungrammatical (or nearly grammatical) sentences and mark them as violations (show how they are violations). Native speakers have definite intuitions about sentences which are not fully grammatical; they can often interpret them, find them ambiguous, relate them to other sentences, transform them, and so on. Utterances whose grammar is questionable may still provide evidence useful to a syntactician. An adequate cultural grammar must account for (allow interpretations of?) certain sorts of deviant behavior. Not everything everyone does is appropriate, unsurprising, predictable, normal, or acceptable. But deviance does not (always) mark the breakdown of the cultural mechanism or variations in cultural competence (ideocults?). Natives have ways of coming to understand or simply countering mistakes, accidents, and perversity. Just as fluent speakers interpret many ungrammatical sentences in standard ways, I claim that gossips typically apply rules of culture to action outside the rules.

Still, cultural grammars patterned after grammars of language are mechanisms with impoverished capabilities even with respect to their own limited goals. We need to build into such grammars what seems a constantly increasing complexity: inventories of objects, roles, situations, and "scenes" (units and contexts); rankings of priorities, hierarchies, conflicting paths to various ends (ordering of rules); an appreciation for the communicative power of acts (including speech acts), the ability to anticipate action from prior cues (the semantics of behavior), and so on. Moreover, we require a cultural grammar with the capacity for change. The units of the code change: clothing styles change; positions in ritual hierarchies are born and die; occupations, objects, animals, bodies of knowledge come and go. So, too, do the rules change: laws have periods of ascendancy, then fall into disuse; etiquette reforms itself; times change, as every old native can tell you. There is no mechanical problem here: cyberneticians build machines that modify themselves. But our usual cultural grammars are static—or, more exactly, the fragments we extract of such grammars are deeply rooted in the data of one moment.

The prospects for developing even a descriptive mechanism powerful enough to capture this widened cultural competence seem bleak. I suggest, instead, that we can appreciate the nature of this mechanism by looking at gossip. Even without routines for predicting (or anticipating) all behavior, we can satisfy ourselves with the ability to appreciate the import of behavior we see (or are likely to see). The capacity to assess others' actions is essentially the capacity to participate in gossip. I suggest that we aim at untangling a culture's rules at least until we have learned to manipulate them well enough to gossip.[8] (This is at least a necessary condition to having mastered a culture.) What constitutes the ability to gossip?

The most striking fact about this ability (as part of overall cultural competence) is this: it is difficult to distinguish an "ideational" component, which involves knowledge of the general rules of the culture, from knowledge of a wide set of contingencies which are in no sense common to a cultural tradition. We ordinarily have thought of one's cultural competence as composed of codes: conceptual schemata for, say, plants and animals, kinship systems, political structures, and so on. The conceptual schemata have, we assume, an independent existence prior to any particular configuration of animals, any set of actual kin, any actual political operation. (The fact that a man is an only child does not, that is, affect his understanding of words for siblings, or of sibling relationships. Or does it?) But in gossip the nonparticular is irrelevant before the actual; the contingencies determine the general principles—for they are all there is. In gossip, the world becomes more than ideal schemata and codes; it rests on the Who's Who, much expanded, on history, on reputations, on idiosyncrasies, on exceptions and accidents. Gossip exalts the particular. Much of an actor's cultural competence rests on a vast knowledge of contingent fact, raw unconnected trivia—in addition to the understanding of taxonomies and lexical subsystems which we have always suspected to be there.[9] Being able to gossip is part of being a Zinacanteco; thus knowing those particular random facts about other people that render gossip meaningful and interesting is necessary to being a successful Zinacanteco.

Watching people operate on their cultural rules through gossip also shows us the folly of our belief that culture *provides* sets of ideal rules which apply to particular configurations of people, places, things, and events. The contingencies of life themselves restructure the rules, even change them over time. Thus, in gossip people may mouth the same words, may invoke the same rule, and derive different conclusions. They may talk about the same facts, espouse the same standards, and still contradict one another. Here is the source for doubt about modeling the cultural rules so as to predict those occasional troublesome marriages that don't fit the marriage rule, residence choices that violate the accepted norm. A skilled native rationalizer could doubtless reconcile almost any aberration with some rules; and gossip about such aberrations might cut both ways—some will say "freakish and immoral," others "just what one would expect." It is in gossip sessions that people most often confront rules directly; at such times the rules have no independence—one's whole understanding of the cultural code depends on the particular setting, on the configuration of past experiences and knowledge, which is suddenly relevant to the application of rules and standards to the facts in question.

We must not be misled by the fact that people typically state cultural rules baldly and absolutely. Informants could certainly state the traffic rules governing intersections. We know—as competent drivers—that the rules are subject to contingencies, and that we apply them (as I suggested before) other things being equal. Gossip, in looking at past sequences of actual behavior, leads participants precisely to the point where unnecessary details have been shorn. Other things *are* equal: one can apply the rules with an appearance of objectivity and absoluteness. The insignificant variations of fact have been masked by gossip's rhetoric. Gossip continually works toward a verbal representation of the facts amenable to the application of rules, to evaluation, and to mental filing for future reference.

I propose that the native's ability to act appropriately is—though epistemologically on a different level—essentially equivalent to the gossip's ability to understand his action.[10] At least, for purposes of our ethnographic descriptions, we may treat rules as operating after the fact to explain behavior. We have not really learned the rules of a culture until we know how to manipulate them in gossip. Moreover, we are still novices at a culture until we can listen to its gossip with an understanding ear. Finally, I claim that when we crack the gossip that pervades social life we see the cultural tradition in its most dynamic form as it applies itself to the kinds of behavior most interesting to natives. We see people actively speculating about the nature of their neighbors, their lives, and, in short, their world.

Gossip in Taxonomies
of Verbal Behavior
in Tzotzil

Following a suggestion of Abrahams (1970), it appears
useful to locate gossip within a native classification of verbal
behavior, as a particular type of performance, as a speech
genre, at least as a lexically labeled behavioral domain. Such
a procedure would allow the analyst to state the criterial
attributes of what he is going to call "gossip," and to relate
these attributes to the criterial attributes of "gossip" in his
analytical language (in this case, social science English).
Rather than employing ordinary "ethnoscientific" procedures
to produce a taxonomy of "verbal behavior," in chapter 3
I elected to present evidence for a Zinacanteco theory of the
properties of certain sorts of conversation which I claim
resemble gossip. This choice reflects my opinion that artifi-
cially elicited taxonomies (particularly taxonomies of *nouns*)
tell us little about the attributes of actually occurring
behavior, and not much more about how people manipulate words (of various syntactic shapes) to "order their
experience."

Fortunately, various anthropologists have provided
taxonomies of Tzotzil words for speech, and it will be
illuminating to try to discover a domain of "gossip" within
these taxonomies.

Victoria Bricker (1974) reports that standard eliciting
techniques with various informants in Zinacantan produced
apparently divergent taxonomies of *lo?il* ("speech"). These
Bricker was able to reconcile by inviting informants to
elaborate on what seemed incomplete responses and to
clarify responses which seemed to confound relations of
contrast and inclusion.[1] The resulting "suggested composite
speech taxonomy" (1974, p. 80) is presented in figure 10.
The position of a domain resembling that of English "gossip"

in this scheme is not clear. Bricker suggests that "the term *lo?il* has a general meaning, 'speech,' and a specific meaning, 'gossip'," (1974, p. 75, note 6), where *lo?il* ("stories") about nonverbal behavior are thus "gossip." (One of Bricker's informants gave, as one answer to the query, "What are the names of the kinds of speech?" the following: "speech called 'the man who quarrels with his wife because he has a mistress'.") We should expect that several of the categories on Bricker's taxonomic tree would include gossiplike behavior: certainly much gossip is frivolous (although much is dead serious); much gossip is lies; and "stories about people" are presumably as often gossip as they are, say, news reports.

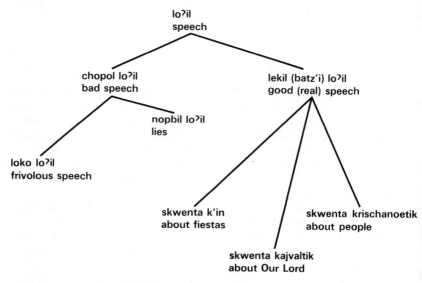

Fig. 10   Suggested taxonomy of speech
for Zinacantan. (After Bricker
1974, p. 80)

Bricker delimits a genre which relates more closely to gossip in a paper on Tzotzil insults (1973*b*). Among other things she is concerned to distinguish "teasing or frivolous talk" (which includes *loko lo?il*) from *labanvanej* ("ridicule") and *?ut bail* ("criticism").[2] All three genres, she says, are characterized by insult;[3] but the insult takes different forms in each genre, and the legal repercussions of insulting someone in one genre or another are quite different. She writes:

> When sober, Zinacantecos do not like to confront each other with explicit insults. Even though insults which are true may be expressed directly in the second person without fear of legal punishment, most Zinacantecos prefer to wait until they can express insults as ridicule to some third party, in the absence of the victim, rather than to confront him with criticism. [1973*b*, p. 196]

These "insults . . . made behind the victim's back" belong to the category of *labanvanej* ("ridicule"); and they seem to fall naturally within behavior we would class as gossip.

Here Bricker appeals to two criteria to distinguish "ridicule" from "criticism." The first criterion amounts to the requirement that "ridicule" never be directly addressed to its victim—a requirement similar to the one I imposed in my working definition of gossip. The second requirement is that insulting remarks about someone which are false, whether directly expressed or not, are *ʔut bail*—and, accordingly, are grounds for legal action (1973*b*, pp. 129–93).

> Whenever an alleged case of defamation is brought before the magistrate, his first concern is to determine whether the insulting accusation in question is true or false. This he does by consulting witnesses. If they say it is true, the case is dropped. [1973*b*, p. 197]

Truth can of course be garbed in more or less insulting ways, and the notions of truth and falsity are in most social discourse themselves negotiable.[4] Doubtless people often fear disclosure of potentially damaging information that is true more than the spreading of fabrications. After two men made a secret deal to trade cargos, one man said to the other: *mu xalabanon* ("don't go and mock me")—in this case, a better translation might be: "don't reveal this [potentially damaging] information about me." But, as I show in chapter 3, this criterion cannot be decisive about gossip, for people consider that gossip may be false but usually must contain a *grain* of truth. And gossip is not often grounds for claiming damages from the offender at the town hall.[5]

Gary Gossen (1974) bases a slightly different taxonomy of the usage of neighboring Chamula on the word *k'op*. The basic first level of contrast may be represented as in figure 11.

> Ordinary language is restricted in use only by the dictates of everyday social situations, and by the grammar or intelligibility of the utterance. It is believed to be totally idiosyncratic and without noteworthiness in style, form, content or setting; it is everyday language. Pure words, in contrast, include all of the stable genres that comprise Chamula oral tradition; they have formal and contextual constraints of many kinds. Chamulas view pure words as "closed" in certain respects and ordinary language as "open," for the latter can be used freely for other kinds of communication; pure words are "bound" in that they are destined to be performed only in specific social settings. [Gossen 1974, pp. 47–48]

The position of "gossip" within this classification is particularly revealing.

> What we would call "gossip" is in Chamula a form of pure words because it reports a single event in a predictable way in a predictable setting. It is not, in theory, idiosyncratic or original, as is language for people whose hearts are heated. Gossip is classified as true recent narrative, a genre of pure words, for it is a significant segment of information, known by several people and potentially available to everyone, which is told in a familiar narrative style in a predictable setting. For example, the gossip

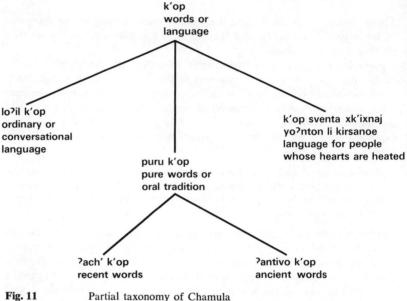

k'op
words or
language

lo?il k'op
ordinary or
conversational
language

puru k'op
pure words or
oral tradition

k'op sventa xk'ixnaj
yo?nton li kirsanoe
language for people
whose hearts are heated

?ach' k'op
recent words

?antivo k'op
ancient words

Fig. 11 Partial taxonomy of Chamula *k'op*. (After Gossen 1974, pp. 50–51)

among women at a waterhole about the presidente's oration to the Chamulas at the past Festival of San Juan is true recent narrative, a form of pure words, whereas the oration itself is not, because no one knew exactly what the presidente was going to say, only how he would say it and where. [1974, p. 52]

Here we find a rather static view of gossip—as true, more or less, standardized recounting of (actual) recent events—which contrasts rather sharply with the picture of gossip that emerges from Zinacanteco native theory I expound in chapter 3.

I managed to elicit a rather different taxonomy for *k'op* and *lo?il*. In conversation, I discussed the meanings of various types of *lo?il* and *k'op* which appear in Gossen's and Bricker's taxonomies. It became obvious, for example, that most of the labels applied to verbal genres in Chamula were unfamiliar to Zinacantecos—despite the fact that these communities are geographically close, situated on the opposite sides of a ridge and valley. At the end of these conversations I asked a Zinacanteco friend to name the different "types" of *k'op* and *lo?il*,[6] and to arrange cards with the different names into piles by similarity of meaning.[7] I then had him arrange piles into two large groups corresponding to a basic taxonomic split in the domain (see fig. 12).

I shall consider each category in turn. Figure 12 is headed by *k'op* ("word") and roughly divided into *chopol k'op* and *lekil k'op*—though these terms, in these contexts, were specially coined to label the two groups.

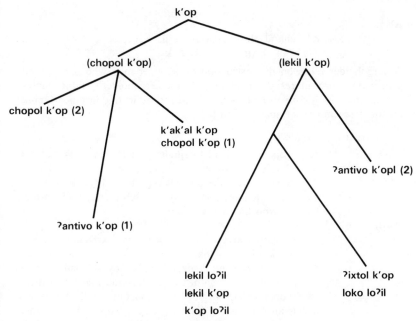

Fig. 12   A taxonomy of *k'op* in Zinacantan. (Suggested by Chep
K'obyox ta ʔApas, 7 May 1971)

Chopol k'op means "bad *k'op*," and *lekil k'op* "good *k'op*." Under the
category of "good words" my informant listed the following types and
offered the following explanations:

a. "good   *lekil k'op*
    words"   lek tuk' chloʔilaj, lek rason
               "When people just talk straight together; when they talk
               sensibly."
Lekil k'op seems to imply ordinary conversation with some purpose. (People
in Zinacantan do not talk, or indeed, socialize, *aimlessly*.) In such conversations people make decisions or discuss questions in seriousness.[8]

b. "good talk"   *lekil loʔil*
               Tzjak'beik k'op tzjak'beik rason much'u snaʔ rason k'u
               chaʔal totil-meʔil, k'u chaʔal ʔoy stot-smeʔ jpas-ʔabtel jaʔ
               tzkoʔoltasbe sk'op.
               "This is when one asks another for advice about the wise
               course of action, about the proper way—when one asks
               some wise person like a ritual adviser; as when a cargoholder
               agrees with his ritual adviser about how things should be
               done."

Also:

K'u cha?al chlo?ilaj totil-me?il.
"The way a ritual adviser talks."

A cargoholder relies on the instruction of an elder man who has learned proper ritual procedures; this man becomes the cargoholder's "father-mother" (ritual adviser) for his year in office. *Lekil lo?il* is in this instance typified by the wise counsel of such a man.

c. "current   *k'op lo?il*
    stories"   ?Oy k'op ?oy lo?il mi ta sjunlej parajel, ?oy yech slo?iltael ?antz bu ?ep sa? yajmul.
                "There are words, there is talk—perhaps throughout a whole hamlet; sometimes there may be such stories told on a woman who has many lovers."

Also:

Mi ?ep tzobol krixchano, xu? xal li yan krixchanoe mi slak'-na k'usi, tol alabal-k'op alabal-lo?il, mi ?o much'u slo?iltaik mi tzeb mi ?antz mi vinik, ?oy sk'oplal chkaltike.
"If a lot of people gather together some may say—their neighbors, perhaps—'You have too much talk, too much discussion.' That is if they are telling stories on someone, whether it be a girl or a woman or a man—someone who has a reputation as we say."

K'op lo?il seems to refer to circulating gossip: stories which spread around a hamlet.

Grouped along with categories (*a*) – (*c*) was one variety of *?antivo k'op.*

d. "ancient   *?antivo k'op* (2)
    words"   ?Oy to much'u sna?be smelol k'utik x?elan sbiinoj li totil-me?il ta jteklum, meltzajem ?eklexya, batem krixchano ta Nibak—ja? ?antivo k'op chalbeik.
                "There are still people who know the stories about how the ancestral gods in Zinacantan Center got their names, about how the church was created, about how people first went to Ixtapa—that is what people call 'ancient words'."

Such *?antivo k'op* are clearly mythical accounts of past events (cf. Wasserstrom 1970).

Two joking genres were also grouped on the side of "good" verbal behavior.

e. "banter"   *?ixtol k'op*
               Much'u tztzak ta yech no?ox lo?il, ?ak'o mi lek tuk' chlo?ilaj cha?vo? krixchano, li june muk' xa lek stak'—?ixtol k'op xa xtak'av.
               "[This is what is done by] someone who engages another in purposeless conversation; suppose two men are talking

together properly, but one of them no longer answers appropriately—he has started to tease the other."

This genre of speech is similar to what Gossen (1974) describes in Chamula as *batz'i ʔixtol loʔil* or "Real Frivolous Talk." In the midst of an apparently innocuous conversation one party begins to twist, pun on, or otherwise intentionally misunderstand the other's words so as to mock or tease him.[9]

f. "joking   *loko loʔil*
   talk"
         Naka loko loʔil, koʔol yech stak'be sbaik.
         "Just crazy talk: both people answer each other the same way."

From this brief description we suppose that *loko loʔil* is like *ʔixtol k'op* except that both parties to the exchange are consciously funny and/or insulting as they talk. Bricker (1973b, p. 189) suggests that the following expressions are, in fact, all used interchangeably: *loko loʔil, ʔixtol loʔil, ʔixtol k'op*. These she finds to mean "teasing or frivolous talk," following Laughlin (1975, p. 63).

By contrast to these categories, my informant grouped the following genres under the heading of "bad words."

g. "heated   *k'ak'al k'op*
   words"
         Bu kapem chk'opoh tajmek.
         "When someone speaks with great anger."
         The way a man talks when enraged is characterized by low pitch, lengthened vowels in expletives, and shortened vowels in ordinary words.

h. "bad   *chopol k'op* (1)
   words"
         Jaʔ k'u chaʔal mi ʔoy ʔutbail ʔoy chukbail ʔoy jmilvanej—
         jaʔ yech chalik li krixchanoetik, mi ʔo avaʔi mi yech ti ʔoy
         chopol k'op ta ʔankostura.
         "This is when there is a fight when people are jailing each other, or when there is a murder. Then people will ask, for example, 'Have you heard, is it true that there is bad talk in Angostura?' "

I believe that *k'op* in this sense is best not translated as "word" at all, but better as "dispute." Thus *chopol k'op* (1) refers to *trouble*.

Categories (*g*) and (*h*) were grouped together and then more loosely grouped with the last two genres.

i. "bad words"   *chopol k'op* (2)
         Naka ta pentejo, yuʔnox chal pentejo li much'u chʔilin,
         jaʔ k'u chaʔal pentejo, kavron.
         "These are words like *pentejo*, since someone who gets angry says things like 'asshole' or 'bastard'."

This is a category relating to swearing or to vulgar or obscene language. The words in question are loans from Spanish: from *pendejo* ("stupid", lit., "pubic hair") and *cabrón* ("cuckold, bastard").[10]

j. "ancient   ʔ*antivo k'op* (1)
   words"   K'u chaʔal xk'opojik toʔox voʔne moletik yaʔel.
                 "The way people long ago talked."

This category refers to phrases which were once in use to describe or refer to norms or customs. My informant grouped them under "bad talk" because the examples which came to his mind had to do with punishment and cruelty.[11]

I have offered this taxonomy not because I believe it depicts the essence of Zincanteco conceptualization of verbal behavior (indeed, I know this is not the case). Instead, I mean to suggest that a hierarchial structure of nominal forms will be of little use in characterizing such conceptualization. For one thing, we should probably have more success if we concentrated on speech *verbs* (like *loʔilta, laban, loʔilaj, k'opoj*, etc.). How to delimit the distinctions within such a set is a problem with no obvious solution. If we are determined to find a taxonomically structured domain, our informants will doubtless oblige by offering convincing labels for the various tree nodes we offer them. But, as I remarked in chapter 3, we are unlikely to be able to use the resulting labels for eliciting. Moreover, there are good grounds for doubting that labels which appear in the various taxonomies we have sketched govern *domains* at all; that is, that they refer to conceptual classes of behavior.

When we suggest an illustrative situation, an informant—being fluent in his language—is able to produce a phrase to describe it. Such a phrase may not be equally fortunate when applied to another example. For instance, when I asked my informant to reconcile the taxonomy of figure 12 with the kind of talk that went on during Who's Who sessions—in which a group of Zinacantecos discussed particular absent Zinacantecos' reputations in front of a tape recorder—he was unable to pick any labels as appropriate descriptions. Who's Who sessions were *k'opetik noʔox, kapal lek kapal chopol yaʔel* ("just words, both good and bad mixed, I guess").[12] Yet the sort of talk that occurred at Who's Who sessions was, to all appearances, exactly the sort of conversation most common among Zinacanteco men.

More specifically, though the taxonomy of figure 12 contains the category *k'op loʔil*, which resembles the category labeled "gossip" in English, we should be unsuccessful trying to elicit gossip by asking for examples of *k'op loʔil*; nor should we be inclined to limit our investigation of gossip to examples of speech which could be unambiguously labeled *k'op loʔil*. The terms which appear in this and similar taxonomies do contrast with one another; but the contrasts operate only in certain contexts, for certain purposes. And it is only with reference to such contrasts (within "sense systems") that these terms convey any information at all.[13]

There is certainly a point to trying to delimit carefully the possibilities of contrastive expression made available by a lexical set, or to propose precise definitions of terms for analytical purposes (see Paine 1970 for such distinctions between "gossip," "rumor," and "scandal"). It has been suggested to me[14] that what is distinctive about gossip is that it characteristically conveys derogatory messages about its victims, and that it often tells one a good deal more about the motives and personality of the gossip than about the protagonist. It may often be true that gossip promulgates information about people that they would rather not have spread about (and note the imagery of such words as "spread," "circulate," "leak out," and so forth, that describe gossip); but it is important in this connection that there are cultural and situational constraints on what sorts of information are potentially damaging. Thus, clearly, what is damaging in one context ("Petul is very rich, so why doesn't he do a cargo?") may be innocent or praiseworthy in another ("Petul is rich, so why is his younger brother such a lazy lout?"). Thus, if gossip is venom, we still need to discover and describe why one man's poison is another man's meat.

Table 1 shows the most highly developed Who's Who category list. The first categories have to do with a man's performance in the religious and civil hierarchies and their peripheral posts. About each man we asked

Mi ʔech'em ta ʔabtel?
"Has he passed through any *work*?"

"Work" in this context is always understood to mean "religious *cargo*," and the question would prompt informants to recount the man's whole *cargo* history. The first category in table 1,

1.   j-pas-ʔabtel
"cargoholder"

elicited the names of men in a hamlet currently serving in a religious office or known to be expecting such a post at a definite future date. Most hamlets have at least one

2.   pasaro
"*pasado*" (man who has passed through all four levels of the cargo system)

who is a respected older man. Occasionally a man who has decided to retire from the system after only three (and sometimes two) cargos may be called a *pasaro*.

If the cargo system is a mechanism for securing (buying) prestige, then a man will be interested in comparing his own success in the system with that of others. One might hear the following exchange in a discussion of someone's cargo career:

"Wasn't his second cargo *San Pedro Martir?*"
"Yes, I remember hearing that it was just a *small* cargo [*bik'it noʔox yabtel iyak'be*]."

The speaker betrays his feeling that the cargo was just a little one: inex-
pensive and inferior. Zinacantecos may keep track of—and gossip about—
other men's cargo records, since such records are explicit models against
which they can test their own success.

Some older men are also known to be

3.   totil-me?il
            "father-mother" (ritual adviser to cargoholder, or for other
            ceremonies)

These men are well-versed in the dtails of correct ritual performance and
thus guide their charges through ceremonies.

A fairly young Zinacanteco who had passed through two cargos before he
was thirty-five told me why he had refused a request to be ritual adviser to
one of his relatives.

"I guess I know the proper way to perform a cargo. I am not afraid of
performing badly. But I do not want to be criticized and scolded by the
elders. Even if the cargo holders were older than I, since my head would be
red [wrapped in a red kerchief as a sign of office] I could not bow to them.
I would be ashamed to bow as a ritual adviser. No, I am too young yet."

Two categories relate to performance beyond the ordinary bounds of the
religious hierarchy:

4.   ch'ul mol
            "holy elder"
5.   j-k'echnomal
            "saint-bearer" (or "pallbearer")

The Six Holy Elders are *pasaroetik* who serve for life, and whose most
significant ritual function is nailing the Christ image to the cross on Good
Friday (Vogt 1969, p. 259). The bearers carry Christ nailed to the cross
during Lenten processions; they are senior cargoholders.

Two further important classes of people are at the periphery of the religious cargo system.

6.   pixkal
            "sacristan"
7.   Chk'ot ta ch'omil.
            "He goes as someone borrowed." [i.e., he serves as a helper]

Nowadays, it is usually young men literate in Spanish who serve as *sacristanes*; they care for the church, opening and closing the doors, ringing
the bells, and so forth. During their terms they acquire ritual expertise;
cargoholders cultivate them as useful allies and advisers. At the same time,
rumor has it that *sacristanes* tend to steal from offerings to the saints and
to seduce cargoholders' wives.

Men also become well known for serving frequently as helpers to cargoholders. Helpers are responsible for assembling and carrying ritual parapher-

nalia, or for managing a cargoholder's supply of liquor. In this capacity
they learn proper ritual form.

One elicits names of men who have served in the civil hierarchy by
asking about

8.   ?abtel ta kavilto
                "work at the town hall,"

though, alternately, people often ask whether a man has *?ech'em ta melt-
zanej-k'op* ("had experience at settling disputes"). Zinacantecos can name
past *presidentes* or *agentes* (hamlet-level magistrates; see categories 9 and
10) more often than they can remember lesser civil officials, who are sometimes just called *kavilto* ("town hall people").

Finally, in response to the most general question,

                Mi ?o k'usi tunem ?oe?
                "Has he served as anything at all?"

members of the panel gave a wide range of hamlet-level officials, temporary
fiesta offices, officials associated with short-term projects (electrifiication,
potable water), and so on. Table 1 retains only the most frequent such
categories (11–15). Most of these positions are minor, though being on the
ejido or education committees may represent a first step toward political
power.

Several categories refer to auxiliary personnel in the cargo system. There
are positions which must be filled by old women.

16.   j-chik' -pom
                "incense burner" (who is responsible for keeping the
                incensario lit during ceremonies).
17.   j-jap-kantela
                "candle-bearer" (for elders during Lent)

Only a few women are qualified to serve in such positions, and these are
the first *women* to be named in a Who's Who session. Other ritual specialists
include the musicians;

18.   j-vabajom
                "stringed instrument player"
19.   j-?amarero, j-tampolero
                "flutist," "drummer"

Musicians not only provide the musical entertainment for *kajvaltik* ("Our
Lord") during ceremonies, but also are known for their joking ability (see
Haviland 1967). In Who's Who discussions, informants distinguished
between those musicians who were good enough to play for cargoholders
in Zinacantan Center and those who played only in their own hamlets.
Furthermore, people would often identify a man as a musician and immediately comment upon his haughtiness, general tractability, and willingness
to serve as a musician when asked.

A well-known musician, Chep, had agreed to serve as musician for a cargoholder; but for three successive weeks he failed to show up for the ceremony.

". . . so you see how haughty he is. Who knows what the trouble was— maybe he wasn't fed or given liquor to drink, I don't know."
"Ahhh, no, it was simply uncooperativeness. Couldn't he have spoken up if there was something wrong? Even if he couldn't simply say that the cargoholders gave insufficient gifts, he could have told them he was busy, that they must look for someone else."
"Yes, so he should; the cargoholders could have made other plans then."
"That's the way it should have been."
"But the way he did it was deceitful; he lied when he agreed to perform."
"But he hasn't been abandoned as a musician. He was old Jvakin's violinist just last year. So I guess he's still good for something."
"It's just that he is very unreliable, but I guess that can be endured."

The rosters of available ritual specialists like these (as well as the names of qualified cannon-tampers who set off thundering blasts which accompany a cargoholder's retinue) must be public knowledge; a man's skills must accrue to his reputation if he is to be recruited.

People are known in Zinacantan for special skills outside the religious or civil hierarchies. There are the medical practitioners (categories 21–23)— both men and women (though men are ordinarily not midwives). The public always strives to discover which practicing curers are the most powerful, the most successful, those with the most recent debut. Gossips speculate about the likelihood of people' claims to curing power or the circumstances under which such power was (allegedly) acquired.

A Zinacanteco named Palas was subject to attacks of epilepsy (*tup' ?ik'*). Curers reported that this was a symptom of his curing abilities, and that he himself should become a curer.

"Palas was elated, because he would become a curer and would be able to enjoy meals of chicken (eaten at curing ceremonies); also he would recover from his sickness. . . . So he carried his staff and prayed the way curers do; but it sounded as if he had learned the prayers—he didn't just know them himself, because he wasn't a real curer. He had only been told that he was; and he didn't know this was just trickery and deceit because he had a simple soul. . . . His epilepsy got worse. When he finally recovered, people began to think that they would ask him to serve as their curer. For they knew that a *new* curer has more success in relieving sickness. But when Palas heard that he was going to be asked to cure he just fled; he didn't let anyone even catch a glimpse of him."

Another set of categories relates to verbal skills and talents as a mediator in disputes.

24.   Sna? smeltzan k'op.
             "He knows how to settle disputes."

25.   Snaʔ rason.
             "He knows the proper way to do things; he is wise."

Community elders are often called upon to settle disputes. Jane Collier characterizes such elders as:

older men, known for their wisdom in settling conflicts, who can be aproached by a person involved in a dispute. Such elders are usually leaders of their own descent groups, but affinal, *compadrazgo,* and political ties allow them to extend their range of influence. . . . In a few hamlets there is one paramount elder who handles most of the hamlet disputes. Such men are powerful political leaders, have extensive compadrazgo ties, and are known as men who look after their hamlets. [1973, p. 26]

There was usually little doubt in an informant's mind which few men were the best mediators in each hamlet; to attribute "reasonableness" or ability at settling disputes to an elder is to speak as much about his actual political power as about his bargaining skills.

About some Zinacantecos it may be said that

26.   Xtojob ta k'opojel.
             "He is successful at talking."

This may mean that

27.   Snaʔ k'op ryox.
             "He knows how to talk to saints [i.e., to pray],"

or, more likely, that he is a good "mouthpiece": that he is a useful ally in any dispute because he is a convincing talker. In particular, there are the "Zinacanteco lawyers" who negotiate with ladino lawyers and legal officials (Freeman 1974). Thus, knowing Spanish is a related ability.

28.   Snaʔ kastiya.
             "He knows Spanish [i.e., can speak it fluently]."
29.   Snaʔ vun.
             "He is literate [in Spanish]."

Though many men of all ages can speak and understand some Spanish, literacy is almost totally confined to men under the age of thirty; the percentage is low in any case. Knowing how to read and write is not a highly valued skill in Zinacantan, but there are enough occasions when Zinacantecos need documents read or written that it is important to know who can do it (Haviland 1974*a*).

Only older men with certain ritual skills are asked to be godparents at weddings (table 1, category 30). The godfather must instruct a newly married couple in marital obligations, and he becomes responsible for the success of the marriage after the wedding. It is his "duty to mediate between the couple in serious disputes" (Jane Collier 1973, p. 188; and cf. Jane Collier 1968). The choice of wedding godfather is important for the couple and for the families of both bride and groom; only a few men have the reputation of being often wanted for the role.

Particular Zinacantecos are known for their special abilities—knowledge of adobe-making and house-building, ability to make traditional hats, Zinacanteco violins, and so on (see table 1, categories 31 and 32)—and when these abilities are important to others, they are frequently mentioned in conversation. Hence, one asks which of one's neighbors are competent masons when one intends to build a new house.

Though Zinacantecos rarely identify others by explicit reference to wealth (or poverty), they are certainly aware of which men are

33.   j-k'ulej
             "rich"

and which are just *j-k'ulejtik* ("moderately rich") or *ta leklektik no?ox* ("just so-so"). Conversations often revolve around the economic fortunes and misfortunes of others.

Old Manvel was reputed to be one of the richest men in Zinacantan, having inherited wealth from his father, who in turn stole money from the Earth Lord. But now he has lost his considerable fortune from unwise lending.

"*Kere*, the money he used to have—lots, they say!"
"He's just spread it all around, I understand."
"But it is never repaid, that's why the old man himself must now go into debt."
"*Puta*, but that is bad."
"That old man just seems to have lost everything."
"Why do you suppose that is?"
"I guess it is because he just distributed his money."
"It was just like giving it away."
"He treated it as if he had as much as he wanted—just as if he could pick it [as one picks peaches], just as if he could manufacture it. So he just gave it away to other people."

Zinacantecos frequently have occasion to borrow money, whether for cargo expenses or more immediate needs. Men can ordinarily approach their kinsmen or *compadres* for such loans; when they need larger amounts they may ask wealthy Zinacantecos, some of whom charge interest.

38.   [Lek] xak' ta ch'om stak'in.
             "He [willingly] lends his money."
39.   Xak' ta jolinom stak'in.
             "He lends money at interest."

Zinacantecos gossip about how willingly men lend the money they have. There is a certain presumption that wealthy people *will* lend, especially for cargo costs or the expenses of a curing ceremony. Knowledge of which men demand high interest and which are good-hearted about lending is a crucial part of the common store of information.

Other economically motivated categorizations have to do with notable things people own (categories 34–37), especially when they represent nontraditional uses of wealth: trucks, kerosine-powered corn mills, stores, and so forth. Similarly, since most Zinacantecos still support themselves by growing corn, mostly on share-cropped land, it is significant to make one's living in any other way.

40.   j-chon-ʔatz'am
             "salt-seller"

41.   j-ʔekel -ʔixim, -turasnu, -nichim
             "reseller of corn, peaches, flowers"

42.   Snaʔ slakan pox.
             "knows how to distill liquor"

A few families have traditionally supported themselves by selling salt from Ixtapa throughout the highlands (in many faraway *municipios* any man in Zinacanteco clothes is taken for a salt vendor). Recently some young men have begun to derive nearly all their income from trade in fruit and flowers between the highlands and the lowland and coastal regions, a return to a pattern common before the Mexican Revolution. Finally, it is still possible (though rare in Zinacantan) to earn extra money by dealing in bootleg liquor.

The last categories on the Who's Who lists distinguish people with undesirable character traits or abnormalities.

43.   ʔOy sryox.
             "He has a [talking] saint."

Saint images and certain other objects in Zinacantan and throughout the highlands are often reputed to have the power of speech, as well as, for example, the ability to diagnose and cure disease or to help barren women become pregnant. Nativistic movements in the highlands have been inspired by such oracles (see Gossen 1970, pp 61 ff.; Reed 1964; Gossen 1974, pp. 280–81, and Vogt 1969, pp. 21 ff.).

Zinacantecos consult these talking saints, called *j-k'opojel ryox* ("talking saint") or more commonly *kuxul ryox* ("living saint"), about diseases, difficult pregnancies, and so forth. Some saint owners call themselves curers but acknowledge that their powers are due to their saints. There is always a fee for a saint's services, and a patient is expected to sponsor small ritual meals and to give candle offerings to the saint. In Who's Who gossip sessions talking-saint owners are objects of considerable scorn; none of my informants seemed to be a believer, though I know that at least one has consulted a talking saint recently.

Witches are unambiguously thought to be evil.

44.   j-ʔak'-chamel
             "witch" (lit., "giver of sickness")

Jane Collier (1973, pp. 113–25) distinguishes six or seven witchcraft techniques, two of which appear in table 1.

45.   snaʔ xchonvan ta balamil
             "knows how to sell people to the Earth Lord"

46.   sna? xk'opoj ta balamil
           "knows how to pray to the Earth Lord" (e.g., to ask that
           sickness be sent to other Zinacantecos)

Notorious witches are feared throughout Zinacantan; they are given a wide
berth and are not to be crossed.

47.   jmilvanej
           "murderer"
48.   jmak-be
           "highwayman, assassin"

If a man commits murder in Zinacantan, or seems implicated in a murder,
his impulse is to flee. If he is caught, he will be sent to San Cristóbal to be
dealt with by ladino authorities. Instead, many a murderer would rather
endure several years of self-imposed exile, after which he may "return
quietly to beg pardon of the close relatives of his victim, of the elders of his
hamlet, and of the new *Presidente*. If he is successful in approaching all
these men, he can return to live peacefully in Zinacantan, enjoying a
reputation as a man not to be angered" (Jane Collier 1970, p. 133). That so
many men living in Zinacantan are known murderers testifies to the fact
that one can not only get away with murder in Zinacantan but in some
senses profit by it.

"Highwaymen" ambush people on the trail at night, usually to rob and
murder them. Since any sort of roaming about after dark is suspicious,
people who seem to be unaccountably absent from home at night expose
themselves to gossip as assassins or witches. In fact, the concept of "highwayman" seems to be a relic of past times when Indians made long journeys
on foot to other *municipios* and hamlets. Old men alive today claim to
have met *jmak-be* in their youths.

"As far as the highwayman is concerned, old Antun was walking along,
and he looked over by the side of the road where he saw a man dressed in
long pants."
"In the daytime?"
"That's what he says. He said to himself, 'What is that person up to?
Perhaps he is getting a drink of water.' So he started to pass by.
"Suddenly the man stood up. 'Let's go!' he said. He had an old horse with
him. *Puta*, that's when old Antun saw the others coming out. About five or
six of them gathered together.
" 'Where are you going?' they asked."
" 'I'm going home,' he said."
" 'Do you have any tortillas?' they said."
" 'None,' he said."
" 'You bastard!' they said. 'If you have no tortillas, then let's play awhile'."
" 'I don't care,' said old Antun, 'But I don't know what kind of a game
you have in mind.' They started to play [i.e., to fight]. 'I took a bad machete
blow,' old Antun told me later. 'But when I hit him with my machete, he
couldn't dodge the blow, and his head landed far away. He fell to the
ground'."

"Then up came another of them, and three or four all tried to get into the act together. Old Antun said, 'Listen, we are not women. We should only play one at a time. If I get killed, then you can carry me away. If one of you dies then another can try, too.' "

"Well, then they began fighting each other one at a time. Up came one—zap!—down to the ground with the highwayman. Another—zap!— down to the ground. He claims to have killed five or six right there on the path. Then he dragged one over and threw him into the creek."

" '*Kabron*, why should I carry them?' he said to himself. 'What good is the horse anyway?' So he tied the other dead men to the horse and dragged them off into the woods."

"Ah, you see, that old man drags people around by horse. (Ha ha ha)."

The label "thief" (category 49) is applied to people who have been caught by ladino authorities stealing some large item (e.g., a horse) and thrown in jail, and to the poverty-stricken, pitiful old women and lazy youths who steal chickens and household goods. One man had the nickname *takwatz* ("possum") because of his reputation for chicken-stealing. Stealing in Zinacantan is something one is ashamed of and can be openly mocked about.

Zinacantecos are aware that certain people readily involve themselves in court disputes. In large factional disputes in the hamlet of Nabenchauk there have indeed been certain troublemakers who have *-tik' -ba* ("stuck themselves into") nearly every controversial issue (see Rush 1971). Such people seem, literally, to be looking for a pretext over which a dispute can be brought to court.

50.   j-saʔ-k'op
             "troublemaker" (lit., one who looks for a quarrel)

Zinacanteco theory on the subject of troublemaking holds that such aggressive people are as likely to be jailed themselves as they are to win their disputes.

Moreover, to have the reputation as

51.   j-chuk-van-ej
             "one who jails people"

or

51*a*.   pukuj yoʔon
             "evil-hearted"

is to be known for mercilessness. Such people take every opportunity to throw someone—whether it be debtor, political enemy, or hapless potential son-in-law—in jail.

Similarly, some people

52.   ʔep sta chukel, lek xaʔi pus
             "are often jailed" or "enjoy the sweatbath."

Being jailed is always *saʔbil* ("sought after"); hence, to say that one enjoys the "sweatbath," that he longs for the cooler, reflects the orthodox Zinacanteco view that a reasonable man restrains himself from behavior which is likely to end in jailing.

All ritual and, in fact, nearly all social intercourse in Zinacantan is accompanied by drinking. Every request is accompanied by a gift of liquor; every agreement is sealed with a bottle.

53.   jyakubel
             "drunk"

There are alcoholics who drink more than ordinary social life requires. Zinacantecos recognize that excessive drinking impairs one's ability to work, as well as one's moral sense. They therefore consider perpetual drunks both laughable and self-destructive. A man's drinking habits and capacity are subject to public scrutiny, and people may label a man a "drunk" if he is especially noticeable when intoxicated, even if it happens rarely.

The inverse of category (38) is

54.   Mu sut yuʔun yil.
             "He can't repay his debts."

Some people are notoriously bad risks for a loan. It is difficult to refuse a persistent borrower outright without being patently rude; thus one tries to avoid relationships which would ordinarily let such people ask for loans. Everyone clucks publicly over the man who doesn't repay loans and shuns his creditors; as a rich gringo I was considered an easy touch for a loan, and the largest amount of unsolicited gossip and advice came from Zinacantecos who wanted me to know which men *not* to lend to. Conscious of the financial condition of their neighbors, Zinacantecos know when men are *tzinil ta ʔil* ("stuck tight in debts"). Having unpaid debts is considered as much a matter of poverty as of bad will.

55.   meʔon
             "poor"
56.   ch'aj, mu snaʔ xʔabtej
             "lazy" or "won't work"

Some men are said not to be able to feed themselves or their families; such men are unlucky or unskillful farmers. Even when they work they get no return. Other men are unabashedly lazy.

"Her son is terribly lazy."
"What do you mean?"
"Well, once I went to him with a bottle of liquor. 'Please, will you work for me in Hot Country,' I said. But he didn't go. 'Please, work for me near ?Atz'am,' I told him.
" 'All right,' he replied. 'I'll be there.' But until this very day he hasn't showed up. That was a year ago. He just drank my liquor for nothing."
"Has he a wife?"

"No, no. He is too lazy. He doesn't want work. He is still young, but even if the work is nearby, even if it is only for one day, he doesn't want to do paid labor. He just stays there, hanging around his house, or sitting on his haunches sunning himself."

The last few undesirable characteristics involve madness and feeble-mindedness.

57.   chuvaj
           "madman"
58.   jvoviel
           "madman"
59.   xchujil
           "dim-witted person" (lit., runt)

There are Zinacanteco madmen who wander around with tattered clothes and wild, unruly hair, muttering to themselves. They are harmless, though bizarre, and they probably come under the category of *chuvaj*. There are also people who begin to rave, strip themselves naked, and run about wildly like rabid dogs; mad dogs and madmen are called *jvoviel*. Finally, there are individuals whom informants seem unwilling to call crazy who are nevertheless clearly considered subnormal, dim-witted. They are likened to the runt of a litter, or a stunted peach, *xchujil*. Such people grow old without marrying and are unable to work or feed themselves. Several other minor forms of mental incapacity appear.

60.   sonso
           "stupid"
61.   sovra
           "leftover, worthless person"
62.   ʔumaʔ
           "dumb person, speechless person"

A man may be reputed to be *sonso* if he is simply good, that is, not distinguished by particular wrongdoings. Or he may be identified as either stupid or worthless if he has never done *anything* to distinguish himself, if he has little contact with his neighbors.

"But he's not very well known."
"No, he hasn't served any office."
"He is just a hidden person; we never see him leave his house."
"Nope. One has nothing to ask him and nothing to tell him."
"We never see his face."
"When the whole hamlet gathers together, or when public decisions are to be made, he still doesn't come out. He stays hidden in the house just like a girl."
"Then he is just a little leftover, as we say. . . ."
"What do you mean? He's a good man; he works. It is on purpose that he hides himself, that he doesn't let other people see him."
"But in any case he doesn't want to be good for anything."

"You must admit he acts like a worthless person; he isn't a fully good man."

Finally, a person who can't talk is often considered to be mentally deficient; a speech impediment is also a serious social impediment in a culture which places such emphasis on verbal interaction.

In what follows I give a brief description of the sort of thematic material that is categorized under each of the subject headings by which the corpus of gossip stories was indexed. I also show the frequencies associated with each category.

Category	Frequency	Explanation
10.	23 anger	Stories including mention of great anger or fury, people who get angry when drunk or act angry when they talk. Key roots: -*kap*, -*ʔilin*.
	3 envy 1 jealousy	Stories that use the root -*ʔit'ix*, ("envy") with respect to either things or people.
11.	2 omens	Stories involving predictions: e.g., a man correctly predicted his own death when he could not get his cigarette to light.
	31 belief	A category including all references to *kreyensya* (Sp. *creencia*, "belief") of the old people, or having to do with the residual category of "bizarre" notions. I have included, among other things, stories about the hot or cold properties of foods, about buried treasure, about the healing properties of certain

		herbs, about loss of potency through sexual mismatch (*-lok' -chon*, "lose one's animal"), and so on.
12.	11 borrow 14 lend	Stories which contain reference to the institutionalized lending of money.
	22 debt/repayment	Stories which emphasize something about a person's reputation for repaying loans: bad risks, honest hardworking men who always repay, etc.
13.	57 cabildo 10 settling disputes	Stories which include scenes of conflict settlement, either at the town hall or elsewhere.
	5 settler of disputes	Stories about people's capacities for settling disputes, especially if they are bad at it.
14.	38 cargo performance	Stories dealing with such things as incomplete or improper cargo performance, one's cargo career and its pecularities, the requirements for success, the difference between passing religious and civil offices, complete cargo service, etc.
	11 cargo expenses	Stories dealing with the costs of religious office and the equipment necessary. (One story, for example, mocks a man for not having built himself a suitable house for his cargo.)
	5 cargo request	Stories dealing with the circumstances by which individuals gain or enter cargos.
	11 cargo lost 4 no cargo career	Stories about people who fail and flee their cargos, or fail to enter them for some reason; or about men who grow old without ever taking religious office.
	28 cargo helpers	Stories about the duties and performance of various

auxiliary personnel: scribes, *sacristanes*, musicians, ritual advisers, etc.

15.	8 childless 2 barren 4 sterile	Stories about couples without children, as well as men or women who are unable to have children.
	10 impotent/inadequate	Stories about impotent men, or women who fail to have sexual satisfaction.
16.	19 civil office	Stories typically about a man's performance in the civil hierarchy.
17.	11 clothes 1 appearance	Stories which mention a person's tattered, dirty, old, or otherwise peculiar dress or looks.
18.	15 courtship–OK	Stories which remark on successful courtships.
	8 bad performance 10 suitor rejected 7 abandoned 11 third person interferes 11 elopement 3 girl flees	Stories in which courtship fails for one of the reasons indicated.
	13 bride-price	Stories focusing on the financial aspects of courtship.
19.	40 curing power	Stories about curers and their particular propensities and abilities. (For example, several stories contrast the abilities of a curer whose talents are God-given with those who learn to cure from talking saints.)
	15 curing practices	Stories which detail curing ritual.
	3 bonesetting, midwifery	Self-explanatory.
20.	24 deceit	Stories involving actions describable with the roots *-lo?lo* ("trick") or *cho?* ("betray, fool"), and involving some sort of broken agreement or chicanery.

21.	7 disrespect 8 disobedience	Stories about people who do not properly *p'is ta vinik* ("measure as a man") their elders; or who do not -*ch'un mantal* ("obey orders").
22.	132 drunken behavior	
23.	29 factions	Stories which detail the factional alignments of individuals on particular divisive questions.
	11 enemies	Stories about particularly unfriendly relations, especially long-term enmities.
24.	39 fighting 33 beating	Stories in which instances of violence represented by the verb -*maj* ("hit") occur.
25.	50 fleeing	Stories about the causes and incidence of fleeing Zinacantan, or a particular *paraje*: e.g., running away from cargo; running away to avoid punishment for crimes or witchcraft; running away to avoid marriage; etc.
26.	12 good man	Stories which focus on virtuous, sin-free men.
	8 good in appearance only	Stories which deal with the irony of evidently respected, virtuous men who have secret past crimes or misadventures.
27.	24 gossip	Stories about the origins and effects of gossiping.
28.	6 haughtiness	Stories about people who act uppity, who -*toy* -*ba* ("raise themselves") and are uncooperative.
	4 bragging	Gossip instances in which a speaker uses the gossip sessions as occasions for self-aggrandizement.
29.	20 identity change	Stories about Indians who become ladinos, Chamulas who became Zinacantecos, etc.

30.	30 illegitimate child 9 paternity problems	Stories about women who bear children out of wedlock, and about men accused of fathering them.
31.	83 illicit sexual relations 21 incest 6 caught in the act	Various kinds of sexual offenses: premarital, extramarital intercourse; affairs with godchildren or *comadres*; lovemaking with one's mother-in-law; being discovered in a compromising position; etc.
	6 age mismatch	Sexual relation between people of different ages (usually leading to sickness and loss of potency).
32.	89 jail 12 punishment	Stories in which someone is jailed or subjected to some other sort of punishment: fines, forced labor, being made into low-ranking *mayol* for a year, etc.
33.	3 joking ability 18 lewd joking	Stories about the joking ability of protagonists; or gossip which is characterized by long exchanges of lewd jokes between participants.
34.	9 ladino ways, things	Stories which discuss articles and institutions from the ladino world, or from gringoland, e.g., medicine.
	15 ladino connections 12 ladino government	Stories in which Indians become involved with ladinos, especially with organs of the government: soldiers, Instituto Nacional Indigenista projects, etc.
35.	33 ladino law	Stories involving appeals to non-Indian legal institutions.
36.	32 laziness	Stories which characterize people as *ch'aj* ("lazy") or feature characters who *mu sna$^{\gamma}$ x$^{\gamma}$abtej* ("won't work").
37.	14 luck	Stories involving the notion of "luck" (roots like *-ora* or *-yaxal*), especially with respect to bad luck or loss of

		luck (i.e., loss of the ability to make money, to grow things).
38.	20 madness	Stories in which people are mad, feebleminded, or epileptic. (Tzotzil: *chuvaj, -chujil, vov*).
39.	4 *manya*	("wickedness, mischievousness"). Attributions of the concept *manya*.
40.	18 marriage 2 civil marriage	Stories of weddings, the ramifications of marriage; especially when these stories involve aberrations: forced marriage, marriage to a Chamula, marriage at a young age, etc.
	5 sexual incompatibility 5 age incompatibility	Stories whose interest derives from the sexual problems arising from an unfortunate marriage.
	20 wife-beating 4 husband-scolding	Stories of marital difficulties of one kind or the other—these two being the most recurrent themes.
41.	39 mocking	Stories about mocking (Tzotzil root: *-laban, -loʔilta*), either between protagonists or by participants in gossip sessions; for example, in a Who's Who session the men spent fifteen minutes making jokes about a man who lived off his wife's money.
42.	54 murder/killing	Stories involving not only actual murder but also murder conspiracies and attempts; also stories about highwaymen in the older days.
43.	14 musician	Stories about musicians and their failings: typically, haughtiness or lack of piety.
44.	46 nickname 11 reputation	Stories which detail people's nicknames, or which dwell on salient features of their

		reputations (or toss them off in short remarks).
45.	27 old age	Stories which talk about the failings of old age: old men who have spent useless (i.e., cargoless) lives; who are senile; who look older or younger than they are; who are impotent with age; etc.
46.	14 owner	Accounts of the various large items certain people own: mills, trucks, cattle, horses, etc.
47.	32 past times	Accounts of conditions in the past, and notable events: the famine (*viʔnaltik*), the flood in Nabenchauk, and so on.
48.	6 physical injury 21 physical abnormality	Accounts of accidents and disabilities, of lameness, light skin, deafness, dirtiness, heavy beards, horns, etc.
49.	10 serial polygamy 12 polygyny	Accounts of people with many spouses, whether all at once or one after the other.
50.	48 promiscuity (female) 15 womanizing (male)	Gossip and joking about excessive sexual appetite, whether of men or women, and the reputations for looseness accorded to different individuals.
51.	17 property rights	Accounts of disputes over land, land frauds, attempts to borrow money from banks using other people's land as collateral, etc.
52.	19 *pukuj* 6 *pukuj*	("ill-tempered") ("demonic, devilish, super-naturally evil") Stories either (*a*) about unpleasant people; or (*b*) about supernatural goats and other demons that roam about.
53.	47 rape	Stories of rapes, completed or attempted.

54.	11 *rason*	("reason, correct thinking") Stories about the lack of, the acquisition of, the nature of *rason*—the ability to think clearly and correctly on a subject.
55.	90 kin disputes—various types	Stories in which people can't get along with their relatives, near or far.
56.	3 religious behavior 7 irreligious behavior	Stories of such things as blasphemy and improper demeanor in churches.
57.	22 residence change	Stories in which, for one reason or another, a protagonist changes his domicile: whether he goes from one *paraje* to another or moves permanently to Hot Country or Tuxtla Gutiérrez.
58.	52 scolding 7 quarreling 2 insulting	Stories involving some sort of verbal abuse and hostility, often represented by the Tzotzil root -*ut* ("scold, say something to someone"), either singly (meaning "scold"), or in reflexive form (meaning "quarrel").
59.	29 selling	Stories in which protagonists trade in some goods, typically cane liquor, hats, corn, flowers, peaches, firewood, charcoal, salt, or peanuts. Selling salt is an old Zinacanteco tradition in certain families. Selling charcoal or firewood is a mark of poverty.
60.	25 sex-role reversal	Stories about unusually aggressive women, men who live off their wives, etc.
61.	61 sexual desire, advances 29 sexual perversion	Stories which relate to the extraordinary sexual desires of old ladies, corn resellers; and on such perversions as homosexuality, bestiality, looking at genital organs, etc.

62.	17 shame	Stories with occurrences of the root *k'exl-* ("shame, embarrassment").
63.	45 sickness, death 14 VD, *xok*	Stories about long illnesses, strange deaths, itchiness, worms, various kinds of rot and venereal disease.
64.	8 soul, dreams	Stories in which dreams are recounted or containing exploits of peoples' *ch'ulel* ("souls"), which are believed to roam around during dreams.
65.	13 *sovra*	("leftover, worthless person") Stories about such people.
66.	8 special skills 5 lawyer skills	Stories which display the special talents of individual Zinacantecos: house-building, butchering, liquor-making, water-divining; and especially the good talking abilities of Zinacanteco "lawyers."
67.	14 Spanish	Tales involving skill at speaking Spanish.
68.	14 spells, potions, medicines	Stories containing recipes for various concoctions with healing powers, or powers to make people ill or amorous.
69.	3 spouseless woman 16 wifeless man	Stories dwelling on the curious people who live alone.
70.	60 stealing 10 embezzling	Stories of theft, whether of private goods or public funds.
71.	10 stupid/smart	Stories which characterize protagonists by such Tzotzil roots as *sonso* ("stupid") *p'ij* ("clever"), or *bivo* ("lively, smart").
72.	22 supernatural	Stories in which supernatural creatures appear: witch/goats, bells in the earth, blackmen, snakes, devil-women, jaguars, etc.

73.	23 talking saint	Stories usually dealing with the fraudulent nature of most saint images which talk, predict, and cure.
74.	11 treasure	Stories about buried treasure and such supernatural objects as *me²tak'in* (lit., "mother of money"—a treasure which replenishes itself).
75.	43 troublemaking	Stories about people who get into, search for, and otherwise stir up disputes: *sa² k'op* ("look for trouble").
76.	39 violence/arrest/weapons	Violence characterized by grabbing people or using weapons other than fists: usually rifles.
77.	92 wealth/poverty	Stories having to do with extremes of either wealth or poverty; also stories that deal with squandering wealth or unnatural sources of wealth; and stories about selling children and land because of extreme poverty.
78.	65 witchcraft	Stories about actual cases of witchcraft.
	5 belief in witchcraft	Gossip sessions in which participants speculate about witches and their alleged powers.
79.	74 adultery	Stories of those particular illicit sexual relations which are adulterous.
80.	87 divorce 9 reconciliation 15 child support	Stories about those particular marital disputes which end in divorce; also stories about the ramifications of divorce such as child support; the problems of eventual reconciliation.

These categories are not intended as reflections of any native Zinacanteco classificatory scheme. Nor can I claim that the various similarities which cause us to group particular stories together would strike Zinacantecos as similarities at all. Instead, this list of subjects is a quick index of material which occurred in the gossip collected.

In this book I use a practical orthography for Tzotzil based on ordinary Spanish orthography. I hope that such an orthography will eventually find some use in promoting pan-Tzotzil literacy and solidarity. A description of Tzotzil phonemes is to be found in Colby (1963) and Laughlin (1975). I use the following special conventions:

ʔ   for glottal stop
j   for x (voiceless glottovelar fricative)
ch   for č (voiceless alveopalatal affricate)
x   for s (voiceless alveopalatal spirant)
tz   for ¢ (voiceless alveolar affricate)
'   to represent glottalized consonants (except for b), i.e., k', ch' (č'), p', t', and tz' (¢')

The letter *b* may be thought of (synchronously) as a glottalized *m*, hence as a voiced bilabial glottalized stop, sometimes implosive.

Glottalized consonants are strongly glottalized in word-initial position; intervocalically they are strongly glottalized, slightly preglottalized, and engender slight lengthening and nasalization of the preceding vowel. Elsewhere (before a consonant and at the end of a word) they are strongly pre-glottalized and engender lengthening and nasalization of the preceding vowel. Hence, one finds:

k'ok'   ʔ*abtel*
[k'õ:ʔk]   [ʔã:ʔmtel]
bot   *tzeb*
[b'ot]   [¢e:ʔm]
lobol
[lõ:(ʔ)b'ol]

In the following text, transcribed from a Who's Who gossip session, the participants discuss the loose and dangerous behavior of a certain old woman. During this session most of the men were reduced to tearful laughter and ribald guffaws.

M: Jlikel ismilbe ʔech'el noxtok ti yajnil P——.
"She quickly killed off P——'s wife, too."

R: Mi la icham xa ti yajnil P——?
"So is P——'s wife dead already?"

C: Icham la aʔa.
"Yes, I hear she's dead."

R: Kere.
"Boy!"

M: Mi la mu jaʔuk yok'al ti icham L——?
"Wasn't that at the same time L—— died?"

C: Mi muʔnuk koʔol iʔoch ta ch'en xchiʔuk li L—— cheʔe?
"Weren't she and L—— both buried at the same time?"

R: Muk' bu xkaʔi, jaʔo batemon ʔox ta ʔOlon ʔOsil taj k'al icham L——.
"I didn't hear about it; I was down in Low Country when L—— died."

C: Mi la mu teuk xa ikaʔi tal ta ʔOlon ʔOsil ʔuk ʔun?
"Well, didn't I too only hear about it coming from Low Country?"

J: K'usi tzpas? Mi chak' chamel?
"What does she do? Is she a witch?"

C: Yuʔun jaʔ taj snaʔ xchonvan ta balamil ʔune.
"She knows how to sell souls to the Earth Lord."

M: . . . Yuʔun la jaʔ stiʔojbe ʔech'el taj yajnil ta ʔalel ʔune. Yuʔun icham xa taj ʔune.

215

". . . She is the one who is supposed to have witched away the wife. She has died, after all.

Yuʔun jaʔ tzk'elbe ʔelav.

"She enjoyed the wife's demise.

Jaʔ ti muʔyuk xʔik'e chavaʔi stuk ʔune.

"For she herself wasn't married, you see.

Jaʔ noʔox iʔak'bat yol ʔune.

"She was just made pregnant."

C: Yuʔun jaʔ muk' xʔik'e.

"It was because she was never taken in marriage."

M: Yech noʔox iʔak'bat yol chavaʔi ʔune.

"She was just made pregnant with no recompense, you see.

Muk' bu iʔik'e ʔune.

"She was never married [by her lover].

Yech'o jaʔ nan koʔol ʔo iyaʔi ʔun.

"That's perhaps why she was so displeased."

C: Jaʔ skrem ti mol C—— ta Nabenchauk taj yajmul taj meʔel ʔune.

"It was old C——'s son, from Nabenchauk, who was that old woman's lover.

Solel kremkrem tajmek yaʔel li kreme.

"The boy was quite young indeed."

R: Krem toʔox, pero voʔne xa ʔun.

"He used to be young, but that was long ago."

C: Pero ʔali meʔel ʔune, yuʔun xa ʔox meʔel ʔun.

"But the old lady was already fairly old by then.

Muk'tik xa ʔonox skremotik yaʔel ʔun.

"Her sons were already grown by then."

J: Jiii.

"Oh."

C: Vaʔi ʔun, taj ʔali skrem taj mol C—— jaʔ krem toʔox

"So, that son of old C—— was just a boy then.

Isk'upin krem jkaxlan xkaltik taj meʔel K—— ʔune.

"And that old lady K—— desired a young ladino, as we say.

Iʔayan jun xch'amal ʔun.

"And one child was born [as a result].

Muk' xa xch'amal.

"That child is now grown.

Jutuk xa nan mu koʔoluk syijil xchiʔuk liʔ ʔune. . . .

"He's probably about the same age as this guy here. . . ."

M: ʔOy xa yajnil taj xch'amal K—— aʔa.

"Yes, old lady K——'s son has a wife of his own now."

C: Vaʔi ʔun, isaʔ yajnil liʔ ta Jobel ʔune.
"Anyway, the lover sought his own wife here in San Cristóbal."

J: A bweno.
"Ah, good."

C: Pero yuʔun leklek li ʔantz iyik' ʔech'el yaʔel ʔune.
"But she was a good woman, that he married and took away with him [to Nabenchauk]."

Jnaʔtik mi yech ti yuʔun jaʔ iyak'be chamel mi ixchon ta balamil k'u chaʔal taj meʔel K——— ʔune
"Who knows if it's true that she witched her or that she sold her soul—old lady K———, that is.

Pero xinulan, xinulan taj yajnil ʔune.
"But she was a ladina, the man's wife was a ladina."

R: Isaʔ yantz taj P——— yuʔun krem toʔox.
"So P——— got himself a mistress, in his youth.

Pero taj jmemeʔtik ʔune, meʔel ʔun.
"But the old lady was already old."

J: Jaʔ meʔel xa ʔun.
"Ah, so she was old already."

R: Ispas sba ta tz'itz'irin taj P——— ʔune ti voʔne ʔune.
"Yes, P——— acted like a young cock back then.

Lek la yij ʔinyeksyon yuʔun tajmek li P——— ʔune.
"And they say he had a good thick injection-giver.

Iyal to la ʔun.
"She even said so, later:

"Li porkirya leʔe ʔanimal noʔox yij sil ʔat ʔi ʔanimal nat.
" 'That disgusting thing—his damned penis is terribly thick and terribly long.

Pero meʔelon xa.
" 'But I'm already an old woman.

ʔEp xa koltak.
" 'I already have many children.

Pero batz'i xitaʔet xa.
" 'I'm completely worn out and exhausted.

Ikuch kuʔun tajmek.
" 'I have endured a good deal.

Batz'i lek stzininet iyak' tajmek," xi la ʔun.
" 'But he just gave it to me nice and snugly,' she said."

All: "Ha ha ha ha."

C: Ilaj to svok'an baketik xi la.
"It just smashed up one's bones, she said."

R: Pero ta yut chobtik la ta xak'beik ʔech'el tajmek.
"But they used to fuck away out in the cornfield.
Te ta tiʔtiʔ nabtik ʔun.
"Just at the edge of the lake."

M: Ta yut chobtik la aʔa.
"Yes, in the cornfields. . . .
"ʔA sk'el tz'iʔ la taj yil P——.
That stupid P—— would say he was going out to look for dogs."

R: Li mol P—— yuʔun ba sk'el xchob ta tiʔ nab.
"Old P—— supposedly went to watch his cornfield by the lake."

C: Yuʔun chlaj la ta tz'iʔ yajan.
"Because, he said, dogs were getting at his *elotes*."

M: Pero ta meʔ tz'iʔ chlaj ʔun.
"But they were *female* dogs doing the eating! (Ha ha ha.)"

R: Pero k'al ta xak'beik ʔune, jaʔ la yikoh li chobtik ʔune.
"But while they were fucking, they bumped against the corn.
Jaʔ yikoj ta xich' ʔinyeksyon ʔun.
"They grabbed the plants while getting injections.
Bweno, komo ʔoy jchanvunetik ʔune . . . K'alal chlok'ik ta rekreo li jchanvunetik ʔune, Jaʔo nan k'alal xchanoj vun li jchiʔiltik leʔ ʔune . . .
"Well, since there were schoolchildren nearby . . . when the students got out for recess . . . maybe our companion here was in school then. . . ."

M: Je juta, yuʔun me jaʔ sk'eloj iyak'beik ʔun taje . . .
"Hell, yes, he watched them fucking. . . .

C: ʔAn mi mu yechuk ti iyak'beik ʔuliʔ sbek' yate cheʔe . . .
"Say, isn't it true that they shot him in the balls with a slingshot? . . ."

R: Jiiiʔ, pero mala to ʔun . . .
"Yes, but wait a minute. . . .

All: "Ha ha ha ha ha."

R: Vaʔi ʔun, li jchanvunetik ʔune ta xbatik ʔun,
"So, listen, the school kids went out,
Ta saʔik mut,
"They would hunt birds.
Ta xlok'ik jlikel ta rekreo ʔune.
"They would go out for a while at recess,
Ta xbatik ta yut chobtik ʔun,
"They might go into the cornfields,
Jaʔ ti bu xvaʔetik ʔune . . .
"Wherever they happened to wander . . .

Jiii, k'alal iyilike,
"Oooh, when they saw them,

isk'elik ta jilail chobtik ʔun,
"when they looked down between the rows of corn,

te yolel ta xak' ʔinyeksyon li P——— ʔune.
"there was P——— in the midst of giving injections.

Slok'oj la li svex ʔune.
"He had taken off his trousers, I hear.

Xvinaj li sbek' yat ta spat ʔune,
"You could see his balls from behind,

ʔiyak'be la ʔech'el ʔun.
"as he fucked away."

C: "Kabron, pero k'u tzaʔ ti buy xjipjon sbek' yate, xiik la ʔun.
" 'The bastard, what is he up to there, swinging his balls
about,' said the kids."

All: "Ha ha ha ha ha."

D: Pero batz'i xmut'lij xa jnaʔ ʔun . . .
"But I'll bet he really jerked [when he felt the stone]. . . ."

C: ʔOra nan isbotz' lok'el ta ʔanil ʔun.
"He probably yanked it out in a hurry."

N: Muk' xa jal xixtalan li mol ʔuk ʔun.
"He didn't keep playing for long."

C: Jal la te chotol xiik ʔun.
"They say he just sat there for a while."

R: Pero mu la bu istabe li sbek' yate.
"But they didn't actually hit him in the balls."

Ta xchak la ik'ot.
"Instead they got him on the ass, I hear.

"ʔAy!" xi la li P———.
" 'Ouch!' said P———.

ʔAli meʔele, ʔanil la ivaʔi.
"The old lady stood up quickly.

"K'usi apas?" xi la.
" 'What happened to you?' she said.

"Mujnaʔ," xi la, yaʔuk xa la sk'el.
" 'I don't know,' he said, and started to look around."

C: Ibat xa ʔox li jʔak'-ʔuliʔ ʔune.
"But the slingshot-shooters had already left."

R: Li jchanvune, ibat la ta ʔanil ʔun.
"The schoolchildren had gone off in a hurry."

All: "Ha ha ha ha ha."

R: Li jchanvune, ʔiʔoch ·xa ʔox ta ʔiskwela,
"The students had already entered school again,

ta xchan xa vun.
"they were back hard at work.

Mu me jna? much'u ti jkobel yak'oj ?uli? ?une . . . .
"I just don't remember which kid shot the slingshot . . . .

Pero ka?yoj to ?ox, pero mu xa jna? much'u ?un.
"I heard once, but I can't think who it was."

N: Kuxul to nan li j?a?yele,
"But I presume this person is still alive?

mi ichone van ta balamil?
"Or was he perhaps sold to the Earth Lord?"

R: Mi?n ta sna? ?un. . .
"How could she know who it was?"

N: Mu nan bu ivinaj ?onox.
"Perhaps it was never discovered."

R: Pero ta tz'akal to ilo?ilajik li jchanvun ?une. . .
"No, later on the schoolchildren joked about it."

N: "Pentejo tajmek li kitz'ine," xi li mol Pru———— ?uk ?une.
" 'My younger brother is very stupid,' says old Pru————.

"Muk' ta sk'el ?osil kabron," xi ?un.
" 'He isn't circumspect, the bastard,' he says."

C: Pero muk' xa skrem ta P'ij ?uk li mol Pru———— ?uke."
"Yes, but old Pru———— himself has a grown illegitimate son
in P'ij."

N: Mol nan a?a.
"He does at that.

Pero yu?un muk' xlaj ta ?uli? nan sbek' yat nan cha?i ?uk
?une.
"But then he's never been shot in the balls with a slingshot,
or so he figures it.

Yu?un yich'oj kwenta ?un.
"He pays attention to what he's doing,

Yech'o pentejo li kitz'ine, xi li jkobel ?uk ?un.
"and that's why he calls his brother P———— stupid."

M: Pero ?o la xich' ?inyeksyon ta yan ?o ?un.
"But that old lady has also gotten injections from others."

R: Ja? taj yak'el k'al ta x?ilolaj a?a.
"Yes, she gets it when she is curing."

C: Ja? ka?yoj a?a.
"Yes, I've heard about that.

K'al tzut tal ta sna li jchamel ya?ele,
"When she returns home from the patient's house,

bu chbat ta ?ilole,
"where she has gone to perform a curing ceremony,

ta xich' ?inyeksyon ta be.
"she gets injections on the path."

R: Komo ta xyakub ?une.
"Because, you see, she gets drunk.

?Ali much'u ta xtal ?ak'vanuk ?une
"The person who accompanies her home

ta xak' komel ?inyeksyon noxtok ?un.
"leaves a few injections behind when he leaves."

N: Pero muk' bu xlaj ta ?uli? sbek' yat. . .
"But he doesn't get shot in the balls with a slingshot."

C: Komo ?ak'ubaltik chava?i ?une,
"Since it is nighttime, you see,

?O la ta be no?ox chak' ?inyeksyon,
"sometimes they give injections right on the path.

Mi mo?oje, ?o la ta batz'i yut xa sna.
"If not, sometimes they even do it right inside her house.

Chak'beik mas li poxe,
"They give her more liquor,

yo?o ta xlom ?o ta lum.
"so that she'll pass out and fall to the ground.

?Ora mi ilom ta lum ?une,
"As soon as she has fallen to the ground,

Lek xa chak'ik ?inyekseyon li jkobeletik ?une.
"then the fuckers give her a good injection."

All: "Ha ha ha ha ha."
N: Jkobel . . .
"Damn . . . !"

Notes

Chapter 1   A Plea for Gossip

1. Certain kinds of skills, categories, and objects that figure in "cultural codes" certainly never enter gossip at all. I do not suggest that we can know *nothing* interesting about a society if we cannot grasp its gossip. Various suggestions about what a "cultural grammar" ought to include are to be found in Kay 1966; Keesing 1970, 1971, 1974*a*.

2. Whorf (1956) suggests, perhaps tongue in cheek, that, at least in fire insurance claims, the words people use to describe a situation literally determine what the situation is. It is a commonplace of the sociological study of institutions that institutional descriptions of situations (e.g., "X is insane") are definitive; that is, they define the facts (and institutions ordinarily guarantee their definitions by applying sanctions).

3. Peter Wilson's (1974) convincing reinterpretation of the Makah case suggests that certain traditions and values *appeared* to Colson to persist in gossip, because the Makah used gossip against their neighbors but aimed precisely at the ethnographer as (a particular sort of) outsider. "Gossip among the Makah appears to have been used as a stratagem to confuse or divert an outsider whose enquiries are quite innocently aimed at an especially sensitive area, namely status and descent" (1974, p. 99).

4. Cox (1970) applies the term "information management" to gossip, following Goffman (1959). And, as we all know, managing information is no simple matter; rather, "the tactical use of these clues to convey an impression, to manage a situation, to boost a friend or to bring down a rival generates a quite formidable sophistication and com-

plexity" (Bailey 1971, p. 13). The linguistic clues Bailey has in mind include the subtleties of gossip and slander.

5.   Don Handelman (1971, 1973) argues persuasively that it is difficult to claim that individuals simply manage information through gossip, since success at passing information depends on features of the interaction which may well not be individually manageable. "It is quite misleading to state only that gossip does or does not occur within the social settings of a particular social order when the medium of information transmission is the encounter, and when forms of encounter differ in their capacity to sustain the successful passing of gossip" (1973, p. 212). Handelman gives a particularly telling example of the *control* of information in his dissertation (1971, p. 409): a woman manages to exclude another woman's interjections and amendments to one version of a story because she "appeared to have all the relevant, previously closed, information about the event she was describing"—even though the other woman was a principal protagonist in the story.

6.   See Haviland (1974*b*) for an account of such a recent political dispute involving a newly built road in the hamlet. In this case, gossip circulated about greed, fights between kinsmen, jealousy, and so forth; but little conversation hit on what seemed basic political forces at work in the dispute.

7.   See also Szwed 1966.

8.   Garfinkel's (1956) treatment of "degradation ceremonies" speaks of such manipulations (redefinition of events, transformations of "event" and "perpetrator" by locating them within particular "schemes of preferences") as *conditions* for the success of degradation ceremonies.

9.   During these conversations I myself was the interlocutor; my ineptness in that role may well have impoverished the resulting sessions. Cf. chapter 4.

10.   The Who's Who lists contained a revelation about naming. Collier and Bricker (1970) have demonstrated not only that the system of *nickname*s in Zinacantan is the most efficient of the naming codes (most likely to give each individual a unique, unambiguous label) that operate within a hamlet, but also that nickname groups correspond to significant lineage segments. Hence, as lineages fissure over time, nickname labels are institutionalized as ordinary surnames marking the resultant groups. The Who's Who sessions indicated that nicknames not only operate at the level of the hamlet but function as the only names in common use to describe individuals throughout the *municipio*. Occasionally an informant would announce what a man's "real name" was; the others would reply "But we don't understand that; we don't know who that is." The extent of *municipio*wide knowledge about nickname *groups* is not clear.

Chapter 2   The Ethnographic Context

1.   Vogt (1969) intends these units to have greater importance ritually and socially than I accord them here. He defines the *sna* as "the grouping

that is composed of one or more localized patrilineages" (p. 140). Ordinary Zinacanteco usage, however, does not necessarily entail genealogical relations of this kind. Moreover, patrilineages and identifiable lineage segments are not always localized, though there is a preference for patrilocal settlement after young men marry. Cf. G. Collier (1968), especially pp. 12–17.

2.   The situation is complicated by recent introductions: all-weather truck roads, electric light posts and lines, standpipe water, long-lasting house-building materials, and so forth. Waterhole ceremonies in Nabenchauk, where potable water is available from standpipes, have virtually ceased.

3.   For example, in the area of the hamlet of Vo? ch'oj vo? called *stzelej* or *mina carbon*, individuals associated with both the hamlets of Nachij and Paste? are to be found.

4.   In fact, neighborhood integrity can outweigh hamlet boundaries politically. In a recent government reorganization in which each hamlet was made an *agencia* with its own set of civil officials, the section of the hamlet Paste? known as Xul Vo? became a separate political entity in its own right. The people of the area had functioned before as a separate social unit, and according to report had "quarreled with their fellows," prompting a more definitive division.

5.   I shall have considerably less to say, throughout this book, about what Zinacanteco women know and say of their neighbors and acquaintances. My wife Leslie deserves the credit for enlightening me about women's gossip.

6.   In chapter 6 I consider the cargo system in some detail.

7.   The man was soon preempted by those same ladino authorities and given a job in the federal office that oversees such *ejido* colonies. The move effectively defused the man's personal power in his own communities and confused his allegiances.

8.   See Haviland (1974*b*) for an account of such a dispute and a characterization of the hamlet leaders involved.

Chapter 3   The Domain of Gossip

1.   As Handelman (1973) points out, all that is really necessary in most societies for gossip to occur is that the protagonist (victim) be established as a nonperson for purposes of the interaction. This rule explains the so-called third person invisible. ("Look at him sitting there. He doesn't touch his soup that I slaved all day to make for him.")

2.   Paine (1970) proposes a useful set of critical definitions for distinguishing such concepts ("gossip," "scandal," "rumour," etc.). And see F. G. Bailey 1971, pp. 284ff. Several of my colleagues have complained about what they consider to be my overly broad definition of gossip, suggesting that gossip, unlike ordinary news reporting, accounts of past events, speculation about future events, and so forth—all of which may well fall within the broad range of phenomena I consider—has certain distinctive properties. For some, what is crucial about gossip is the evaluative component it

manifests, allowing participants to manipulate "values" and opinions among their interlocutors. Other critics have suggested that what is distinctive about gossip is the nature of its subject matter, said to consist of news about the absent third party that is somehow damaging to him or her, or which was meant to be confidential. Consider an innocent conversation that begins by telling the news about absent X but which soon turns to more delicate topics, prompting remarks like: "We shouldn't be talking like this." Or: "*Now* we're *gossip*ing!" I examine such definitional questions with respect to Tzotzil usage in somewhat more detail in Appendix 1.

Precision with these words, and careful definition, are presumably necessary for some tasks, but not particularly so for the purposes of my present argument. Moreover, it may in fact be true that gossip, in any restricted sense, is not a universal feature of human intercourse (or even a desirable one), whereas broader sorts of conversation *are* ubiquitous and hence constant sources for ethnographic investigation.

3.   Roger Abrahams (1970) argues that an important way to approach gossip is "to understand gossip in the context of the range of speech acts of a community" (1970, p. 290). That is, of a wide range of communicatory behavior, gossip or something like it may have its own rules, may be a special sort of verbal performance, which can be delimited either explicitly as a native category or—as in this chapter—by reference to implicit native theorizing.

4.   Bricker (1968, pp. 108–10) presents some of the derivational material I am concerned with, though she provides only English glosses for most words. I am indebted to Dr. Bricker for the insight that Tzotzil derivational morphology can shed conisderable light on the inner workings of the Zinacanteco mind.

5.   Note that the particle *la* represents "quotative evidence" (Jakobson 1957, p. 4); that is, it qualifies a sentence to the effect that the speaker cannot vouch for its truth: it is hearsay.

Note further the possibility that *loʔil* and *loʔlo* ("deceive, trick") are etymologically related; Laughlin (1975, p. 215) lists the two stems under a common root. Perhaps the language suggests that talk is potentially deceitful; that gossip may trick the listener.

6.   Several of my colleagues have suggested to me that it is a criterion of gossip that it should always recount stories which cast its protagonists in an unfavorable light—that otherwise we should be disinclined to call it gossip. Such an observation may well lead to profitable lines of inquiry (and see Allport and Postman's well-known *Psychology of Rumour,* 1947) about why gossips engage in such activity. These issues are tangential here, however. Cf. Haviland (1975).

7.   Tzotzil, like other Mayan languages, employs couplets in ritual speech: prayer, formal petitioning, scolding, etc. Texts are composed of pairs of lines identical except for the last elements, which are often nearly synonyms —metaphorically, if not literally. With respect to Zinacanteco song, such

couplets are enumerated in Haviland (1967). Gossen (1970) reports similar phenomena throughout ritual speech in Chamula.

8.   That is, the root *k'op* occurs frequently in conversation with verbs which may be glossed as indicated.

9.   Note here that *k'op* is counted with the numeral classifier -*p'el*, used for a word, a shout, the crow of a rooster, etc.

10.   This usage contrasts with a more artificial sense for the phrase *lekil k'op*, which appears in various formally elicited taxonomies. See Appendix 1.

11.   I am indebted to Robert M. Laughlin for this example. Consider also the usage *muk' sk'oplal* ("there is no plan about it"), meaning "that has not been arranged" or "it doesn't matter."

12.   This I take to be a conversational *rule*. That is, while we *can* in principle talk about anything we wish, no matter how normal or unmarked (or dull) it may be, we are ordinarily constrained from doing so by the conversational presumption that by mentioning something we are pointing out something *worth* mentioning. Cavell's remarks about "voluntary" (1958) suggest to me a similar moral, as do Grice's well-known ideas about conversational postulates.

13.   Garfinkel (1956) notes that for a degradation ceremony to succeed, the events which are denounced "must be removed from the realm of their everyday character and be made to stand as 'out of the ordinary' " (p. 422). A similar condition holds on *successful* gossip (Handelman 1973).

14.   Bricker (1973*b*, pp. 191ff.) gives a rather different treatment of the word -*laban*. I provide more details in Appendix 1.

15.   It has been suggested to me that if I want to claim that there are "rules" which govern so-called gossiplike behavior then there must be rules which enable Zinacantecos, in turn, to decide whether particular talk *is* gossip. How, asks this critic, can there be rules for gossiping if we don't know what gossiping is? The criticism conceals a mistaken notion of how rules govern behavior at all—there is a certain sense in which a rule applies to a given situation only by virtue of the fact that we decide to apply it (see chapter 8). But surely the claim that only a well-defined activity can have its own rules is mistaken. There are rules of conversation ("We don't tell lies to our friends. We tell the whole truth") which don't govern all conversations; there are rules of gossip ("We don't tell stories about people to their faces") which conflict with other precepts ("You shouldn't talk about someone behind his back"), and none of which depend on deciding first whether a given situation is or is not gossip or "conversation with a friend," etc. Similarly, rules of etiquette as much define a situation as are brought into play by one.

16.   Few people are literate. Radios are little more than articles for prestige: Zinacantecos fluent in Spanish listen mostly to the radio announcements of the correct time, by which they can set their wristwatches. Tzotzil

announcements, mostly of the public-service variety, are very recent innovations.

17.   I am indebted to David Maybury-Lewis for this phrase. Such stories can be unlikely to both native and ethnographer, though perhaps for different reasons. There is, of course, a brierpatch of unresolved questions here into which I am unwilling to be thrown. Cf. Needham (1972), Hahn (1973).

Chapter 4   The Structure of
                              Zinacanteco Gossip

1.   These participants are not named in Tzotzil, nor is there a name for what the interlocutor does. He does not simply *tak'* ("respond") or *tak'av* ("answer"). It is interesting to note the similarities between the situation in Zinacantan and that in the Saramaka village of Kadjoe, Brownsweg, Surinam, where I worked in the summer of 1968. There the positions of storyteller and listener are formal and invariant; in fact, once the headman of the village, wanting to make a formal speech to me, had to go out and find a "listener" before he could talk at all—since I myself was unable to "listen" with the appropriate responses. Recent sociolinguistic work describes similar situations closer to home (Schegloff 1968; Labov 1972).

2.   See Gossen (1970, pp. 195–96) for examples of such fillers in Chamula narrative.

3.   Tzotzil syntax allows noun phrases, which are indexed on the verb, to be dropped. In the face of the obvious potential confusion, transitive sentences with human subject and object must often be disambiguated to mark one person as actor, the other as patient. Tzotzil syntax provides a passive to query object, and an antipassive to query subject. See Haviland (1976) for details.

4.   Zinacantecos employ the same device for snubbing someone as we do: they do not answer when he talks, and he soon stutters to a halt.

5.   Robert M. Laughlin has remarked to me that a similarly outstanding feature of dreams in Zinacantan is that they are filled with dialogue. Characters in dreams always talk to one another.

6.   I do not pretend here to offer a generalizable sociolinguistic scheme or even a complete presentation of the relevant variables of the particular speech interaction represented in a gossip session. An applicable and exhaustive set of variables can be found in various familiar formulations of Dell Hymes—for example, his paper in Gumperz and Hymes 1972.

F. G. Bailey sketches a somewhat different but useful schematization of gossip or scandalous interaction (1971, pp. 284–86) with special attention to the selection of "code" for transmitting a message, including overt marks which show "the degree to which S commits himself to a moral interpretation of the news he is giving" (p. 286)—for example, when a man begins a disclosure with the words, "I tell you this in the strictest confidence . . ." (one of Bailey's examples), or "I shouldn't be telling you this, but . . ."

7.   Popper writes: "Because all our dispositions are in some sense adjustments to invariant or slowly changing environmental conditions, they can be described as *theory-impregnated*, assuming a sufficiently wide sense of the term theory. What I have in mind is, that there is no observation which is not related to a set of typical situations—regularities—between which it tries to find a decision" (1972, p. 72). (See also Ryle's related usage [1949, pp. 280ff.].) Of course, the ethnographer carries with him his own theory (of the world, of action, of everyday life) which informs his observations; and this theory may be perfectly good, even if unlike the native's. But it may also happen that the ethnographer will observe behavior which fits *in no* way into the sets of regularities he is prepared to choose between— for which, for example, he has no label or description (e.g., "X is talking with the ancestors," etc.). Thus, while a sensitive behavioral scientist may see a good deal more in behavior than the natives do, the reverse is also commonly true.

These I take to be anthropological commonplaces, though many behavioral scientists seem to accord some special status to observations impregnated with current "scientific theory." There may indeed be some special status to such observations (which Marvin Harris misleadingly calls "etic"), but they leave out a significant portion of what is going on: what the natives observe.

8.   I use such a word despite the critique of Needham (1972). With special reference to an application of Quine's work to anthropological investigations of belief see Hahn (1973).

9.   There is an underlying color imagery here, since some people with similar palm designs do not suffer the repeated loss of their spouses. They are said to exhibit *yaxal tzek* ("a green [blue] scorpion"). Compare the expressions *yaxal ?ora* ("good [lit., green] luck, long life") vs. *tzajal ?ora* ("bad [lit., red] luck, short destiny").

10.   There is a parallel point to be made. There is no reason to suppose that, say, accounts of events accurately reflect even native theories of events (if this is a sensible notion). In a seminar dealing with Tahitian theories of disease, Tony Hooper brought out the point nicely: Does it follow from the fact that gossip about accidents (and the resulting injuries) often draws morals like "Well, he deserved to fall off his bicycle [and sprain his arm], because yesterday he beat his child" that, on the native theory, all accidents have *causes* (of the sort shown)? It seems, on the contrary, that naturally occurring accounts of events include moralizing, evaluation, rationalization, and so forth—and that all these cannot be taken to constitute (native) explanations of events (native theory of causes).

11.   Thus, the commonplace of our own native theory of gossip: that it tells us a good deal more about the person gossiping than about the person gossiped about.

12.   These are partly definitional matters. Gossip may employ the "third-person invisible," as I remarked in chapter 3, to treat the object of gossip *as if he or she were absent.* And a narrator may explicitly intend his gossip to be passed on from interlocutor to a wider audience. Gossiping therefore has affinities to, among other things, open mocking or denunciation and to *spreading* gossip or rumour or news. Very little hangs on the exact choice of words in this particular case: narrators and interlocutors (audiences) clearly size each other up carefully in all these activities.

13.   Consider the parallel with what Jane Collier calls "rational settlement" of a legal dispute: "A legal procedure can only produce a rational solution when an attempt is made to resolve the conflict in terms of norms and procedures regarded as valid by both parties" (1970, p. 21). Gossip *rationalizes* the past behavior of others in the sense that it tends to produce agreement between parties to the gossip about the applicable norms and standards and the appropriate judgments involved. But see chapter 8.

14.   Cf. Peter Wilson: "When a person gossips to another he takes someone's good name (a reputation has many facets, each of which can provide plenty to talk about) and he distorts it—not necessarily willfully and often only out of the bias implicit in any selection of information from a repertoire. At the same time the gossip's good name is, hopefully enhanced unless the listener can recognize the distortions. When similar stratagems utilising the same subjects are adopted by many persons towards one person, or group of persons, then the group may be said to gossip and the totality of information purveyed to the listener is riddled with contradictions, ambiguities and confusion" (1974, p. 100).

Chapter 5   The Content of Zinacanteco
                                 Gossip

1.   Bricker (1968) suggests that much humor in Zinacantan is based on violations of a cluster of norms having to do with "Self-Image"—clothing, appearance, demeanor. People are certainly *identified* by their physical abnormalities, visible or invisible. Cf. Bricker (1973a, pp. 147ff.)

2.   Cancian (1965, pp. 183–84) points out that having waiting lists for cargo positions allows a man to sign up for a cargo far in the future, thus fulfilling the social demand to expend wealth on religious service but avoiding the cargo itself through a convenient calendrical game.

3.   I am extremely indebted to George A. Collier and the Stanford Anthropology Department for making available their resources at the Stanford Computer Center, where I began indexing this material.

   In compiling an index to the corpus of gossip I abandoned a formal content analysis in favor of a more flexible coding and retrieval system. Bricker (1968) used the *General Inquirer* to index the Tzotzil humor texts she had gathered according to various ethnographic categories. For example, the cluster she calls the "Self-Image Complex" (1968, p. 54) includes such categories as Clothing, Filth, Awkwardness, Caught, Losing, Violence, and Drunkenness. Her dictionary (according to which the computer scans text) might, for example, have assigned Tzotzil roots meaning "drunk" and "tipsy" to the category of Drunkenness. Unfortunately, Bricker's dictionary, though doubtless adequate for her purposes, was too restrictive for the range of material in the corpus of gossip. To create a suitable dictionary which included all appropriate categories would have been to survey the range of subjects in the whole corpus—in short, to complete the content analysis. In any case, I was unwilling to convert the voluminous texts and conversations I had recorded into a form suitable for the computer's maw.

Since the gossip I recorded was natural conversation, I was able to code not only subject matter (e.g., all gossip having to do with divorce, or with drunken behavior) but also certain other metalinguistic variables. I marked exchanges as joking speech, as insult, as bragging, as mocking, and so on. Similarly I used certain frankly imposed categories to index statements of beliefs, statements about personality and temperament, accounts of super-natural events, and others; such categories facilitated later retrieval of stories. I let my impressions themselves create a coding system with the help of a simple computerized routine. As I read and reread the gossip and divided it into discrete items, I associated with each story a set of ethno-graphic categories (topics) and metalinguistics properties (e.g., "lewd joking"); I also entered occurrences of certain Tzotzil expressions for later retrieval (see chap. 7). By continually reexamining and collapsing the categories which resulted from this haphazard process I arrived finally at the subject-matter category list which appears in Appendix 3.

I cannot claim that the resulting categories resemble native behavioral domains (though nothing serious depends on such similarity; the index of stories is merely a convenient device for retrieval and exposition). I put cases of wife-beating with other cases of wife-beating, instances of divorce with other instances of divorce, and so on. Stories in which similar things happen are grouped together under a heading which represents that sort of happening. But two instances of what I called aggressive female behavior (e.g., a woman who seeks a lover and a girl who actively solicits a fiancé) may not strike a Zinacanteco as at all the same sort of thing.

4. I am only half serious about "counting" discrete gossip stories at all. First, a single story can figure in more than one category; for example, a story in which a woman divorces her habitually drunken husband might be listed under the categories both of "drunkenness' and "divorce." Moreover, the unevenness of the corpus complicates coding. Some conversations I alone had with a single Zinacanteco cannot be compared with full trans-criptions of Who's Who gossip sessions; and two-minute stories are hardly comparable to two-hour accounts of complicated events, though my index counts each as a single unit. Fortunately, very little rests on the numbers here, as the frequencies of various topics do give a relative idea of Zina-canteco gossips' preoccupations.

5. This will not be a fair test since my work in the field benefited from the previous ethnographic work of Jane Collier on law and of Victoria Bricker on humor. I freely acknowledge that in creating the category system by which I "counted" gossip themes I drew heavily on organizational principles these other researchers developed for their own work. Since I base comparison between, for example, the things people gossip about and the things they joke about on individual stories, however, the interdependence of sorting categories is only tangentially a problem.

6. Neither Collier nor I, so far as I can tell, tried to organize cases or gossip stories on the basis of some native Zinacanteco classificatory scheme. Hence, while I have a "drunkenness" category, for example, Collier associates "drunken insults" with aggression and "drunken destructiveness" with neighbor disputes—on the basis of the rules called up to justify settlements of the corresponding disputes. It would be possible, though tedious, for an informant to sort gossip stories or law cases by "similarity" and thus to exhibit whatever native classificatory dimensions there may be for organizing such things. I cannot claim to have made such an experiment. Note that J. Collier (1973) employs a slightly different set of categories.

Chapter 6   Gossip and the Cargo
                                                System

1. Cancian chose to work in Spanish (though Francesca Cancian, his wife and fellow fieldworker in Zinacantan, concurrently became competent in Tzotzil), and he did not find this a handicap (see Cancian 1965, p. 198). Moreover, he worked from formal interviews designed to sample cargo histories and to measure economic status from a variety of informants. My work, by contrast, was conducted in Tzotzil, and with the exception of the Who's Who material described in previous chapters is wholly based on interaction that was as informal as possible, given my presence. (For some doubts about whether one can dismiss the ethnographer's presence as irrelevant, see Peter Wilson's paper (1974), "Filcher of Good Names".) I made no systematic attempt, for example, to verify people's cargo records other than recording what people said. Cancian, on the other hand, tried to get somewhat beyond the hearsay on which I relied.

2. In fact, the nature of these positions has changed drastically from their beginnings as *cofradias* introduced at various stages after the Conquest by Dominican missionaries, through various transformations wrought by Mexican civil law and internal pressures. The current historical work of Robert Wasserstrom will doubtless provide the details.

3. The numeral classifier (Berlin 1968) used to count grades in a cargo career is *koj* ("level"), also used to count, among other things, rungs on a ladder, layers on a mountain range, and songs from the fixed cycle of ritual music. Verbal forms of the same root mean "to sit astride," "to be on top of," "to get to the top of [a peak, a mountain, a difficult trail]," "to pile on top of," and so on. To trace a man's progress through the

hierarchy by counting the *koj* in his service is thus reminiscent of the English idiom of success "getting to the top."

4. Tzotzil provides some fairly subtle distinctions here. Regular verbal forms on the same root ʔ*abt-* never seem to apply to cargo work but rather refer to ordinary labor for gain. Cargo work is expressed verbally through compound expressions based on the noun ʔ*abtel* ("[cargo] work"). Thus, to pass a cargo is to -*pas-*ʔ*abtel* (lit., "do work") or to -ʔ*ech' ta* ʔ*abtel* (lit., "pass through work"); a cargoholder is *j-pas-*ʔ*abtel* ("work-doer"), whereas *j*ʔ*abtel* is, instead, "laborer." Hence:

> Mi snaʔ xʔabtej?
> "Does he know how to work [or is he lazy]?"
>
> Mi snaʔ {spas-ʔabtel?
> {xʔech' ta ʔabtel?
> "Does he know how to do cargos [or does he lack the interest]?"

5. Not all cargos called ʔ*alperes X* (where *X* is a saint-name) belong to the second level of the hierarchy, the level labeled ʔ*alperesal*. Not every cargo that counts at the ʔ*alkalteal* level is called ʔ*alkalte*. The terminology, and Zinacanteco usage, invites a confusion which ethnographers of the cargo system have not entirely avoided. There are fourteen cargos called ʔ*alperes*; the men serving these positions from a natural group who perform ritual together. Similarly, the four cargos called *rejirol* and the two ʔ*alkaltes* (a senior or "large" ʔ*alkalte* and his junior [or "small"] counterpart) function together in both ritual and administrative capacities as the *moletik* ("elders"). But two of the ʔ*alperes*-named cargos now belong to higher levels of the hierarchy. (It seems likely that at some past time the situation was more regular—with all ʔ*alperes* positions being second-level cargos. Cancian attributes the alleged change to "supply and demand" (1965, p. 29), that is, to the need for more cargo positions at the third and fourth levels). ʔ*Alperes kajvaltik ryox* is a third-level cargo which, according to my informants and pace Cancian, cannot be served as a second-level cargo. Thus, despite its name, and despite the fact that its holder performs together with other ʔ*alperesetik*, the cargo counts as *rejirol*. Similarly, ʔ*alperes santorominko* is a common alternate final (fourth) cargo, more or less equivalent in prestige to *muk'ta* ʔ*alkalte* as a way of ending one's career.

No single label will encompass all the possible first cargos, which may be arranged into several natural groups. At the most expensive and prestigious end of the scale there are the *martomoreys*, who perform ritual jointly with the *mexon*s in the Hermitage of Señor Esquipulas. There is also a group of *martomo* cargos, arranged in senior/junior pairs and each attached to a particular saint name. There are the lowly *mayol*s, whose tasks are little more than those of an errand boy for the civil officials and higher cargoholders. Finally there are various short-term cargos with performance limited only to particular fiestas (e.g., *kapitan*, or *paxyon*), as well as a growing number of cargos serving local hamlet-level churches. There are many ways to begin a cargo career, though further progress is more restricted. Zinacantecos refer generically to this first level of cargo service by asking about a person's *sba-ʔabtel* ("first work").

Cancian claims that *ʔalperes santorominko* can be a second-, third-, or fourth-level cargo. I have no case in the entire Who's Who of a man passing this cargo as a second-level position. Informants admitted the formal possibility that someone might request this cargo at the second level in extraordinary circumstances; this possibility, however, immediately prompted another far-fetched suggestion: that a man with great ambition, considerable wealth, and a very long life might pass *ʔalperes santorominko* as a fourth cargo, and then go on to the unprecedented move of doing *muk-ta ʔalkalte* as *fifth* cargo! Such a career has never, to my knowledge, occurred; indeed, it would never have occurred in the old days when people strove to avoid cargos and their expenses and were drafted into service by the elders. Judging by reported careers, the rule seems to be for *santorominko* to come as third, more often fourth, cargo, and for *kajvaltik royx* to occur only at the third level. At least one man reportedly did *ʔalperes santorominko* twice, as both his third and fourth cargos.

6.   Ordinarily the cargo of *mexon* is a first-level cargo involved in ritual, together with the *martomorey*, in the Hermitage of Señor Esquipulas.

7.   Cancian (1965, p. 162) suggests that in the past the position of *mayol* did not belong to the cargo hierarchy at all. It is, even now, a virtual dead end in the system, formally the beginning to a career but pragmatically a damper on future ambitions.

8.   Cancian notes these two cases as exceptions in the order of progression; one he calls only an apparent exception, the other a "true exception" to the rules as Zinacantecos conceive them:

> The Alcalde Shuves is always a terminal cargo. That is, a man who has passed it is considered to have completed his service and is not eligible for further cargos. It is a minor post and carries little prestige. The typical incumbent is a very old man who passed a minor first level cargo in his youth and then avoided further service in the hierarchy: too old and too poor to consider normal progression through the system, he is given this cargo and allowed, in effect, to slip away from the course of a normal career. . . .
>
> The only true exception in the system is often made with respect to the junior of the two fourth level Alcaldes Viejos [i.e., the *bik'it ʔalkalte*]. This position is sometimes served by a man who has passed only two cargos previously. It is my idea that most men who have had the resources and endurance to pass three cargos will not settle for the junior post on the fourth level. Thus the cargo has few takers. [Cancian 1965, pp. 31–32]

Cancian claims that only the latter case is "seen as [an] exception by Zinacantecos," though he does not describe how Zinacantecos distinguish between the two cases.

9.   *Atole* is a corn drink which the *alferez* presents to the public when he enters his cargo. The *bik-it* ʔ*alkalte* does not give this drink.

10.   An alternate Tzotzil name for the cargo, *bik'it mol*, is itself almost an ironic joke: *bik'it* = "little," *mol* = "elder"; hence, the whole expression suggests: "an elder, but just a little one."

11.   An example is the current (1975) senior musician in Zinacantan, who last cargo was first-*rejirol* (in 1966)—a high-ranking third-level cargo —but who plans not to do another cargo. Of him people say *lek xa tunem*—"He has already served well."

12.   Cancian (1965, pp. 111–14) provides statistical evidence that men who pass early cargos of high prestige are also those who go on to distinguished, ultimately complete cargo careers. Summarizing the argument, he writes: "I have shown how men who reach the top level of the system usually begin with the relatively high prestige lower level positions. . . . This pattern is not based on any explicit Zinacanteco ritual practice or rule; rather, it is a behavioral tendency that reflects stratification in the community" (1974, p. 166). The pattern in the late 1960s, however, seemed somewhat different. Cancian's 1967 data "show that mobile individuals have held onto the traditional pattern, while nonmobile people have compromised to avoid the delays and frustrations brought by population growth, economic prosperity, and the consequent over-demand for expensive, prestigious cargos" (1974, p. 171). Such people have accomplished this by taking "a lower ranking second level cargo that is available immediately and that speeds them on their way to higher level service and the ultimate in . . . prestige" (1974, p. 171).

13.   The *sakramentu* is the most senior *mayordomo*, literally the chief of the twelve *mayordomos*, whose duty is to make sure the others perform their duties.

14.   One learns, however, only a limited amount about a person from his performance of cargo ritual. Cancian (1965, p. 34) points out that in ritual (and, in fact, in almost all circumstances during a cargo year, and for periods beforehand) people "use the name of the cargo, not the name of the person," and hence may not even know the full names of people with whom they have served for a year.

15.   During the Christmas season, the *martomoetik* take turns dressing in special costumes to play with another man dressed as a bull (Cf. Vogt 1969, pp. 522–36). This is one of the highlights of a *martomo*'s year in office.

16.   Ritual advisers and senior cargoholders second-level and above (as well as grooms at weddings) wear special costumes that include a red *pok'* which is tied turbanlike around the head.

17.   Conversation about cargo choice and career planning clearly shows that strategic choices are subject to complex reasoning, not simply obvious from the premise that Zinacantecos will seek to maximize their prestige

from cargo performance, given certain economic constraints. A *compadre* of mine was scheduled to be *muk'ta ʔalkalte*, the most senior-ranking cargoholder, for a given year. He decided to switch, to pass instead the cargo Alferez Santo Domingo as a fourth cargo. Cancian reports that both cargos can be equally described as "very prestigious" (p. 92) and ought therefore to be equally desirable, other things being equal. (He goes on to claim that "Junior Alcalde Viejo"—the *bik'it mol* I have argued above to be a booby prize at the end of an undistinguished cargo career—"is simply prestigious" [p. 92]—a claim I suggest cannot be substantiated). In fact, the cost differential is great; during the year in question, the *muk'ta ʔalkalte* cargo was anticipated to involve expenditures of roughly 4,000 pesos; the *ʔalperes santorominko* cargo, on the other hand, was certain to cost at least 12,000 pesos, largely because of the increase in the price of beef. My *compadre* justified what seemed an economically unwise change in cargo plans by the following argument: "If I were *muk'ta ʔalkalte* I would have to spend the entire year in Zinacantan Center, with official duties every week. Being *ʔalperes* may cost more, but I am only busy then during fourteen fiestas during the year. I can have time to do my own corn farming. If I do not farm, who will take care of my fields?" This man had only very young sons who could not take full responsibility for the farming operation without their father's help. Thus he preferred to spend three times the money on a slightly lower-ranking fourth cargo in order to leave himself time free from cargo duties to oversee his farming operation in the lowlands.

18.   The position involved, *martomorey*, ranks first on Cancian's Prestige Scale for first-level cargos (Cancian 1965, p. 87, table 10).

19.   It is sometimes permitted to pour shots of liquor given in ritual events into one's own personal storage bottle (carried expressly for this purpose) rather than to drink it on the spot. Such liquor can be taken home. Some especially active ritualists collect large amounts of liquor, albeit mixed from various sources, in this way. But the quality of poured-off liquor is understandably suspect.

20.   People requesting cargos give bottles of liquor to the elders, whose scribes then check the waiting lists to determine when cargo positions are free. Accepting a petitioner's bottle signifies accepting his request.

21.   *Jch'ul-meʔtik* is listed by Cancian as the Mayordomo Virgen del Rosario, the second most prestigious first-level cargo.

Chapter 7   Gossip Words

1.   This is not to suggest that such words are unintelligible or that their use is indeterminate, but only that it is singularly unilluminating to equate their meanings with *referents* (entities to which they refer). However, a good deal of work has been done to show how various concepts which have to do with "mind" in our ordinary discourse have behavioral criteria

of correct use (see especially Ryle 1947). Whether an adequate account of the meanings of such words can be given in behavioral terms is a somewhat different, more troublesome question.

2. This is admittedly a shadowy notion. What makes usage interesting? What divides literal expressions from idioms? Are exotic usages idiomatic, or are they literal uses of exotic words? These are philosophical dilemmas that would take me far afield. How does one state precisely the fascination of learning a new language? One says: What an odd/charming/obvious way to talk!

3. Christopher Boehm has suggested to me in conversation that all people have natural schemata for definition; that is, that in all languages people regularly define words—if only to instruct others in the language. Whether or not this is true, it seems unlikely that—except for philosophers—people ever offer definitions for common words (as, for example, those used in ordinary evaluation). Or, more exactly, one has occasion to define a word ("give a definition") only in quite particular circumstances; it is not, perhaps, the most common (or even most efficient) way to teach someone how to use a word. All of these techniques must be distinguished from offering a gloss (a translation?) for a word. Cf. Weinreich 1962, p. 42.

4. Laughlin (1975, p. 23) provides a classification of roots on operational grounds according to their behavior with certain desinences. Laughlin has remarked to me in conversation that many roots seem to fall into more than one "root class" or are defective in that they show some but not all of the expected forms. My procedures in compiling the groups of expressions in this chapter have been somewhat informal, and I employ slightly different categories from those Laughlin uses (see Haviland 1976). Note, of course, that not all surface adjectives, say, in Tzotzil derive from adjectival roots. The class of so-called positional roots is especially pro-ductive of surface adjectives which may apply to human beings. For example, the adjective *vaxal* comes from a "positional root" meaning "calm, quiet, tame, unmoving"; when applied to humans it ordinarily means "good natured" or simply "good" (i.e., not unruly, troublesome, or wicked).

For the interested reader, I provide some examples of the varying surface words derived from a single root. The italicized words in the following sentences are all associated with the single underlying noun root *k'op* ("word," etc.):

1. Ip'ajik ʔo ta nop-*k'op*.
   "Thus they became involved in *telling lies*."
2. Kechel ʔo *sk'oplal*.
   "The *affair in which he is involved* is still unresolved."
3. Baz'i toj xilim *chk'opoj*.
   "The way he *talks* is completely wild."
4. Saʔoj *yajk'opojel* pero isjoyp'in sba.
   "He found a *lawyer*, but he changed sides."

5. Li mole mu sk'an *k'oponel*.
"The old man doesn't want *to be talked to*."

6. Yu²van xaval ti ²o jset' xchikin *xak'opon*.
"Don't try to tell me that he will listen to you at all if you try *to talk to* him."

7. Lek ²amiko *jk'opon jba* jchi²uk.
"I *talk to him* [treat him] as a friend."

5. The Tzotzil expressions relevant here are

Lek xchi²in sbaik.
"They accompany each other well."
Lek snup sbaik.
"They meet well; they fit together."

Batz'i ko²ol xk'ot.
"They come to the same thing;
they translate the same."

For expressions which do not fit together:

Ch'abal snup.
"It has nothing to match with it, no mate."
Jtos ²o tajmek.
"This is quite different."

Presumably semantic judgments of some kind underlie such pronouncements. The man who performed this sorting task for me, Chep K'obyox of ²Apas, arranged cards into piles, offering as explanation for his choices some phrase like those I have listed. As will be clear below, he solidified the relationships between words sorted together by means of often elaborate stories or examples of usage, a satisfyingly Austinian way of proceeding.

6. Although Laughlin has glosses for all these expressions, in many cases gossip usage seems to require a wider or somewhat different reading.

7. There are many kinds of eliciting tasks that could add further structure to this set of words which I never attempted in the field. For example, I could have asked informants to arrange words according to more complicated semantic relations (into antonymic pairs, for example); instead, the clusters of words represent *likely* coincidences of characteristics in single people or types of people.

8. Note that, although in the diagram several areas are indicated in which no adjectival words occur (e.g., there is no word meaning "law-abiding," no adjective meaning "wealthy"), these gaps are often filled by nominal constructions (*jk'ulej* ["wealthy man"]) or by verbal constructions (*xch'un mantal* ["obeys orders"]). How to bring these syntactically unlike units together into a semantically coherent domain is an operational problem with no obvious solution. One could easily ask informants to sort whole phrases (rather than single words, whether they be adjectives, nouns, verbs, etc.).

Note further that the gaps in the diagram indicate that gossip commonly talks only about a few evaluable properties of its subjects. The paradigm is not defective: the language can describe much about people that is hardly worth saying.

9.   E. Z. Vogt (personal communication) suggests that *batz'i,* when used to modify nouns, points to the most culturally salient or oldest referents of a noun. Hence *batz'i k'op* ("real talk") refers to the Tzotzil language; *batz'i vob* ("real music") refers to traditional as opposed to ladino music (and to the corresponding instruments); and, e.g., *batz'i moral* ("real shoulder bag") refers to an old type of woven bag which has been replaced in recent times by leather shoulder bags.

10.   And, of course, very few indeed are the languages which do not employ body-part metaphor to some degree. Australian languages, including the Guugu-Yimidhirr language of Cape York (Haviland 1972), have particularly rich sets of idioms based on body parts.

Andrea Cousins has done extensive work on similar phenomena in Belizian Carib. In a forthcoming publication I shall explore some of this extremely powerful metaphor based on a universal human source—the body.

Chapter 8	Rules in Gossip

1.   I benefited from criticisms of an earlier version of this discussion by David Maybury-Lewis. I expect that he would disagree with a good deal of what remains here.

2.   See especially the enlightening discussion by Peter Winch (1958), to which I refer below. H. L. A. Hart's well-known *Concept of Law* (1961) suggests that a great many difficulties in defining a legal system can be elucidated by attention to the notion of rule. Landesman (1965, 1972) points out some difficulties with Winch's use of the notion "rule" while acknowledging the central importance to accounts of action and institutions of the (problematic) idea of "rule-regulated behavior."

3.   Cf. Wittgenstein, *Philosophical Investigations* (1953):
Sec. 224. The word "agreement" and the word "rule" are *related* to one another, they are cousins. If I teach anyone the use of the one word, he learns the use of the other with it.
Sec. 225. The use of the word "rule" and the use of the word "same" are interwoven.

4.   Wittgenstein (1953, sec. 291): "What we call *descriptions* are instruments for particular uses."

5.   The difficulty in claiming, as Winch (1958) seems to do, that all human behavior (or all meaningful behavior) depends on rules, somehow understood, is that here the notion of a "rule" is asked to bear too much weight. It may be argued that social institutions (and the actions which occur within the framework of such institutions) are underlain in some essential way by rules; but only an elucidation of different sorts of occasions when we would say that someone was "following a rule" or "invoking a

rule" (or, equally, "violating a rule," "ignoring a rule," etc.) can lend substance to such a claim. That we must look at these expressions rather than, say, at "rule" (as a noun) is a lesson drawn from Wittgenstein, although I am afraid that my discussion does not observe the moral consistently. (See 1953, sec. 199 "a note on the grammar of the expression 'to obey a rule' ".)

6.   "It is doubtful that anything to which the summary conception did apply would be called a *rule*. Arguing as if one regarded rules in this way is a mistake one makes while doing philosophy" (p. 323); and, I might add, when one tries to find rules in regularities in doing anthropology.

7.   It is not clear, among other things, whether rules define a practice, or whether the existence of a practice is what enables us to talk about rules. The phrase "act as if . . . one is obeying the rules," I suggest, makes sense only within the context of a well-defined practice. (In what circumstances would we ask, or try to discover, whether someone was "actually obeying a rule" or "just acting as *if* we were [or pretending to be] obeying the rule"?) These considerations derive from my reading of certain passages in Wittgenstein, especially 1953, secs. 82–85, 100, 162–64, 199–208.

8.   Diggs points out that there will certainly be many borderline cases in which a game has become so interwoven with the instrumental activities of a society that it is hard to distinguish the object of the game from some independent goal (1964, p. 39, footnote 18). And, of course, it is possible that a game may engender rules of strategy, which are instrumental maxims having to do with how best to attain the "object of the game." Similarly, the rules of a game as a whole may well have a *point* which allows us to characterize particular rules and conventions of the game as *superfluous* (with respect to the object of the game). This is Wittgenstein's point at 1953, secs. 563–64.

9.   Diggs writes of the third type, "Rules of this kind are found in very different institutions. Some are rules of a 'job' in the ordinary sense. Others apply to anyone who voluntarily assumes a 'role,' such as 'automobile driver.' Others characterize a position which one is obliged to take by law, for example, that of private in the army. The goals which the rules are designed to serve may be ordinary products of labor, such as houses, steel beams, etc.; or fairly specific social goals such as 'getting vehicles to their destinations safely and expeditiously'; or goals as general as 'the national defense' (1964, p. 33).

10.   It is possible to quarrel with Hart's dichotomy here, and I do not suggest that the classification is either exhaustive or particularly well-defined. What is there to exclude the possibility of tertiary (or higher-order) rules governing secondary rules, and so forth? (In this connection see Wittgenstein 1953, secs. 86 ff.)

Moreover, it is not clear that all the sorts of rules Hart mentions as secondary (rules of recognition, rules of change, power-conferring rules, rules of adjudication, etc.) are in fact *rules*, rather than, say, conditions on social arrangements that allow us to speak of rules being in force at all. Nonetheless, it seems useful to point out Hart's dichotomy because Zinacanteco gossips do in fact spend a good deal of time discussing not simply rules of conduct but the standards of their appropriate application and scope.

11.   I offer these as hypothetical rules only. That is, I do not guarantee that the facts they suggest are true in Zinacantan.

12.   I thank my wife Leslie for pointing out this practical maxim.

13.   I have deliberately omitted from consideration here the sort of rule most characteristic of, for example, a grammar: a characterization of a certain abstract object (say, a string of symbols) which bears various relations to actual speech and which may not be conscious or formulable to native speakers.

14.   This remains true even though, as is certainly the case, there are general sources of conflict within a society—some perceived, others invisible—which result in similar conflicts of interests and parallel disputes among many people.

15.   We apply rules and perform this sort of conceptual twisting whenever we talk: we use words to talk about the world by virtue of "rules" (about the mapping between word and object, or, more accurately, about the *world* itself) which govern all speech. It is precisely this operation of fitting the observed to the preconceived that is at the heart of consciousness (the consciousness we have of our world and our lives).

16.   Notice that Winch's account does not claim that all mistakes are violations of rules, only that if someone is claimed to be "following a rule," then it must be possible for him to make a mistake. See Landesman (1972, p. 47), who argues that, for example, a man falling off his bicycle is a "mistake" that cannot be construed as a violation of a rule or convention. Perhaps not, but it is unclear that such a mishap is, indeed, in any ordinary sense, "a mistake" (see, again, Austin 1961). To see that this is so, imagine that we see the man fall and rush up to him asking "What happened?" He may reply, but if he says "I made a mistake" he will be referring to something other than falling off the bicycle. Perhaps he will mean, "I thought you pedaled backwards to make it go, but I was mistaken"; or perhaps, "I thought I knew how to ride a bicycle, but I made a mistake [about that]." And in these cases, it is not so easy to say that here are no rules or conventions involved (underlying judgments that turn out to have been mistaken). (See also Winch's slightly different formulation of 1958, p. 58.)

17.   Charles Landesman (1965, p. 345): "For the existence of certain actions presupposes the existence of various institutions and social practices, in the sense that the actions could not bear just the descriptions they do if those institutions and practices did not exist. . . . A satisfactory philosophy of mind requires an adequate theory of institutions; and here we see why

the concept of rule-regulated behavior represents not a solution but a problem."

18. Cf. Wittgenstein 1953, ca. sec. 650, and Cavell's remarks on "voluntary" (1958).

19. And, of course, as Robert Laughlin has pointed out to me, natives are occasionally surprised, baffled, confused, and puzzled. Rules may fail, and words along with them.

A good deal of ethnomethodological work has focused precisely on the process of *rationalizing* behavior through appeal to rules. Consider, for example, the following: "Ethnomethodological studies of the employment of criteria have found that the use of such ad hoc procedures as elaborating the sense of a rule so that how the rule fits in this case can be seen, reconstructing some feature of an event so that it can be seen that it fits the prescriptions of the rule, ignoring some aspect of an event that does not fit the rule, and proceeding to classify an event while some 'critical' aspects are left undetermined are essential, unavoidable practices. Whenever persons are confronted with having to make a choice and cannot rely on leaving this case in the status of undecided they will employ these practices" (Wieder 1970, p. 129).

20. I have in mind here more than a communication (Goffman 1959, p. 1967) of the facts of self and situation through interactive behavior. I claim that the rules and conventions governing behavior lend meaning to the choice between culturally appropriate alternative acts in specific situations—for example, the choice between bowing and shaking hands in greeting. Rules define the semantics of behavior.

21. Wittgenstein (1953, sec. 88): "But has this exactness still got a function here: isn't the engine idling?"

22. See especially Winch's discussion of learning what motives are (1958, pp. 80–83); and consider: "The concepts in terms of which we understand our *own* mental processes and behavior have to be learned, and must, therefore, be *socially* established, just as much as the concepts in terms of which we come to understand the behavior of other people" (ibid., p. 119). The concept of "following a rule" is just such a concept. I have learned a good deal from Winch's later essay on similar topics (1964, reprinted in 1972).

In a slightly different vein, Peter K. Manning writes: "In effect, then, the meaning of a rule resides in the practical procedures by which they are administered. . . . Rules within organizations, like grammatical rules and rules of logic, take on an indexical quality, that is, they can be understood only contextually, as practical problems that themselves arise out of those people, facing those problems, in those periods of time" (1970, p. 242).

Chapter 9   Cultural Competence

1. See Keesing (1972) for an able review of some of the underpinning of early cognitive anthropology, based on linguistic analogies.

2. "What the linguist does when he describes a language, English for example, is to construct a model, not of actual language-behavior, but of the system of regularities which underlie that behavior (more precisely of that part of language-behavior which the linguist defines by methodological decision to be "linguistic," rather than "non-linguistic" . . .)—a model of what I am calling the *language-system*" (Lyons 1972, p. 57–58). Lyons goes on to consider in some detail the (admittedly controversial) stages of "idealization" that allow the linguist to extract from actual utterances objects of the sort amenable to grammatical analysis (roughly, sentences).

3. On questions of prediction and anticipation I have benefited from discussions with George A. Collier.

4. Nor is this a matter we can *ask* our informants about. Wittgenstein speaks to this point: " 'How am I able to obey a rule?'—if this is not a question about causes, then it is about the justification for my following the rule in the way I do. If I have exhausted the justifications I have reached bedrock, and my spade is turned. Then I am inclined to say: 'This is simply what I do.' " (1953, sec. 217). We can imagine cases (though it is a mistake to expect a *precise* line dividing them from the normal case) in which we should be tempted to say: "but here people are not following rules at all." Perhaps we will say, "They are just making up rules as they go along." This is, of course, the point of Achilles' conversation with Lewis Carroll's tortoise.

5. See the paper by Michael Wolff in Birenbaum and Sagarin 1973, and also Goffman's discussion of the same study (1971, pp. 26–40).

6. Controlling totally automated vehicles in traffic is, of course, already a possibility. Simulation of human decision-making, however, is of a different order of complexity; and simulation by computer of human perception remains primitive at best. See Rose 1969; Kessing 1974*a*, p. 92.

7. Unremarkable, that is, in that they do not draw the gossip's attention. It is no doubt the case that many of these skills do more to defy our powers of explanation and understanding than do more clearly intellectual skills. Computers prove theorems more readily than they recognize patterns (Keesing 1974*b*, p. 261)—something a Zinacanteco does continually, and with ease, as he hoes his corn. Calling cognitive skills more remarkable, or more complex, may be simply an artifact of our own analytic ignorance of less striking but evolutionarily prior abilities.

8. Cultural interpretation will certainly go beyond gossip. At the very least, it may involve a kind of supracultural gossip, a sort of translation which brings some clarity to what, in Geertz's Moroccan example, is called "a confusion of tongues" (Geertz 1973, p. 9): a metagossip about someone else's ground rules for gossip.

9. Factoring context out of utterances is a theoretical as well as a methodological problem in linguistics, too. As Lyons notes: "Utterances are typically *context dependent*, with respect both to their meaning and their grammatical structure" (1972, p. 61).

To relate such context-dependent utterances to context-independent sentences requires the addition of various sorts of information (perhaps, simply certain sentence elements, presuppositions, indexical particulars, etc.) available from context and necessary to proper analysis. But knowledge of context and how it relates to utterances, what must be called pragmatic knowledge (Silverstein 1974), presumably belongs to a native speaker's knowledge of his language, just as analogous knowledge of the particular is inevitably part of what a gossip draws upon to interpret action.

Again, ethnomethodologists, following an insight of Schutz, have anticipated a similar conclusion. Schutz suggests that typification characterizes all our social relationships with others except those in which we confront one another face to face. In such a direct social relationship, "fugitive and superficial as it may be, the Other is grasped as a unique individuality (although merely one aspect of his personality becomes apparent) in its unique biographical situation (although revealed merely fragmentarily)" (1962, p. 17). But in gossip the direct acquaintance with Other and his biography becomes paramount (even if typified). Moreover, even typifications change, and gossips frequently manipulate typifications and channel changes. "The ideal types that are constantly being constructed in everyday life are subject to constant adjustment and revision on the basis of the observer's experience, whether the latter is direct or indirect" (Schutz 1967 3:193).

Manning suggests, furthermore, that the degree to which various members of a society (or speakers of a language) have mastered various techniques —hence, the degree to which they are themselves "competent"—is variable. "We have suggested that the ability of sepakers and hearers to make sense of conversation—when it is truncated, when "words fail," or when people speak ironically . . . , or by glossing . . . , by synecdoche . . . , or by analogy . . . —has reference to a source that clarifies the course of events. This source, however, is not equally distributed: sediments of experience in the organization [or society], biographically accumulated knowledge, and situational constraints (can't say what I mean here because of the audience) introduce barriers to socialized, fully acceptable conversational understandings and, hence, to role imputations, typifications, normal events, and the rest" (1970, p. 51).

10. I am indebted to an unpublished paper of Nancy Jay (n.d.), who points out the similarity between what I am arguing here and Garfinkel's initial premise: "The activities whereby members produce and manage settings of organized everyday affairs are identical with members' procedures for making those settings 'accountable'" (1967, p. 1).

Appendix 1   Gossip in Taxonomies of
                             Verbal Behavior

1. Bricker suggests that standard ethnoscientific eliciting procedures can go wrong for several reasons (including informant boredom; 1974, p. 73, and note 4); in particular she suggests that questions like "What are the kinds of ———?" are ambiguous in that they do not specify

a level of contrast or the nature of contrast by which to distinguish cases. There is a more radical difficulty, of course; namely, that such a question is drastically misconceived. Different kinds of things may not have *names* at all (Berlin, Breedlove, and Raven 1974). Moreover, for people to be able to classify things in practice it is not necessary that there be consistent or complete criteria for such classifications in the abstract. These issues are important, but they are too complicated for me to review here. Bricker notices an important phenomenon when she points out "informant variability," but she does not carry the implications far enough.

2. The difficulty of working with nominal forms is especially apparent here. The underlying forms in question here are *verbs* (unsurprisingly, since Bricker is talking about *activities*). Many derivational contortions are required to produce these nominal forms; namely:

laban	transitive verb, "to mock [someone]," "to ridicule [someone]"
labanvan	"antipassive" of the above [i.e., intransitive—"to engage in scolding or mocking people"]
labanvanej	"deverbal noun," "mocking of people" (the transitive deverbal noun—*labanel*— also occurs: *slabanel*, "the mocking of him")
-ut	transitive verb, which, with an animate object, means "scold, upbraid, criticize [someone]" (the word also means "say")
-ut -ba	reflexive/reciprocal of -*ut*; hence, "scold self" or "scold one another"
ʔut bail	deverbal noun from the above; hence "scolding of one another" (a phrase which in normal usage implies either that people were trading insults or that there was a good deal of shouting and scolding going on). The nonreflexive deverbal noun *ʔutel* ("scolding") also occurs, rather frequently to mean "angry words." Bricker's remarks seem somehow more naturally applicable to this word, although she does not choose to treat it.

3. A difficulty pervades Bricker's treatment here, in that she simply assumes the notion of "insult" as unproblematic. There is, so far as I know, no Tzotzil word which corresponds precisely to English "insult." And not all joking, scolding, or ridicule is necessarily insulting, although this is a strong presumption in North American usage. The difficulty is that Bricker ignores the fact that an utterance about a victim will be called "criticism" or "ridicule" or "insult" (and the same is true of the Tzotzil glosses for these terms) only if the utterance has a certain character (roughly: derogatory); and Bricker assumes but does not describe this character. I shall return briefly to this issue at the end of this appendix.

4. It is hard to reconcile Bricker's remarks about "truth" in Zinacanteco legal discourse here with what Jane Collier has to say about the irrelevance of truth for the settlement of disputes (J. Collier 1973, pp. 97–98).

5. In a forthcoming paper I describe just such a case in which gossip about a man prompted him to seek redress in court. However, the incident that precipitated the legal action was not gossip, but a direct insulting confrontation on the path between the man and the one who was spreading gossip about him. And the underlying issues, which surfaced decisively at the court hearing, were substantive and did not hinge on gossip at all (see Haviland 1974b).

Note that Bricker's use of Laughlin's (1975, p. 215) glosses for words based on the root loʔil again ignores syntactic and derivational facts. See Haviland (1976). Bricker distinguishes loʔiltabe ("gossiping") from loʔilta ("discussing") (1973b, p. 194). In fact, the basic stem here is just loʔilta, a two-place transitive stem, from loʔil ("story"), meaning "tell a story about [someone]". The longer stem employs a syntactic formative which transforms the two-place transitive into a three-place transitive which can accommodate an "indirect object"—canonically, a noun phrase which is the "possessor" of the direct object. The best gloss for loʔiltabe then will be "tell a story about someone's_____." An example will clarify the point:

Chasloʔilta.	"He tells a story about you" (Second-person direct object).
Chasloʔiltabe latzebe.	"He tells a story [on you] about your daughter" (second-person indirect object, possessed noun direct object—"your daughter").

The implication is that gossip about someone with whom you have a connection is gossip that also touches you.

6. Tzotzil tos is a numeral classifier used for "kind of" and for "group"; Bricker used this root to elicit taxa as well.

7. In this sorting task I used instructions similar to those I detailed in chapter 1 (see chap. 7, note 5).

8. This is far from the ordinary use of the phrase *lekil k'op*, which is discussed in chapter 3. See example sentences (32a)–(32c), chapter 3.

9. My informant felt that people had only recently learned to joke in this way. (*?Ach to tajmek stamoj yech krixchano*). Two short exchanges my informant offered by way of example follow:

A:	*Mi chabat?*	("Are you going?")
B:	*Chibat.*	("Yes, I'm going.")
A:	*Ta chukel chkale.*	("To jail, I would say.")
A:	*Mi chavak'bon?*	("Will you give it to me?")
B:	*Chakak'be.*	("Yes, I'll give it to you.")
A:	*Lachak chkale.*	("[You'll probably give me] your ass, I expect.")

In my experience such joking is less common than exchanges in which Zinacantecos create puns on one another's words. See especially Bricker 1968, chap. 7, pp. 106–58).

10. My informant thought that women were most likely to use the phrase *chopol k'op* to describe vulgar language. Women, he said, are likely to be angered by continual swearing and will remark:

> Naka ta chopol *k'op* sna? xk'opoj, naka ta yan x?elan k'op, mu?nuk lek xk'opoj.
> "He only knows how to talk with *bad words*, with disgusting words; he doesn't speak well."

11. For example, the saying

> makob ka?   ("covering for a horse")

refers to the load of corn young men were formerly made to carry to encourage them to learn to walk strongly and bear heavy loads.

Similarly, the expression

> pat p'in chkom   ("he ends up like the outside of a cooking pot")

refers to the appearance of a youth's back after he is whipped. In the olden days, according to the informant, boys and girls caught in illicit relations would be beaten by four or five men who used both hands to wield tumplines; after the whipping the victim's back would be "black as the outside of a pot."

12. *Chopol* ("bad") in figure 12 seems to label two features of speech: (*a*) that it is angry, unpleasant, ill-tempered speech; or (*b*) that it deals with misbehavior or disputes.

13. In different contexts, words sometimes contrast and sometimes complement one another. For example, *lo?ilta* ("tell stories on . . .") and *-laban* ("mock . . .") both contain elements of the English "gossip about . . ."; yet the words are neither synonyms nor antonyms. When the two words occur together in a couplet, the meaning of *-lo?ilta* stretches to include an element of mocking. Yet to describe the shrewish public ridiculing of a man by his wife, the choice of *-laban* ("She wanted the world to know how awful he was; that she wanted nothing more to do with

him. So she mocked and ridiculed his behavior") over -*lo^ʔilta* ("She let everyone in on his transgressions") is significant.

14. I have been enlightened in these matters by seminar comments of Derek Freeman, Anthony Forge, and Meyer Fortes.

Bibliography

Abrahams, Roger D. 1970. A performance centered approach to gossip. *Man* (n.s.) 5:290–301.

Allport, Gordon W., and Postman, Leo. 1947. *The psychology of rumor*, New York: Russell and Russell.

Austin, John L. 1961. A plea for excuses. In idem, *Philosophical papers*. Oxford: Blackwell.

Bailey, F. G., ed. 1971. *Gifts and poison*. Oxford: Blackwell.

Barth, Fredrik. 1967. On the study of social change. *American Anthropologist*. 69:661–69.

Beals, Alan R., and Siegel, Bernard J. 1966. *Divisiveness and social conflict: An anthropological approach*. Stanford: Stanford University Press.

Berlin, Brent. 1968. *Tzeltal numeral classifiers: A study of ethnographic semantics*. The Hague: Mouton (Janua linguarum—series practica, no. 70).

Berlin, Brent; Breedlove, D.; and Raven, P. 1974. *Principles of Tzeltal plant classification*. New York: Academic Press.

Birenbaum, Arnold, and Sagarin, Edward, eds. 1973. *People in places: The sociology of the familiar*. London: Nelson.

Boissevain, Jeremy. 1974. *Friends of friends*. Oxford: Blackwell.

Bricker, Victoria E. Reifler. 1968. *The meaning of laughter in Zinacantan: An analysis of the humor of a highland Maya community*. Ph.D. diss. Harvard University.

———. 1973a. *Ritual humor in highland Chiapas*. Austin: Texas University Press.

———. 1973b. Three genres of Tzotzil insult. *In Meaning in Mayan languages*, ed. Munro S. Edmondson, pp. 184–203. The Hague: Mouton.

250   Bibliography

————. 1974. Some cognitive implications of informant variability in Zina-
canteco speech classification. *Language in Society*. 3:69–82.
Cancian, Frank. 1965. *Economics and prestige in a Maya community: A
study of the religious cargo system in Zinacantan, Chiapas, Mexico.*
Stanford: Stanford University Press.
————. 1974. New patterns of stratification in the Zinacantan cargo system.
Journal of Anthropological Research 30:164–73.
Care, Norman S., and Landesman, Charles, eds. 1968. *Readings in the
theory of action.* Bloomington: Indiana University Press.
Carroll, Lewis. 1960. *Through the looking glass,* ed. Martin Gardner.
London: A. Blond.
Cavell, Stanley. 1958. Must we mean what we say? *Inquiry* 1:172–212.
Chomsky, Noam. 1965. *Aspects of the theory of syntax.* Cambridge:
M.I.T. Press.
————. 1968. *Language and mind.* New York: Harcourt, Brace and World.
Colby, Lore M. 1963. *Zinacantan Tzotzil sound and word structure.* Ph.D.
diss., Harvard University.
Collier, George A. 1968. *Land inheritance and land use in a modern Maya
community.* Ph.D. diss., Harvard University.
————. 1975. *The fields of Tzotzil.* Austin: Texas University Press.
Collier, George A., and Bricker, Victoria E. R. 1970. Nicknames and social
structure in Zinacantan. *American Anthropologist* 72:289–302.
Collier, Jane F. 1968. *Courtship and marriage in Zinacantan.* New Orleans:
Middle American Research Institute, Tulane University, pub. 25.
————. 1970. *Zinacanteco law: A study of conflict in a modern Maya
community.* Ph.D. diss., Tulane University.
————. 1973. *Law and social change in Zinacantan.* Stanford: Stanford
University Press.
Cox, Bruce A. What is Hopi gossip about? Information management and
Hopi factions. *Man* (n.s.) 5:88–98.
Diggs, B. J. 1964. Rules and utilitarianism. *American Anthropological
Quarterly,* vol. 1. Reprinted in *Readings in the theory of action,* ed. N.
Care and C. Landesman, pp. 341–72. Bloomington: Indiana University
press, 1968.
Douglas, Jack D., ed. 1970. *Understanding everyday life.* London: Rout-
ledge and Kegan Paul.
Frake, C. O. 1960. The ethnographic study of cognitive systems. *Anthro-
pology and human behavior,* ed. T. Gladwin and W. Sturtevant, pp.
72–85. Washington, D.C.: Anthropological Society of Washington.
Frankenberg, Ronald. 1957. *Village on the border: A social study of religion,
politics and football in a North Wales community.* London: Cohen and
West.
Freeman, William. 1974. *The lawyers of Zinacantan.* Harvard College
honors thesis, Department of Anthropology.
Garfinkel, Harold. 1956. Conditions of successful degradation ceremonies.
American Journal of Sociology 61:420–24.

————. 1967. *Studies in ethnomethodology.* Englewood Cliffs, N.J.: Prentice-Hall.

Geertz, Clifford. 1973. *The interpretation of culture.* New York: Basic Books.

Gluckman, Max. 1963. Gossip and scandal. *Current Anthropology* 4:307–16.

————. 1968. Psychological, sociological and anthropological explanations of witchcraft and gossip: A clarification. *Man* (n.s.) 3:20–34.

Goffman, Erving. 1959. *The presentation of self in everyday life.* Garden City, N.Y.: Doubleday.

————. 1967. *Strategic interaction.* Philadelphia: University of Pennsylvania press.

————. 1971. *Relations in public.* Baltimore: Penguin.

Goodenough, Ward H. 1957. Cultural anthropology and linguistics. In *Language in culture and society,* ed. Dell H. Hymes, pp. 36–39. New York: Harper and Row.

————. 1961. Comment on cultural evolution. *Daedalus* 90:521–28.

————. 1965. Rethinking status and role. In *The relevance of models for social anthropology,* pp. 1–22. London: Tavistock Publications (Association of Social Anthropologists of the Commonwealth; ASA Monographs, 1).

Gossen, Gary Hamilton. 1970. *Time and space in Chamula oral tradition.* Ph.D. diss., Harvard University.

————. 1974. *Chamulas in the world of the sun.* Cambridge: Harvard University Press.

Gumperz, John, and Hymes, Dell, eds. 1972. *Directions in sociolinguistics.* New York: Holt, Rinehart and Winston.

Hahn, Robert. 1973. Understanding beliefs. *Current Anthropology* 14: 207–29.

Handelman, Don. 1971. *Patterns of interaction in a sheltered workshop in Jerusalem.* Ph.D. diss., University of Manchester.

————. 1973. Gossip in encounters. *Man* (n.s.) 8:210–27.

Hannerz, Ulf. 1967. Gossip, networks and culture in a black American ghetto. *Ethnos* 32:35–60.

Hart, H. L. A. 1961. *The concept of law.* Oxford: Clarendon.

Haviland, John B. 1967. *Vob*: Traditional instrumental music in Zinacantan. Working paper, Harvard Chiapas Project, Harvard University.

————. 1970a. Review of B. Berlin, *Tzeltal numeral classifiers. American Anthropologist* 72:194–96.

————. 1970b. Son of ethnographic semantics: A new look at a dying subject. Specials paper, Department of Social Relations, Harvard University.

————. 1972. Guugu-Yimidhirr body part metaphor. Paper presented at meetings of Australian Institute of Aboriginal Studies, Canberra, A.C.T.

————. 1974a. El problema de la educación bilingüe en el área Tzotzil. Paper presented to the Anthropological Symposium in honour of Fray Bartolomé de las Casas, San Cristóbal de las Casas, Chiapas, Mexico, August 1974.

————. 1974*b*. Tzotzil language and Zinacanteco identity. Paper presented to meetings of the American Anthropological Association, Mexico City, November 1974.

————. 1975. Espionage begins at home. Mimeographed.

————. 1976. Sk'op sotz'leb; el tzotzil de San Lorenzo Zinacantán. Mimeographed.

Heath, Shirley B. 1972. *Telling tongues*. New York: Teachers College Press.

Hotchkiss, John C. 1967. Children and conduct in a ladino community of Chiapas, Mexico. *American Anthropologist* 68:711–18.

Hymes, Dell H., ed. 1964. *Language in culture and society: A reader in linguistics and anthropology*. New York: Harper and Row.

Jakobson, Roman. 1957. Shifters, verbal categories, and the Russian verb. Cambridge: Harvard University, Department of Slavic Languages and Literatures, Russian Language Project.

Jay, Nancy. (n.d.). Culture ex machina: Anthropologists' accounts of informants' accounts; or, An account out of context is a no-account account. Brandeis University. Mimeographed.

Kay, Paul. 1966. Ethnography and the theory of culture. *Bucknell Review*. 14:106–13.

————. 1970. Some theoretical implications of ethnographic semantics. In *Current directions in anthropology*, ed. Ann Fischer, pp. 19–31. Special Publication of the American Anthropological Association.

Keesing, Roger M. 1970. Toward a model of role analysis. In *A handbook of method in cultural anthropology*, ed. Raoul Norall and Ronald Cohen. Garden City, N.Y.: Published for the American Museum of Natural History Press.

————. 1971. Simple models of complexity: The lure of kinship. Paper read to the Anthropological Society of Washington, 19 Jan. 1971.

————. 1972. Paradigms lost. *Southwestern Journal of Anthropology* 28:299–332.

————. 1974*a*. Theories of culture. *Annual Review of Anthropology* 3:73–97.

————. 1974*b*. Transformational linguistics and structural anthropology. *Cultural Hermeneutics* 2:243–66.

Labov, William. 1972. *Sociolinguistic patterns*. Philadelphia: University of Pennsylvania Press.

Lakoff, George. 1965. *On the nature of syntactic irregularity*. Report no. NSF–16, Mathematical Linguistics and Automatic Translation, to National Science Foundation. The Computation Laboratory, Harvard University.

Landesman, Charles. 1965. The new dualism in the philosophy of mind. *Review of Metaphysics* 19 (1965–66):329–45.

————. 1972. *Discourse and its presuppositions*. New Haven: Yale University Press.

Laughlin, Robert Moody. 1962. *Through the looking glass: Reflections on Zinacantan courtship and marriage*. Ph.D. Thesis, Harvard University.

———. 1975. *The great Tzotzil dictionary of San Lorenzo Zinacantán.* Smithsonian Contributions to Anthropology, no. 19. Washington, D.C.: Smithsonian Institution Press.

Lyons, John. 1963. *Structural semantics: An analysis of part of the vocabulary of Plato.* Oxford: Blackwell (Philological Society of London, publications no. 20).

———. 1972. Human language. In *Non-verbal communication,* ed. Robert A. Hinde, pp. 49–85. Cambridge: Cambridge University Press.

Malinowski, Bronislaw. 1965. *Coral gardens and their magic. Vol. 2. The language of magic and gardening.* Bloomington: Indiana University Press. (First published 1935.)

Manning, Peter K. 1970. Talking and becoming: A view of organizational socialization. In Douglas (1970), pp. 239–56.

Nash, Manning. 1958. Political relations in Guatemala. *Social and Economic Studies* 7:65–76.

Needham, Rodney. 1972. *Belief, language, and experience.* Chicago: University of Chicago Press.

Paine, Robert. 1967. What is gossip about? An alternative hypothesis. *Man* (n.s.) 2:278–85.

———. 1968. Correspondence: Gossip and transaction. *Man* (n.s.) 3:305–8.

———. 1970. Informal communication and information management. *Canadian Review of Sociology and Anthropology* 7:172–88.

Parsons, Elsie Clews. 1936. *Mitla: Town of souls.* Chicago: University of Chicago Press.

Popper, Karl. 1972. *Objective knowledge.* London: Oxford University Press.

Quine, Willard Van Ormand. 1960. *Word and object.* Cambridge: Technology Press of Massachusetts Institute of Technology.

Rawls, John. 1955. Two concepts of rules. *Philosophical Review,* vol. 64. Reprinted in *Readings in the theory of action,* ed. N. Care and C. Landesman, pp. 306–40. Bloomington: Indiana University Press, 1968.

Reed, Nelson. 1964. *The caste war of Yucatan.* Stanford: Stanford University Press.

Rose, J., ed. 1969. *Survey of cybernetics: A tribute to Norbert Weiner,* New York: Gordon and Breach.

Rush, Timothy. 1971. Disputes in Nabencauk: The social basis of factions in a Mexican Indian village. Senior honors thesis, Committee on Degrees in Social Studies, Harvard College.

Ryle, Gilbert. 1947. *The concept of mind.* New York: Barnes and Noble.

Sapir, Edward. 1944. Grading: A study of semantics. *Philosophy of Science* 11:93–116.

Schegloff, E. 1968. Sequencing in conversational openings. *American Anthropologist* 70:1075–95.

Schutz, Alfred J. 1962. *Collected papers. Vol. 1. The problem of social reality,* edited by Maurice Natanson. The Hague: Martinus Nijhoff.

————. 1967. *Collected papers. Vol. 3. Studies in phenomenological philosophy*, edited by I. Schutz. The Hague: Martinus Nijhoff.

Silverstein, Michael. 1974. Shifters, linguistic categories, and cultural description. Mimeographed.

Szwed, John F. 1966. Gossip, drinking and social control: Consensus and communication in a Newfoundland parish. *Ethnology* 5:434–41.

Vendler, Zeno. 1967. *Linguistics in philosophy*. Ithaca: Cornell University Press.

Vogt, Evon Z. 1969. *Zinacantan: A Maya community in the highlands of Chiapas*. Cambridge: Harvard University Press, Belknap Press.

————. 1970. *The Zinacantecos of Mexico: A modern Maya way of life*. New York: Holt, Rinehart and Winston.

Wasserstrom, Robert F. 1970. Our Lady of the Salt. Senior honors thesis, Department of Anthropology, Harvard College.

Weinreich, Uriel. 1962. Lexicographic definition in descriptive semantics. In *Problems in lexicography*, ed. Householder and Saporta, *International Journal of American Linguistics*, part iv, 28(2):25–44.

Whitten, Norman E., and Whitten, Dorothea S. 1972. Social strategies and social relationships. *Annual Review of Anthropology* 1:247–70.

Whorf, Benjamin L. 1956. *Language, thought, and reality: Selected writings*. Edited and with an introduction by John B. Carroll. Cambridge: Technology Press of Massachusetts Institute of Technology.

Wieder, D. Lawrence. 1970. On meaning by rule. In Douglas (1970), pp. 107–35.

Wilson, Peter J. 1974. Filcher of good names. *Man* (n.s.) 9:93–102.

Winch, Peter. 1958. *The idea of a social science*. London: Routledge and Kegan Paul.

————. 1964. Understanding a primitive society. *American Philosophical Quarterly*, vol. 1. Reprinted in *Ethics and action*, ed. Peter Winch, pp. 8–49. London: Routledge and Kegan Paul, 1972.

Wittgenstein, Ludwig. 1953. *Philosophical investigations*. Translated by G. E. M. Anscombe. New York: Macmillan.

Wolf, Eric. 1966. *Peasants*. Englewood Cliffs, N.J.: Prentice-Hall.

Zimmerman, Don H. 1970. The practicalities of rule use. In Douglas (1970) pp. 221–38.

Index